CALIFORNIA POLICY CHOICES

CALIFORNIA POLICY CHOICES

Volume Six

John J. Kirlin and Donald R. Winkler, *Editors*
Peter Asmus and Nora Harlow, *Assistant Editors*

Katrina Burgess
Bruce E. Cain
Jeffrey I. Chapman
Tim Duane
Eugene C. Lee
Abraham F. Lowenthal
Chester A. Newland
Beryl A. Radin
Michael B. Teitz
Fernando Torres-Gil
Linda A. Wray

UNIVERSITY OF SOUTHERN CALIFORNIA
SCHOOL OF PUBLIC ADMINISTRATION
Los Angeles/Sacramento/Washington, D.C.

Founded over fifty years ago, the School of Public Administration of the University of Southern California now ranks among the top three such schools in the nation. It is also the only school of its kind with permanent facilities and resident faculty in three governmentally significant locations: the Los Angeles campus, the Sacramento Center, and the Washington Public Affairs Center in Washington, D.C. As a result, the school's faculty and its more than 1,600 students are in a unique position to engage intergovernmental policies.

The School of Public Administration also seeks to develop models for joint action between the public sector and those non-governmental organizations and individuals who are crucial to achievement of any public purpose. The faculty brings to bear the knowledge of varied disciplines upon critical issues facing this nation and the world. In all of the school's educational programs there is a focus upon theory and research combined with strong commitment to integrating these into policy making and administrative practice.

California Policy Choices is a multi-volume series of contributions by individuals from universities, colleges, and research institutions in California. These volumes seek to improve public policy making in the state by analyzing the consequences of choices already made, increasing knowledge of the forces shaping California, and examining choices available for the future.

Publication of the first six volumes of *California Policy Choices* is supported by a grant from the William and Flora Hewlett Foundation to USC's School of Public Administration. Opinions expressed are solely those of the authors of each chapter and should not be attributed to the institutions with which they are affiliated, the University of Southern California, or the William and Flora Hewlett Foundation.

The editors of *California Policy Choices* are assisted by an advisory board, whose primary role is to identify chapter topics and potential authors. The assistance of the following board members is appreciated:

Wayne Bartlett, Merrill Lynch White, Weld Capital Markets Group
Don Benninghoven, League of California Cities
Elizabeth G. Hill, Legislative Analyst, State of California
William G. Hamm, World Savings and Loan
Jesse Huff, Department of Finance, State of California
David Lyon, The Rand Corporation
Ex-officio: *Clint E. Smith*, William and Flora Hewlett Foundation

CONTENTS

ANALYTICAL CONTENTS

TABLES

FIGURES

CALIFORNIA POLICY CHOICES

1

John J. Kirlin and Donald R. Winkler

California Policy Choices seeks to improve the process of public policy making by increasing citizens' and policy makers' understanding of the choices to be made. Contributors to this multi-volume series assess and describe the impacts of past choices on options currently available and identify and evaluate strategies for achieving public goals. This chapter reviews the contents of this sixth volume of *California Policy Choices*.

This is the sixth volume of *California Policy Choices*, which is published annually under the auspices of the University of Southern California School of Public Administration with the support of the William and Flora Hewlett Foundation. This volume includes eleven analyses of public policy issues important to the future of California. Included are chapters analyzing growth dynamics, long-term health care, air quality, the initiative process, electricity regulation, and reapportionment, among other topics.

California is a great state, large in population and economic activity, with a vibrant arts community and natural resources of exceptional beauty. California faces problems that rival its assets. Accommodating growth while maintaining a high quality of life is a challenge encountered over and over—very evidently in providing housing and transportation or ensuring clean air, but also in managing wastes, creating jobs, educating youth, and providing energy and water supplies.

An often reiterated theme in previous volumes of *California Policy Choices* is that the state is not adequately meeting the challenges it faces. Housing is expensive, transportation systems are often congested, air quality is below national standards in most urban areas, basic prenatal health care is unavailable to many poor expectant women, too many children are raised in poverty, and far too many youth fail to graduate from high school.

Equally apparent in previous volumes of *California Policy Choices* is that the fundamental problem is not lack of money or questionable intentions of California public officials, elected or appointed. Total state and local government revenues in California ranked fourth among all states in 1986-87, and increased 5.3 percent in real dollars per capita between 1977-78 and 1985-86. The fiscal capacity of California governments does vary widely. Most significantly, the state has captured increasing shares of all revenues for its purposes, with state government expenditures net of transfers to local governments increasing 26.5 percent in real per capita dollars between 1977-78 and 1985-86, a growth rate five times larger than changes in total state and local government spending.[1]

California public officials remain among the most highly regarded in the nation; simply replacing officeholders or career employees is not likely to improve the situation much. Instead, a common theme in previous volumes of *California Policy Choices* is the need for new policy strategies and reformed public institutions, for fundamentally new approaches to achieving policy goals.

This theme is again found in contributions to this volume. The eleven chapters that follow fall roughly into three categories. Four chapters deal with growth in the California economy and the impacts of that growth. Included here are an historical analysis of growth patterns and examinations of air quality, hazardous wastes, and energy policy. Four chapters examine various facets of the political system, including the initiative process, redistricting, representation of California in the national capital, and earmarked revenues. Finally, three chapters focus on discrete policy arenas, including long-term care, corrections, and California-Mexico relationships.

Growth and Its Impacts

Economic growth issues have received considerable attention in the first five volumes of *California Policy Choices.* These issues have included assessments of changing growth patterns, explanation of citizen attitudes toward growth, analyses of local government growth policies, and discussion of the policy choices facing the state.

---

1. See Gary J. Reid and Donald R. Winkler, "Fiscal Limits and Government Finance," in volume four of *California Policy Choices.*

Several conclusions follow from the analyses published in earlier volumes of *California Policy Choices*. The California economy continues to grow, but its performance has declined relative to other states.[2] Growth in the state's economy and its population has increased the demand for publicly provided services.[3] The failure of the government to adequately meet new demands has resulted in increased congestion and subsequent attempts by citizen groups to enact slow growth initiatives.[4] Since economic and population growth are inevitable in California, state and local governments need to formulate policies that encourage desirable types of economic growth and that successfully manage the adverse impacts of growth. Recommendations for the former include further increasing California's access to and involvement in international markets[5] and stimulating technological development in California industry, in part through making more efficient use of state research funds.[6]

In this volume Michael Teitz continues his contribution to the policy debate on growth by putting economic and population growth of the state in a comparative perspective. Teitz argues on two grounds against alarmist claims that increases in population portend disaster. First, the densities of population in California are substantially below those of the Northeast region of our nation or of Italy, for example. If California today were to be populated at the density of the Northeast of 1980, it would have a population of 47.2 million, more than half again as many as currently live in the state. The "carrying capacity" of California may not yet have been reached.

---

2. California's per capita income and median family income continues to exceed those for the nation as a whole, but the state's ranking in the nation has declined. This reflects, in part, changes in the economic structure, with highly paid manufacturing employment declining while less highly paid service employment has increased. These trends are examined in Michael B. Teitz's "The California Economy: Changing Structure and Policy Responses," in volume one of *California Policy Choices*.

3. See Eric Heikkila, "Impacts of Urban Growth," in volume five of *California Policy Choices*. This chapter describes the nature and magnitude of these impacts and role of the state in managing growth.

4. See Phillip E. Vincent, "Encouraging Economic Growth," in volume two of *California Policy Choices*. This chapter analyzes local government growth policies. Also see John Landis and Cynthia Kroll, "The Southern California Growth War," in volume five of *California Policy Choices*.

5. Walter E. Hoadley, "California and the International Economy," in volume three of *California Policy Choices*.

6. Jonathan Brown and Robert Biller, "Higher Education and R & D," in volume four of *California Policy Choices*.

Second, growth rates tend to moderate over time. This occurred in the Northeast, where the population grew by 36 percent from 1940 to 1980, but hardly at all in the last decade. Overall, population increments in California declined during the 1960s, but increased again through the 1970s and 1980s. Within this pattern of overall growth, however, the experience of counties varied greatly and can be understood as fitting into eight "growth regimes." Some counties, such as Los Angeles, grew rapidly in the 1950s and 1960s, lost population in the early 1970s, and then surged again in the late 1970s and 1980s. Others, such as Santa Clara or Orange counties, peaked in annual increments to population in the early 1960s and have decreased fairly steadily since then. In contrast, Riverside and San Bernardino counties are still on ascending growth curves that started in the late 1970s. This analysis suggests that California is accommodating growth in population by spreading it out to the urbanizing fringes of metropolitan areas and to counties with lower population densities.

This pattern of growth strains infrastructure and leads to perceptions of decreases in the quality of life as undeveloped or agricultural areas are urbanized, long commutes encounter traffic congestion, and air quality deteriorates. Moreover, as the consensus that supported growth in previous decades has eroded, needed infrastructure investments often are not made, with the consequence of greater negative impacts from growth that does occur.

Human activity generates wastes, and an advanced economy generates substantial quantities of hazardous wastes. Managing and disposing of these wastes has proven difficult, with neighbors of proposed disposal and treatment facilities often adopting an attitude of "Not In My Backyard!" Peter Asmus analyzes how California has sought to overcome the NIMBY syndrome through a collaborative state-local policy, commonly called the Tanner process after its author, Assemblymember Tanner.

Implementation of the legislation adopted in 1986 has strained relationships between counties that develop hazardous waste management plans and the California Department of Health Services, which reviews and approves the plans. Only thirteen counties now have state-approved plans, and the plans submitted by thirty-one counties have been rejected. Not a single treatment and disposal facility has been sited. Implementation of an apparently good policy has generated conflict between the state and counties, largely around counties' desire to include "fair share" language in their plans.

Tim Duane analyzes energy regulation, a topic also related to growth. In this policy area a policymaking and regulatory system designed for the energy industry of the 1970s is faltering as the 1990s begin. Previously functional divisions of roles between the Public Utilities Commission and the California Energy Commission now make less sense as the structure of the energy industry has changed. Additionally, air quality management plans, such as that adopted for the South Coast Air Quality Management District, include policies that affect demand for specific forms of energy and that simultaneously control energy generation, with the result that they may effectively set energy policy for the state.

Air quality is the final issue examined in this group of chapters dealing with growth and its impacts. John Kirlin analyzes the effectiveness of incentive-based regulation (IBR) versus the now dominant command-and-control style of regulation (CCR). An example of a CCR policy is mandated emissions limits for automobiles. An example of an IBR policy is basing vehicle registration fees on miles driven and vehicle emissions. IBR strategies are widely recognized as providing incentives for individuals and businesses to control emissions, thereby achieving emission reductions at lower total costs than CCR strategies. They have been little used, however, as policy makers have chosen to mandate particular technologies on vehicle manufacturers, a strategy they apparently believe is easier to implement and more palatable politically.

After an extensive review of the available literature on reducing emissions from vehicles, Kirlin argues that both CCR and IBR strategies are needed to achieve the improvements in air quality required to meet national standards. CCR strategies have helped to improve air quality, but they will be less effective in the future. Appropriately designed IBR policies can build on the progress made to date and result in larger improvements in air quality, less total cost, and less intrusion in the lives of Californians.

Politics and Governance

Problems of politics and governance have been examined by several contributors to earlier volumes of *California Policy Choices*. These authors have examined structural weaknesses in governance and analyzed why state government has failed to demonstrate leadership in confronting major public policy issues and why voters have lost confidence in Sacramento and resorted to the ballot initiative.[7]

The lack of leadership by Sacramento is a frequent theme in the five previous volumes of *California Policy Choices*. The causes of the leadership vacuum are attributable less to political leaders than to institutional factors such as campaign financing, which increases the political voice of special interests, and the weakness of political parties in the state.[8] There is a need for both political campaign finance reform and for political party renewal to limit the influence of special interests and increase the accountability of elected politicians to the citizenry.[9] The failure of political institutions has resulted in a lack of trust, which is immediately reflected in the ubiquitous California ballot initiative.[10]

Analysis of problems of the political system continues in this volume of *California Policy Choices*. As has been noted in earlier volumes, the ballot initiative has revolutionized government finance in California and has brought numerous other policy changes.[11] In this volume Eugene Lee provides a comprehensive analysis of the initiative process and of the sizable industry that has emerged to qualify and campaign for initiatives. Lee concludes that initiatives have many negative impacts as well as some benefits, and argues that the process needs to be reformed if it is to play a constructive role in the twenty-first century. He reviews possible reforms, most of which have been used in other states, favoring those that provide opportunities for technical reviews and public hearings and full disclosure of impacts and of sponsorship. He also advocates placing

7. Analyses of the structure of governance have, in particular, examined the respective roles of the state and local governments, pointing out the need for improvements in regional governance. See John J. Kirlin's "Improving Regional Governance" and Robert B. Hawkins, Jr.'s "Governance: the Case of Transportation," both in volume five of *California Policy Choices*.
8. Walter Zelman, "Political Stalemate and Drift," in volume five of *California Policy Choices*.
9. These conclusions follow from the chapters on campaign finance reform in volumes one ("Reforming Political Finance" by Herbert Alexander) and two ("Political Party Renewal," by Kay Lawson) of *California Policy Choices*.
10. For further comment on this point, see Harry Snyder, "Reviving Citizenship in California," in volume five of *California Policy Choices*.
11. Changes in government finance are evaluated in Jeffrey I. Chapman and Donald R. Winkler, "The Revenue Structure of California State and Local Government: a Framework for Choice," volume one of *California Policy Choices*, and in Gary J. Reid and Donald R. Winkler, "Fiscal Limits and Government Finance," in volume four of *California Policy Choices*.

all initiatives on the November ballot when there is a larger turnout and adoption of an indirect initiative process, in which the legislature considers measures prior to their placement on the ballot.

The redistricting that occurs after every decennial census is of great importance to elected officials. Bruce Cain argues that redistricting has policy as well as political impacts. After setting the context for the upcoming redistricting by considering those of the past, he analyzes criteria by which redistricting can be judged fair, and examines several reform proposals.

Two such proposals, Propositions 118 and 119, were defeated by voters in June 1990. Cain argues that a shift in perceptions of fairness appears to be occurring in the electorate, a shift toward a proportional representation system. Legitimacy will be given to the political system to the extent the outcomes of elections reflect the diverse populations of the state. This standard of fairness can be met partially through redistricting, but increasing sizes of elected legislative bodies and use of semi-proportional electoral processes could also result in outcomes more likely to be judged fair.

Some eighty California public organizations—more than any other state—have representatives in the nation's capital. Beryl Radin catalogs their efforts and analyzes how they work. Despite their numbers, representatives of California public organizations do not feel they are as successful as they would like to be. Because non-Californians view the state as affluent and as the beneficiary of considerable largess from the national government, especially in defense contracting, an "ABC" (Anywhere But California) is believed to disadvantage the state. One proposal to improve the effectiveness of California representatives is to develop a California Institute, modeled on the other state or multi-state think tanks in Washington.

Fiscal System

Since the fiscal system constrains the feasible set of policy alternatives, each volume of *California Policy Choices* has discussed the current fiscal state of government, as well as emerging issues in government finance. Among the issues examined have been the efficiency and equity effects of tax and expenditure limitations;[12] the

---

12. See Chapman and Winkler, *ibid.*

response of local governments to these limitations, especially the rapid increase in municipal user fees;[13] the response of the state to changes and reductions in federal grants-in-aid;[14] and the finance of particular goods and services, including pensions, schools, and public works.[15]

As voter-imposed fiscal constraints have become more binding, special interests have responded by promoting earmarking of revenues for their favored programs. Currently, over half of total state revenues are earmarked, according to Donald Winkler and Jeffrey Chapman in the current volume. The largest of these earmarkings in dollars is the result of Proposition 98, which designates 41 percent of the state's general fund revenues for expenditure on K-14 education.

Earmarking is the result of explicit political choices, and its use by some interests leads to efforts by others to earmark additional funds. This tendency is aggravated in the current context of fiscal stress. While much earmarking occurs in the legislative process, the initiative is increasingly used for this purpose.

Selected Issues

In addition to analyses of economic growth, political institutions, and fiscal conditions, the first five volumes of *California Policy Choices* have examined problems and proposed policy alternatives for a number of discrete public policy dilemmas. These have included policy problems in water supply and pricing, incarceration, juvenile justice, medically indigent health care, public welfare, children's welfare, hazardous waste, all levels of public education, the delta levee system, energy production, transportation, and space. This volume continues the tradition of examining specific public policy issues, including long-term health care, corrections, and California-Mexico relations.

Long-Term Care. Fernando Torres-Gil and Linda Wray analyze long-term care, which they describe as an emerging crisis. Long-term care is a set of health, personal care, and social services deliv-

---

13. See Reid and Winkler, *supra* note 11.
14. Dale Rogers Marshall, "Block Grants: Reagan's, Deukmejian's and Choices for the Future," in volume one of *California Policy Choices*.
15. Jack W. Osman and John M. Gemello, "California School Finance: Policy Perspectives" and James M. Ferris, "Public Pension Policy Choices for California," both in volume one of *California Policy Choices*. Also see Dean J. Misczynski, "The Fiscalization of Land Use," in volume three of *California Policy Choices*.

ered over a sustained period to those who lack the capacity to care for themselves. Included are nursing home care, board and care facilities, and community and home-based services.

Between 1980 and 2020 the long-term care population in California is expected to increase 134 percent, twice the rate of the total population. In 1985 more than a million Californians were estimated to need some type of formal long-term care. The aged constitute about two-thirds of the long-term care population, and their increasing numbers are the major factor in the growing population needing such care.

While California has been seen as an innovator in long-term care policy making, the state faces continuing dilemmas. Despite efforts to integrate programs, long-term care remains fragmented and uncoordinated. Long-term care also suffers from being subsumed in health care programs, which leads to an emphasis on institutional rather than community-based services. And, since long-term care is expensive, funding levels always leave providers strained.

Corrections. Corrections can be seen as a "care" program too, some-times of short and sometimes of long duration. Chester Newland analyzes the current state of corrections in California and policy choices available. Governor Deukmejian has given high priority to prison construction, but facilities remain crowded and are likely to be so well into the next century. As discussed in the first volume of *California Policy Choices*, the major choices in corrections revolve around deciding who goes to prison for how long.[16]

California policy makers have chosen to fight crime by mandating prison for an ever-increasing list of offenses and by legislating longer prison terms. It is increasingly apparent that California cannot build prisons fast enough, or find sufficient funds for their operation, unless incarceration policies are changed. California's corrections leaders have developed an alternative approach that relies on a system of graded and interchangeable corrections options, including prisons and jails, but relying far more on community-based programs and financial penalties. Reform of court procedures and improved information systems also are needed.

California-Mexico Relations. Finally, Katrina Burgess and Abraham Lowenthal of the USC California-Mexico project analyze the chal-

---

16. Barry Krisberg and James Austin, "Dealing with Offenders: the California Prison Crisis," in volume four of *California Policy Choices*.

lenges and opportunities found in California-Mexico relations. Over the past two decades the economic integration of California and Mexico have become more marked, the flows of migrants more important, and the interrelationships of their ecosystems more apparent and critical.

Burgess and Lowenthal believe that the benefits that California receives from its contiguity with Mexico outweigh the costs. Trade, investment, and labor are positive impacts, for example. Pressures on infrastructure and the environment in border areas are among the costs. These authors conclude that improving the future prospects of Mexican immigrants to California is an important strategy for ensuring that Mexico-California relationships remain positive.

Conclusion

California remains a favored place, but the state is, in many respects, coasting on the momentum generated in the period following World War II and consuming the social and physical capital created in that period.

In too many areas of pressing importance, from air quality and energy through long-term care and redistricting, California is frozen into patterns of action established in the past. Policies, institutions, and ways of thinking about issues often are held in a kind of "time warp" defined by the context in which they were first addressed.

The state needs new visions to achieve its potential, and those visions must energize, mobilize, and focus Californians. This can occur only if appropriate choices are made, if public policies and institutions address the pressing issues confronting the state and afford the possibility of improved lives for its residents. Protecting entrenched interests and enshrining outdated policies and institutions will only hasten the decline of California and the impoverishment of Californians.

EARMARKED REVENUES AND FISCAL CONSTRAINTS

Donald R. Winkler and Jeffrey I. Chapman

2

One popular response to constraints on state budgets has been the legal or constitutional appropriation of specified shares of revenues or revenues from specific sources to designated programs, a practice known as earmarking. Earmarking revenues, especially by means of voter-approved ballot initiatives, can ensure that citizens' preferences for government services are reflected in the state budget. However, earmarking tends to create budgetary inflexibility and reduce expenditure control by elected officials, and it can negatively impact unprotected programs when expenditures must be cut. Several examples of earmarking in California are evaluated in terms of selected criteria, and some ways of improving the practice are recommended.

Since 1978 California voters have imposed some well known limits on government revenues and spending. Proposition 13 (now Article XIIIA of the state constitution) and Proposition 4 (Article XIIIB) have been effective in reducing tax liabilities and the size of government at all levels. But reductions in revenue growth have not been accompanied by reduced demand for government services. Voters, to their consternation, have found that reductions in spending growth have come not only from improvements in government efficiency, but from cutbacks in some of the most important government functions. For example, California's rank in capital spending on highways is now close to last among the fifty states, and its ranking in educational spending has fallen precipitously.[1]

California governments have reacted in various ways to reduce costs of service provision and to increase revenues required to meet growing public demands for government services. State government has responded to fiscal stress by reducing fiscal transfers to local governments, which has increased fiscal stress at the local level.

1. Allan Odden, "Elementary and Secondary Education," *California Policy Choices*, vol. 3, Sacramento, University of Southern California, School of Public Administration, Sacramento Center, 1986, pp. 107-49.

Cities have been more creative, dramatically increasing revenues from user fees and charges on formerly subsidized services[2] and introducing new and higher fees on real estate development or requiring developers to provide capital facilities in lieu of fees.

Citizens dissatisfied with the level of services provided by California governments have responded by drafting and approving statewide ballot initiatives either to appropriate a share of existing revenues for high-priority services or to increase taxes with revenue gains dedicated to specific services. The legal or constitutional allocation of specific shares of revenues or revenues from specific taxes to designated programs is known as earmarking.

There are several recent examples of earmarking achieved through ballot initiatives in California. An initiative providing for a statewide lottery was approved by voters in 1984 with profits (revenues less prizes and administrative costs) dedicated to education; a tobacco tax initiative was approved in 1988 that allocates proceeds to health services and natural resources; Proposition 98, also approved in November 1988, allocates 41 percent of state general fund tax revenues to K-14 education; and Proposition 111, passed in June 1990, will significantly increase fuel taxes and vehicle fees with some of the revenues earmarked for mass transit. As a result of these ballot initiatives, at least half of the state's revenues are now earmarked for specific uses.[3] Except for federal mandates and constitutional requirements, the remaining 50 percent of the budget is discretionary, which means that expenditure reductions, when required, must fall on a small number of programs.

Earmarking and Fiscal Stress

Earmarking is one response to growing fiscal stress in the state, but, ironically, it also contributes to fiscal stress, especially for programs not designated as beneficiaries of earmarked revenues. To the extent that state or local earmarking has been accompanied by higher revenues, fiscal stress is reduced in the short run. But in the long run

---

2. Cities increased revenues from fees and charges by over 300 percent between 1978 and 1985. See Gary J. Reid and Donald R. Winkler, "Fiscal Limits and Government Finance," *California Policy Choices*, vol. 4, Sacramento, University of Southern California, School of Public Administration, Sacramento Center, 1988, pp. 11-33.
3. Due to expenditure mandates, discretionary spending is well below half of total revenues; the LAO estimates that as much as 70 percent of the state's general fund budget is now statutorily or constitutionally earmarked for designated programs.

an increase in the earmarked share of the total budget contributes to fiscal stress by reducing budgetary flexibility, especially in times of fiscal deficit, when actual revenues fall short of anticipated revenues or actual expenditures exceed anticipated expenditures. The prolonged and difficult resolution of the state's $3.5 billion budget deficit in fiscal year 1990-91 is in large part attributable to earmarking in the budget and the resulting adjustment costs imposed on non-earmarked programs.

The high percentage of earmarked state revenues and expenditures provides an incentive for further attempts by special interest groups to obtain earmarked revenues for their programs. Indeed, earmarking looks increasingly attractive as the earmarked proportion of the state budget grows,[4] and political negotiations concerning the use (and, in times of fiscal deficit, the reduction) of non-earmarked revenues is likely to become increasingly contentious.

There also may be attempts to use earmarked funds for other purposes during times of fiscal stress. Much conflict over the 1990-91 state budget involved whether or not to reduce funding for K-14 education below the levels required by Proposition 98.

Policy Choices

One basic policy choice confronting the state is whether or not to increase the percentage of the earmarked budget. While economic and administrative efficiency largely argue for reductions in present levels of earmarking in the state budget, political considerations may well lead to further increases.

A second basic policy choice facing the state concerns whether or not earmarking should be permanent. Permanent earmarking, especially in the form of constitutional amendments, makes extremely strong assumptions regarding citizens' future needs and desires. Earmarking with sunset provisions, which reduce or eliminate earmarking after, say, five or seven years, provides protected revenues to specific programs in the short run as well as the flexibility to respond to changing citizen preferences and competing budgetary needs in the long run.

---

4. In the extreme, the entire state budget might be earmarked. In Brazil, where earmarking is widely used, earmarking provisions proposed to be included in a new federal constitution in 1989 comprised well in excess of 100 percent of the budget.

Another policy choice concerns the type of program for which earmarking is adopted. For some programs (e.g., highway construction), a clear association exists with an earmarked revenue source (e.g., gasoline tax). For other programs (e.g., education), no association exists with any particular revenue source. In general, earmarking is a good policy choice when there are clear linkages between the payers of a tax or fee and the beneficiaries of the program for which these revenues are earmarked and a poor policy choice when this linkage is weak or nonexistent.

Is the earmarking of government revenues good public policy? Does it contribute to voter satisfaction by directly linking taxes to benefits? Or does earmarking reduce government efficiency by constraining the flexibility of government officials and elected leaders to reallocate revenues to high-priority needs? Are there ways in which the practice of earmarking could be improved to both increase voter satisfaction and provide the flexibility for government to respond to new needs? These are some of the policy-related questions investigated in this chapter. First we examine the current fiscal status of the state and the need for additional revenues. We then discuss recent growth in earmarking of revenues in California; compare California with similar states and with other states in the region; analyze the effects of earmarking provisions on spending and public administration; and make recommendations for improved revenue earmarking practices.

The Fiscal State of the State

Since fiscal constraints are frequently cited as a principal reason for the growing popularity of earmarking, it is important to examine the fiscal state of the state. In real terms, state and local government expenditures have grown between 1978 and 1988 (see Table 2-1). As a share of state domestic product, however, state and local government spending has remained stable at about 10 percent since 1980.

While trends in aggregate government expenditures do not suggest severe fiscal constraints, the Gann appropriations limit has certainly affected government spending. As shown in Table 2-2, growth in tax revenues has frequently exceeded growth in the Gann limit since 1985. The average annual percentage change in tax revenues between 1985 and 1989 was 9.4 percent, compared to an average

Table 2-1. State and Local Government Expenditures, 1978-88 ($ millions)

Jurisdiction	1978	1980	1984	1988	% change (1978-88)
			Expenditures		
City	7,728	7,361	10,368	12,637	63.5
County	11,326	9,452	10,056	12,568	11.0
State	16,413	21,501	20,771	25,323	55.7
Total	35,467	38,314	41,195	50,527	42.5
Total per capita	1,587	1,647	1,628	1,827	15.1
Total per state domestic product	.14	.10	.10	.10	−35.7

Source: Controller's Reports; Commission on State Finance, *Annual Long Term General Fund Forecast*, Winter 1989-90, Table A-2.

Notes: Fixed weight price deflator for GNP. Counties are exclusive of enterprises.

Table 2-2. Tax Revenues and the Gann Appropriations Limit, 1985-89

Year	Appropriations limit ($millions)	% change in limit	$ change in taxes	Amount under limit	Prop. 98 guarantee
1985	21,740	6.7	5.7	918	—
1986	22,962	5.6	5.7	495	—
1987	24,311	5.9	21.6	(1,138)	—
1988	25,201	3.7	0.0	1,171	—
1989	27,064	7.4	14.1	259	14,678
1990	29,318	8.3	6.5	652	15,823
1991a	31,200	6.4	9.2	143	17,094

Source: *Governor's Budget Summary, 1990-91*, Table 14-1, Schedule 9A, Table 3-9.

a. Projected

annual percentage change in the Gann limit of 5.9 percent.[5] Proposition 111, approved by voters in June 1990, will relax but not remove the Gann limit by modifying the formula and by excluding some spending currently covered by the limit.[6]

In addition to fiscal constraints, the state in recent years has experienced volatility in the balance between general fund revenues and expenditures (see Figure 2-1). Revenues and expenditures have not always grown at the same rate, leading to alternating deficits and surpluses.[7] Frequent deficits have appeared in the state budget despite attempts by a fiscally conservative governor to maintain a moderate reserve fund. The causes of these deficits are not surprising. Usually they involve an unanticipated shortfall of revenues, an increase in the population base of the beneficiaries of programs (e.g., a larger school population than forecast), and/or higher than expected cost-of-living (COLA) increases in particular expenditure categories. The $3.5 billion 1990 deficit reflects these causes. The Legislative Analyst's Office (LAO) estimated that, without changes in revenue and expenditure policies, revenue growth during FY90 to fund increases in state programs was about $1.4 billion, while expenditure growth under existing law and policy would be about $4.9 billion.

After a long and contentious budget confrontation, this approximately $3.5 billion deficit was resolved by a combination of tax increases ($741 million), fee hikes ($102.6 million), program cuts ($1.3 billion), and program delays ($987 million). Although the earmarked Proposition 98 revenues were initially put on the table by the governor, the legislature decisively rejected that approach. The cuts did include a one-year suspension of COLAs for welfare, the aged, and

---

5. To illustrate some of the uncertainty associated with these figures, the LAO argues that average yearly revenue growth has been 8.9 percent, while the governor's office has argued for a 7 percent average yearly growth figure.
6. The old formula used, for a cost-of-living index, the lower of the change in the U.S. Consumer Price Index or California per capita personal income. The new cost-of-living factor is, for the state and schools, the change in California per capita personal income and, for local governments, either the change in California per capita personal income or the percentage change in the jurisdiction's assessed valuation that is attributable to non-residential new construction. The net effect of this is to make the formula less restrictive. Further, the new money for transportation, the costs of meeting natural disasters, and some capital outlay projects are excluded from the limit calculation.
7. The balance between expenditures and revenues gives the best picture of the fiscal state of the state. The general fund balance is required by law to be positive; budget deficits usually are converted to general fund surpluses through accounting changes, one-time revenue increases, and one-time spending reductions.

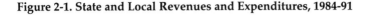

Figure 2-1. State and Local Revenues and Expenditures, 1984-91

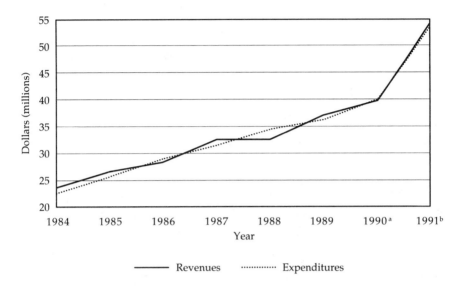

Sources: 1984-89: State of California. Controller's Office, *Annual Report*, 1988-89, p. A-19; 1990: *Governor's Budget, 1990-91*, Schedules 8 and 9; 1991: *Governor's Budget, 1990-91*, Tables 1-1 and 1-2.
a. estimated
b. projected

the disabled, among others. The principal tax change was making the state corporate tax code conform to the federal code.

The evidence suggests that the era of fiscal constraints is not yet over.

Earmarking: an Escape from Fiscal Constraints?

The intentions of California voters in approving the propositions resulting in Articles XIIIA and XIIIB are unclear.[8] One plausible explanation is that California citizens thought government was too large, and this was one means of reducing the size of government. Another plausible explanation is that citizens were not dissatisfied with the size of government but were, instead, unhappy with the composition of government revenues and/or expenditures.

8. For an early attempt to explain these votes, see Jack Citrin, "Do People Want Something for Nothing: Public Opinion on Taxes and Government Spending," *National Tax Journal Supplement*, 1979, pp. 113-28.

Recent actions by the voters are no easier to interpret. Citizens have voted to earmark a minimum share of general fund tax revenues for K-14 education expenditures, thereby either revealing continued dissatisfaction with the composition of state expenditures or demonstrating that they valued K-14 expenditures enough to not want them cut. They have also voted for a lottery, tobacco tax, and gasoline tax increases but earmarked the use of those revenues, thereby increasing government revenues but further constraining the expenditure decisions of elected officials. These votes may reveal some change in attitude regarding the desirable size of government (at least if financed through tax sources that the majority of voters can escape), but they also suggest continued distrust of elected officials in allocating government revenues.

The passage of ballot initiatives that earmark government revenues is likely to continue, as evidenced by the success of Proposition 111. To some extent, interest groups will attempt to garner a larger share of a fixed government revenue pie. It is more likely, however, that both voters and the legislature will use earmarking as a technique to circumvent the revenue and expenditure constraints that have been previously enacted. Earmarking becomes an attractive way to simultaneously increase tax revenues and provide services highly valued by the citizenry.

Earmarking of revenues has one additional use: to promote support for taxes or fees that discourage undesirable behaviors. For example, it is generally conceded that pollution taxes or fees can be a powerful tool to discourage the emission of polluting compounds. Earmarking collected revenues for particular programs may encourage beneficiaries of those programs to support the tax.

Is California Atypical?

The state budget has two major divisions: the general fund and the special fund. The general fund was, until recently, truly general in that revenues accruing to it could be allocated across programs by the joint decision of the legislature and the governor. The special fund, on the other hand, consists entirely of revenues earmarked for specific uses. Of the two funds, the general fund is clearly the larger, representing 85 percent of the total state budget executed in fiscal year 1989 and the same percentage of total revenues projected for fiscal year 1991.[9]

Table 2-3 gives the extent of earmarking in the state budget in fiscal year 1989. As noted above, 100 percent of the special fund was earmarked, including additional revenues resulting from the tobacco tax enacted by Proposition 99 in 1988. In addition, 41 percent of the general fund was earmarked for education as a result of Proposition 98, enacted in 1988. Finally, lottery proceeds, which are not formally part of the budget, were 100 percent earmarked, as a result of Proposition 37, passed in 1984. In total, fully 54 percent of state government revenues were earmarked for specific uses in 1989.

In reality, the discretionary expenditure budget is well below 50 percent. Both federal and state constitutional and statutory mandates and requirements in effect earmark another large share of the general fund. The result, according to the LAO, is that the true discretionary budget represents only 30 percent of the total.[10]

Earmarking at the state level is mirrored at the local level in California, although for different reasons and to a much lesser degree. In particular, earmarking for infrastructure for new development has become popular. This takes principally two forms: fees and exactions imposed on developers either for infrastructure specific to their development or for other infrastructure in the community (such as parks); or the establishment of special assessment districts, which then issue bonds that are paid for by earmarked tax revenues. However, at times the fees collected may be deposited into the general fund with a gentleman's agreement that they will be used to provide the infrastructure for new development. As a result, while it is known that revenues are used for these earmarked purposes, it is difficult to determine the exact magnitude of infrastructure expenditures. In real terms, however, current charges for non-enterprise activity increased by about 25 percent between FY 1978 and FY 1986. The use of special assessment districts, including Mello-Roos districts, has also rapidly grown in the state. In 1982 about $67 million of

9. Legislative Analyst's Office, *The 1990-91 Budget: Perspectives and Issues*, Sacramento, 1990.
10. The governor has argued that only 8 percent of the budget is truly discretionary.

Table 2-3. California Tax and License Earmarking, FY 1989

General Fund Sources	Amount ($ millions)	% Earmarked	Purposes[a]
Taxes	35,647	41	K-14 education
Non-tax revenue	1,306	0	
Total general fund	36,953	40	
Special Fund Sources			
Sales and use tax	74	100	local transit
Motor fuel	1,321	100	local government, transportation
Vehicle license/ registration	3,139	100	local government transportation
Tobacco	397	100	health, natural resources, local government
Oil and gas royalties	90	100	capital investment
Interest on investments	147	100	
Other	1,201	100	
Total special fund	6,369	100	
Off-Budget Sources			
Lottery	1,037[b]	100	education
Unemployment, disability, and employment training tax	3,552	100	unemployment benefits, workers' compensation
Total off-budget	4,589	100	
Total revenues	47,911	54	

Sources: Legislative Analyst's Office, *The 1990-91 Budget: Perspectives and Issues*, 1990; *Governor's Budget*.

a. An additional quarter percent sales tax is earmarked for earthquake relief for calendar year 1990.
b. Estimated for FY 1991.

Table 2-4. Proportion of Tax Revenues Earmarked by State, 1954-88

State	% of Tax Revenues Earmarked				
	1954	1963	1979	1984	1988
Far West					
California	42	28	12	13	12
Arizona	47	51	31	29	32
Nevada	55	35	34	52	40
Oregon	47	36	23	19	53
Washington	35	30	29	26	30
Other States					
Alabama	89	87	88	89	89
Louisiana	85	87	5	4	9
Michigan	67	57	38	39	34
New York	13	10		6	
All States	51	41	23	21	26

Sources: 1954 and 1963: Tax Foundation, *Earmarked State Taxes*, 1965; 1979, 1984, and 1988: National Conference of State Legislatures surveys.

Notes: These figures include only earmarking of specific taxes (excluding earmarking of total general fund revenues) using the Census Bureau definition of tax, which includes vehicle license and registration fees and excludes unemployment insurance tax. Local government add-ons to the sales tax are not defined as a state-earmarked tax, but dedicating a share of total state sales tax revenues to local government is defined as earmarking.

benefit assessment and Mello-Roos debt was sold; in 1989 that figure was over $1.4 billion.[11]

Recent increases in special fund earmarking in California is a reversal of a long-term trend. As shown in Table 2-4, 42 percent of the revenues from specific taxes were earmarked in California in 1954, declining to only 12 percent by 1988 (these calculations do not include the earmarking of general revenues). In this respect California is similar to the rest of the country, where on average earmarking declined from 51 percent of specific tax revenues in 1954 to 26 percent in 1988. On average, the highest degree of earmarking is found in the Southeast, where Alabama still earmarks 89 percent of its revenue, but Louisiana reduced earmarking from 87 percent in 1963 to only 9 percent in 1988. Earmarking in several western states remains higher

---

11. There is also significant earmarking of revenues at the federal level. In FY 1988-89 earmarked revenues accounted for about 48 percent of total revenues (including Social Security). Excluding Social Security, about $278 billion or 26 percent of revenues was earmarked. U.S. General Accounting Office, *Budget Issues: Earmarking in the Federal Government*, GAO/AFMD-90-8FS, January 1990.

Table 2-5. Proportion of States Earmarking Specific Taxes, FY 1984

Revenue Source	% States Earmarking	Purposes
General sales	64	local government, education, highways, pensions
Tobacco	54	local government, education, debt service
Alcoholic beverages	67	local government, education, pensions
Public utility	24	education
Individual income	40	local government, education
Corporation income	35	local government, education
Motor fuel	96	highways, transportation, local government
Motor vehicle registration	84	highways, transportation, local government
Property	23	education
Occupational license	38	regulation
Hunting/fishing license	86	conservation

Source: Tax Foundation, *Earmarking State Taxes*, May 1987.

than in California, with the highest found in Oregon (53%) and Nevada (40%).

California is also similar to other states in the choice of taxes or fees to earmark and the destination of earmarked funds. As shown in Table 2-5, motor fuel taxes and motor vehicle license fees are almost universally earmarked, with revenues typically going to highways and transportation. At the other extreme, a low percentage of states earmark public utility, property, and income tax revenues.

Data do not exist to compare earmarking of general revenues across states, but in its earmarked support for K-14 education, California is not unique in dedicating a high percentage for a specific purpose. Michigan, for example, passed a constitutional amendment in 1978 earmarking 41 percent of its general fund revenues for local government transfers.

Is Earmarking Good Public Policy?

Before evaluating earmarking as a public policy, it is first necessary to precisely define a loosely used term. Earmarking is the constitutional or statutory dedication of government revenues for designated purposes, and it varies in terms of revenue source, linkage to benefits, and targeting of the use of funds.

Revenue source. Either specific fees or taxes or general funds comprised of several specific revenue sources may be earmarked. A vehicle registration fee is an example of the former, and the state general fund is an example of the latter. California earmarks several specific fees and taxes as well as a proportion of the general fund.

Linkage to benefits. The use of earmarked revenues may or may not be linked to the activity that generates the revenues. In effect, a strongly linked earmarked revenue is analogous to a user fee. An example of strong linkage is a gasoline tax earmarked for highway maintenance and construction. It is primarily users of highways who pay the gasoline tax that finances highway maintenance and construction. An example of a weak linkage is the use of lottery proceeds to finance education. The users or beneficiaries of public education are not the ones who generate lottery proceeds; indeed, playing the lottery is likely to vary inversely with educational level. Finally, general revenues are, by definition, not linked to benefits of specific programs.

Targeting. Earmarked revenues can be narrowly or broadly targeted. An example of narrow targeting is the earmarking of tobacco tax revenue to anti-smoking advertisements and health research. An example of broad targeting is the earmarking of tax or general fund revenue to local government with no constraints on use. The extent of the targeting is inversely related to the ease of transferring money from one account to another to circumvent the intent of the law. The broader the earmarking, the greater the degree of fungibility with respect to the earmarked revenue.

In addition to revenue source, benefit linkage, and targeting, earmarking can vary in other respects. For example, it can take the form of a constitutional amendment, which is extremely difficult to change in later years, or legislation, which can be more easily altered. It can also either generate additional revenues through a new or increased tax or reallocate existing revenues. Finally, it can generate revenue for current expenditures, or it can serve as collateral for general obligation bonds; in the latter case funds are not effectively earmarked except in the case of default.

Earmarking revenues must be distinguished from mandating expenditures. Earmarking means that a floor is established for an expenditure category that varies by the revenue collected. Mandated expenditures means that a certain amount of money (or percentage of a budget) must be spent on a particular expenditure category. This also establishes a floor, although there is no reason why the floor should be the same as an earmark-established floor. A mandated floor does not vary by the amount of revenues collected. Examples of different types of earmarking are given in Table 2-6.

Arguments Against Earmarking

The arguments are often made that earmarking misallocates funds, creates budgetary inflexibility and hinders effective expenditure control, and infringes on the policymaking powers of elected officials.[12]

Earmarking has the potential to misallocate funds if activities funded through earmarking are subjected to less rigorous evaluation than activities funded out of general funds and, as a result, may yield lower net benefits. This argument is more true the longer the earmarking requirement has been in effect and less true to the extent that earmarking can be evaded through changing activity names and accounts. The argument may also become more valid as the fiscal condition of the state changes. In the case of worsened conditions, earmarked activities are protected from cuts more than other, potentially higher-return government activities. In the case of increased revenues, additional funds may be allocated to earmarked activities that yield relatively low returns. Earmarking could also lead to inadequate funding of earmarked activities if those activities are viewed as being fully funded from a single revenue source that suffers an unusual change of fortune.[13]

Earmarking creates budgetary inflexibility and reduces expenditure control by locking in expenditures for certain activities, even when citizen preferences change or fiscal conditions worsen.[14] The fact that only 30 percent of the California budget is discretionary means that adverse changes in fiscal conditions are most strongly felt by relatively few activities. This argument is not so much against earmarking *per se* as it is against the degree to which the total budget

---

12. The case for and against earmarking is presented in E. Deran, "Earmarking and Expenditures: a Survey and a New Test," *National Tax Journal*, December 1965.
13. An example is Texas public higher education, which receives earmarked oil royalty revenues, the magnitude of which varies with oil prices.
14. An extreme example of locking in is the continued presence in two states during the 1960s of taxes earmarked for Confederate pensions.

Table 2-6. Examples in an Earmarking Typology

Earmarking Characteristics	Revenue Source	
	Specific Fee or Tax	General Revenues
Linkage to Benefits		
Weak	Lottery proceeds to finance education	n.a.
Strong	Gasoline tax for highway transportation capital investment	n.a.
Targeting		
Narrow	Sales and use tax for local transit	Minimum share of general fund tax revenues allocated to education
Broad	Sales and use tax shared with local government	Minimum share of general fund tax revenues allocated to local government

is earmarked. Critics point out that budgetary inflexibility exists even in the absence of earmarking, resulting from the prevailing practice of incremental budgeting (incrementally changing the budgets of established activities) rather than zero-base budgeting (subjecting activities to full evaluation each year).

Earmarking clearly infringes on the power of elected officials to allocate resources. Whether or not this is desirable depends on the extent to which officials' actions reflect the views of their constituencies. The evidence for California suggests that elected officials are frequently at odds with their constituencies with respect to issues of taxing and spending. Furthermore, while ballot initiatives are frequently cloaked in ambiguous language and misleading arguments, voters are surprisingly consistent in their views, for example, regarding reducing the size of government. Quite clearly, there are circumstances (e.g., natural disasters) when elected officials should have the capacity to reallocate large amounts of resources. Failing these circumstances, it is difficult to conclude that earmarking does a worse job of resource allocation from the perspective of the voters.

Arguments for Earmarking

Arguments in favor of earmarking hold that it more closely ties charges to benefits, generates new sources of revenue, and provides greater stability and continuity of funding, especially important in capital investment. These arguments are all consistent with increased citizen satisfaction and improved resource allocation.

The crux of the argument for earmarking is that it provides a second-best alternative to user charges for government services in cases where user charges are too costly to administer. However, for this argument to hold, the base of the earmarked tax must be related to the amount of the government service used by the taxpayer. This argument supports earmarking where the linkage between a tax and its benefits is strong but not where the linkage is weak.

General fund financing, of course, completely divorces revenues from expenditures. Voters may oppose increases in general fund financing under some circumstances, especially if the distribution of general fund revenues among competing programs is viewed as reflecting the relative strength of political interest groups more than voter preferences. In this situation, which arguably holds true in California, increasing revenues may be politically feasible only when the proceeds are earmarked for uses strongly preferred by voters.[15] This argument holds even when the linkage between a tax and its benefits is weak.

Earmarked revenues can, depending on the tax, ensure a stable revenue stream, especially important for government services that require long-term investments. General obligation bonds can provide the same reliable revenue stream, but a given revenue stream may still serve as collateral for the bonds. For example, the one-half percent increase in the sales and use tax to support local mass transit in some California counties permits long-term planning of and capital investments in mass transit systems that might not be possible were elected officials to decide each budget year on a total transportation budget.

---

15. Alternatively, voters will pass taxes (e.g., Proposition 99, the tobacco tax) where the majority of voters will not pay the tax.

An Assessment of California Earmarking

The arguments given above suggest criteria by which one can evaluate either proposed or actual revenue earmarking. These criteria are expressed in terms of linkage to benefits, locking in, efficiency, targeting, and societal benefits.

Linkage to benefits. Earmarking should be encouraged when it is possible to link fees or taxes to benefits received or services consumed.

Locking in. Since voter preferences are likely to change over time, earmarking provisions, especially those not strongly linked to benefits, should require periodic reapproval. The failure to do this in effect locks in expenditures even after voter preferences have changed.

Efficiency. Since earmarking reduces the extent to which favored program areas must compete with other program areas for funding, favored programs and projects should be subjected to intense evaluation to compensate for the reduced competition.

Targeting. The targeting of revenue use should be neither too specific and narrow (resulting in budgetary inflexibility) nor too general and broad (resulting in weak linkage to benefits and high fungibility).

Societal benefits. Some product-specific taxes are good taxes because the use of the product can harm society. If the tax causes an increase in the price of the product it can lead to a reduction in the product's use. When this is the case, the tax can be of benefit to society, irrespective of the use of the revenues.

California revenue earmarking can be evaluated in terms of these five criteria. Five earmarking provisions are selected for evaluation here—four already enacted and one to be voted on in the November 1990 election. The five provisions are: increase in the gasoline tax (Proposition 111); the state lottery (Proposition 37); the tobacco tax (Proposition 99); earmarking of a proportion of the general fund for education (Proposition 98); and the "nickel-a-drink" alcohol surtax to be voted on in November 1990 (Proposition 134). Table 2-7 summarizes the following discussion.

Table 2-7. Evaluation of California Earmarking

| | Revenue Source | | | | |
Criteria	Gas Tax	Lottery	Tobacco Tax	General Fund/ Education	Alcohol Tax
Linkage to benefits	+ +	−	0	−	+
Locking-in	−	0	0	−	0/−
Efficiency	−	0	0/−	−	0
Targeting	+	0	0	0	0
Societal benefits	+	0	+	0	+

Notes: + is a positive evaluation; − is a negative evaluation; 0 is a neutral evaluation. The fungibility of earmarked revenues from the lottery and tobacco tax means that the locking-in, efficiency, and targeting effects are largely absent.

Gas Tax Increase

Proposition 111 gas tax money comes from an initial increase of $.05 in the per-gallon gas tax, which will be increased by $ .01 each year for the next four years. It also increases commercial vehicle weight fees by 40 percent the first year and by an additional 10 percent in five years.[16] The proceeds are to be spent on highway construction and maintenance as well as mass transit.

Based on our criteria, this is in most respects a desirable earmarked tax. There are direct linkages to benefits, it provides an appropriate level of targeting, and it may reduce pollution and congestion by raising the price of gasoline and thereby possibly reducing its use. On the other hand, it would require another constitutional amendment to change the use of these tax revenues, and there is no provision for improved evaluation of projects to be funded. To the contrary, to the extent that the proposition specifies precise use of the tax revenues (e.g., on fixed rail transit), the result is likely to be reduced efficiency in government spending.[17]

The State Lottery

The state lottery has been in effect since 1985; proceeds from the lottery are earmarked for education.[18] In terms of our criteria, the

16. Proposition 108, also passed in June 1990, changes the appropriations limit formula as well as the rules on how revenues in excess of the limit will be disbursed.
17. Narrowly constraining the use of funds may compel the adoption of projects with low net benefits, thereby adversely affecting the overall efficiency of earmarked programs.
18. For FY 1990-91, estimated net revenues (after prizes and administrative costs) are $1,037 million, which will be allocated to K-12 ($837 million), community colleges ($127 million), California State University ($46 million), the University of California ($25 million), and other ($4 million).

lottery does not fare well. The linkage to benefits is non-existent, earmarked proceeds are locked in, and, to some, the establishment of the lottery legalized an activity that may do social harm. On the other hand, the proceeds from the lottery can be regarded as almost completely fungible, and thus very broadly targeted, especially since they represent a small proportion of spending for any one level of education. Earmarking lottery proceeds for education probably increased the number of citizens voting for its passage, but they did so under the erroneous impression that the earmarked revenues would in fact increase educational spending.

The Tobacco Tax

Proposition 99 was passed in the November 1988 election and took effect on January 1, 1989. It instituted an additional $.25 per pack tax on cigarettes as well as increasing the excise taxes on cigars, chewing tobacco, pipe tobacco, and snuff. The additional money raised is to be allocated as follows: 20 percent for health education, 35 percent for hospital services to treat patients who cannot afford to pay for treatment, 10 percent to pay physicians for uncompensated care, 5 percent for tobacco-related disease research, 5 percent for wildlife maintenance, and 25 percent for the unallocated account, which has been used primarily for general purposes of the state Departments of Health Services and Mental Health.[19] The state forecasts declining cigarette consumption and therefore declining revenues from this tax.

The tobacco tax rates poorly by our evaluation criteria. The linkage to benefits is minimal (except for the 5 percent for tobacco-related disease research), the targeting of revenues is overly specific, and this narrow earmarking is locked in. On the other hand, since tobacco tax revenues represent a small share of total revenues for most of the benefited services, this is another example of a highly fungible earmarked tax.[20] In effect, the tobacco tax increase was an addition to general fund revenues, although voters may have

19. There is an additional $.10 per pack tax, which is allocated to local government (30 percent) and the state general fund (70 percent).

20. For example, health education expenditures from this surtax are less than 1 percent of the Department of Health Services budget but more than 76 percent of the expenditures of the chronic disease program. Hospital service expenditures from the surtax are less than 2 percent of the DHS budget but about 15 percent of the rural and community health program budget.

thought otherwise. In addition, this tax may reduce long-run health care expenditures by increasing the cost of an activity that impairs health.

Guaranteed Revenues for Education

The earmarking of general revenues for K-14 education is an example of effective but inappropriate earmarking. The share of the general fund that is earmarked (approximately 41 percent or about $17.1 billion in FY 91) is large enough to effectively increase resources designated for education. There is no linkage of the general fund to education benefits, the earmarking is locked in, and efficiency in the use of educational funds may decrease as a result of reduced competition for funding.[21] The only valid argument for this type of earmarking is that state legislators value education less highly than do voters. But what is more likely to be true is that legislators understand better than citizens voting on a single issue that increased education spending comes at the expense of other important programs.

Alcohol Surtax

Proposition 134, the alcohol surtax initiative, is already qualified for the November 1990 ballot. This would tax alcoholic drinks at the rate of $.05 per unit, with a unit being defined as twelve ounces of beer, five ounces of non-fortified wine, three ounces of fortified wine, or one ounce of distilled spirits. The taxes are imposed on producers and are expected to be shifted to consumers. The money raised would be placed in five separate accounts: the prevention, treatment, and recovery account, which in addition to funding a variety of treatment and advertising programs will also fund some capital expenditures, including domestic violence shelters; an emergency and trauma care account, which will fund treatment, including physicians services; the mental health account; the infants, children, and innocent victims account; and the law enforcement account.

Once fully phased in, the tax is expected to collect about $760 million in 1991-92, with this total to decline if alcoholic beverage

---

21. For example, the public school system may not be under as much pressure to demonstrate improvements in student test scores or other measures of learning.

consumption declines. The initiative also mandates that existing state funding and per capita levels of service for the funded purposes not be reduced. Depending on how the courts, the governor, and the legislature interpret this, future costs in excess of what the legislature desires may be quite large. For example, the approximate mandated increase in base expenditures for 1991-92 might be as high as $150 million. The most expensive estimate of the mandated costs, assuming that the governor and the legislature would have wanted to eliminate all of the funded programs, is $3.25 billion for base year 2005.[22]

The alcohol tax rates somewhat better than the tobacco tax. The earmarked uses for revenues are at least weakly related to alcohol use, but the benefited programs are narrowly defined, and the earmarking is locked in. Also, as with tobacco, this tax may be desirable in and of itself if increasing the price of alcohol reduces medical and other costs associated with alcohol consumption.

Improving Earmarking

The analysis presented suggests several conclusions and recommendations regarding earmarking policy in California. These can be summarized as follows:

Excessive earmarking. In aggregate, too high a share of the state budget is earmarked, leaving a discretionary budget that is too small and results in a few government services bearing the burden of adverse shifts in fiscal conditions. Earmarking of specific taxes is not excessive in the state. Earmarking of total general fund revenues should be reduced.

Ineffective earmarking. Most earmarking is ineffective because it does not ensure that spending on earmarked programs will be higher than in the absence of earmarking. The smaller the ratio of earmarked revenues to total program funding, the easier it is, especially over time, to substitute earmarked funds for general funds. The result is that what voters passed as an earmarked tax is in effect an increase in the general fund. To the extent that this is true (as is

---

22. To put these numbers in context, the $150 million for 1991-92 would be about .25 percent of the state budget. The estimated 1990 base for these programs is estimated to be about $1.2 billion. Thus the surcharge would increase expenditures on the programs by about 63 percent; however, it would not become part of the base.

likely with the tobacco and the proposed liquor taxes), effective earmarking of revenues may be much smaller than it appears.

Poorly designed earmarking. While there are examples of well designed earmarking (e.g., the gasoline tax), most earmarking in the state fails to satisfy basic criteria. Proposition 98 is a case of especially undesirable earmarking. Future earmarking efforts should more closely follow the criteria specified earlier. In particular, most earmarking should require periodic reapproval by the voters or the legislature.

Inadvertent consequences. The passage of earmarked funds may yield important consequences not fully anticipated by voters. Taxes on undesirable activities (contributing to pollution or traffic congestion, harming the health and well-being of others) may reduce the level of such activities and thereby contribute to general social welfare. This benefit is a result of the tax, however, and not the earmarking of the resulting revenues. The passage of earmarked taxes may also have negative consequences. To the extent that the poor spend higher proportions of their incomes than the rich on lottery tickets, cigarettes, or alcoholic beverages, taxes imposed on these products make the poor worse off and also worsen income distribution.[23]

Missed opportunities. While in aggregate there is excessive earmarking in California, there are situations where additional earmarking is appropriate. These include new or increased user fees where direct beneficiaries of government services can be identified (e.g., water, higher education); new or higher taxes where strong benefit linkages exist (e.g., to retire specific debt instruments); and higher taxes to reduce activity that harms the public good (e.g., pollution or commuter parking taxes) and that can be passed only with the support of special interest groups through the promise of earmarked funds for their programs.

A basic change must occur in California political thinking in order for these recommendations to be enacted. Decision makers must adopt a long-run fiscal strategy for the state. This strategy would include earmarking as one component, but would also address such issues as state-local relations, mandated expenditures, the tax system, and the appropriate role of and expectations for government. The short-run budget solutions in 1990 do nothing to solve the state's

---

23. The state lottery has very high tax rates. Only 50 percent of total sales are distributed as prizes; the remainder (after deducting administrative costs) is earmarked for education.

long-run problems, and it is unrealistic to believe that the optimal
use of earmarking will occur without a thorough examination of the
entire system.

The authors thank Robert Ebel of the Advisory Commission on Intergovernmental Relations,
Martha Fabricius of the National Conference of State Legislatures, Douglas Peterson of the
National League of Cities, and Steve Gold, State University of New York, Albany, for their
helpful comments and advice.

CALIFORNIA GROWTH: HARD QUESTIONS, FEW ANSWERS

Michael B. Teitz

3

California's high rates of growth, long viewed as a positive force for economic development, are coming to be seen as presenting serious problems in the form of land use conflicts, fiscal strains, and a general deterioration in the quality of life. The combination of low taxes and easy access to high-quality transportation, housing, and education to which Californians have become accustomed unfortunately can no longer be sustained.

As growth has continued and problems have emerged, Californians have responded in reactive and limited ways, either passing broad legislation to deal with symptoms of growth or attempting to control growth on a local level. The complexity of issues raised by population growth, and their regional and statewide impacts, suggest that the state should develop and implement a growth management policy that will provide a framework for other levels of government to promote balanced development and economic growth while protecting individual opportunity and environmental quality.

Rapid population growth in California is not new. What is new is that growth is now perceived by many as a problem rather than an advantage. Perhaps for the first time in the state's history, Californians are seriously questioning the value of population growth and urban development. Mainly, this concern is local, responding to traffic congestion and declining environmental quality. But there is also a broader issue, namely the capacity of the state as a whole to absorb and manage growth without significant diminution of the quality of life. This issue has been raised principally by environmental advocates. The opposite question, whether quality of life can be sustained without growth, though less popular, is equally important and is advanced by advocates of business, labor, and development. Confounding both views is the apparently inexorable march of growth itself, which has continued with only temporary slowdowns for over fifty years.

One striking feature of events since the March 1988 publication of *Vision: California 2010* by the California Economic Development Corporation[1] has been the increase both in population and in debate about growth and its local and regional implications. The need for a level of development sufficient to realize the aspirations of California's population, noted in the report, remains. However, it is becoming increasingly clear that a viable strategy for managing growth in the state will also require solutions to some intractable problems of development.

This chapter explores four topics related to population growth in California: growth trends, especially over the last forty years, and projections for the future; attitudes toward growth in California, both present and past, and the assumptions that have underpinned policy and action in the state at different times; successes and failures of responses to growth in the state; and possible policy goals and instruments appropriate for the 1990s.

Growth in California

It is impossible to look at the history of population growth in California and not be struck by its remarkable size and consistency. In the forty-two years from 1947, when the post-World War II boom was just beginning, up to 1989, the state's population tripled, from about ten million people to close to thirty million (see Figure 3-1). The state's compound annual growth rate over that period has been 2.8 percent, more than double the 1.2 percent of the U.S. as a whole. There have been fluctuations in the amount and rate of population growth over time, but at no time has the trend been reversed.[2] Figure 3-2 shows the annual increments in the population for this period. Annual population growth was high, at about 550,000 per year, during the period 1955-64. It fell to a low of 240,000 per year in 1971-72, but in the eighteen years since then the growth increment has increased almost continuously to about 750,000 in 1988-89, the largest total recorded over the whole period. Even in 1979-82, during the most severe recessions since the Depression, population growth scarcely faltered. Such an eighteen-year trend was bound to produce powerful effects, and it raises the question of how long growth at this level can continue.

---

1. California Economic Development Corporation, *Vision: California 2010*, Sacramento, 1988.
2. In the 1970s there was a period when growth slowed in the aggregate with decline in many areas within the state.

Figure 3-1. Total State Population and Growth, 1948-89

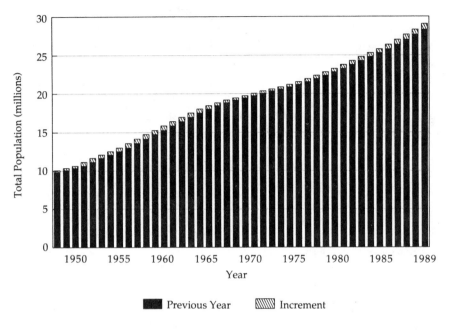

Source: California Department of Finance

Figure 3-2. Annual State Population Growth, 1948-89

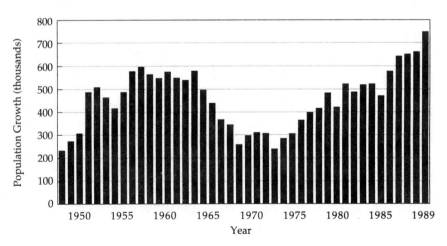

Source: California Department of Finance

History suggests that rapid growth cannot continue indefinitely. But it does not tell us when it will stop or how large the population might become. Is there any limit to California's population? Comparisons can be instructive. New Jersey is an urbanized state that is now growing only very slowly. If California were to equal the population density of New Jersey in 1980, the state would have over 150 million people. That most likely is unrealistic, because New Jersey is the most densely populated state in the U.S. It is small and does not contain large areas of uninhabited land, though there is more than most people realize. It might be more appropriate to compare California instead to the Northeast region of the U.S., comprising the states from Pennsylvania through Maine, an area only 4 percent larger than California, which includes a substantial proportion of mountainous land. At the 1980 density of this Northeast region of the U.S., California would have a population of 47.2 million people. That is 57 percent larger than the state's 1990 population. If past trends were to continue that population would be reached in the year 2030, only forty years from now.

Interestingly, in the forty years from 1940 to 1980, the Northeast's population grew by 36 percent, but by the final decade of that period growth had fallen almost to zero. In 1940 the region's gross population density was 220 persons per square mile (ppsm). By 1980 it had reached 302 ppsm. California in 1980 had a gross population density of 151 ppsm, up from 44 ppsm in 1940. California's gross density was therefore substantially lower in 1980 than that of the Northeast in 1940, and approximately equal to that of New England in 1950.

These comparisons do not tell us what will happen in California. Changes in the region's economy or in that of the world at large may slow population growth, especially from migration. Changes in behavior or composition of the population may slow the rate of births, increase the number of deaths, or change the rate of migration to other states. All of these help to explain the sudden collapse of growth in the Northeast. There may be constraints on growth in California, for example in water supplies or other basic necessities for development associated with the arid character of the state. Such natural constraints have been forcefully argued, but they must confront examples such as Italy, which has a comparable climate and a population of almost 58 million in an area two-thirds the size of California.[3]

There also may be deliberate shifts in policy that affect the growth rate in order to maintain environmental quality and lifestyle. Such policy initiatives are not unprecedented in California. However, in the past, they almost always accommodated or reinforced growth; in this period, they may impede or restrict it.

What the trends and comparisons do tell us is that the dynamics of growth are very powerful. California has been an urbanizing state for a long time. There is little inherent in the state's physical, economic, demographic, or social makeup to prevent growth from continuing if national and world economic, social, and political conditions continue to favor it. Virtually all forecasters of the state's population see no fundamental change over the coming years. They differ in details and in the time horizon to which they are willing to project, but the most widely accepted view is that the state's population will increase by about ten million people by 2010. Population forecasters have been wrong many times, and they will be wrong again. Nonetheless, prudence suggests that these forecasts be taken seriously. The quality of life in California in the next century will depend on actions taken today.

Prospects for the future may be illuminated by looking at where growth has taken us in the past. The simplest way to do this is to examine the changes in population in the state's fifty-eight counties since 1947. Although the counties are not a perfect geographic base for analysis, particularly because some, such as San Bernardino, are so large, they do permit comparisons over long periods of time.

Growth Regimes in California

Some characteristics of growth are immediately evident and well known. The state's population growth has been predominantly urban and metropolitan, primarily in the three metropolitan areas of Los Angeles, San Francisco, and San Diego. Central Valley counties, especially around Sacramento, also have grown rapidly in recent years. In the three coastal metropolitan areas, growth has occurred partly through increasing density, but mainly through extensive

---

3. In fact, Italy is slightly larger than Arizona, but it is not generally perceived as being densely populated.

peripheral development. In the process, it has moved inland—in San Francisco to the inner coastal valleys and now the Central Valley; in Los Angeles toward San Bernardino and Riverside counties, in addition to the enormous growth in Orange County; and in San Diego, into the north and east county areas. These regions have accounted for a major part of the state's total growth in recent years.

The nature of this growth is revealed in the patterns of change over time. These "growth regimes" vary enormously from county to county and among the regions of the state. They show much more precisely what has happened. In a conventional model of development, an area experiencing growth should exhibit over time an S-shaped total population curve, as growth first accelerates then declines as buildable land becomes scarce and further population increases can be achieved only with greater density. Such a pattern would be associated with low absolute growth at the beginning, increasing absolute growth up to some point, and then diminishing growth as the area approaches some population equilibrium. This pattern may be interrupted by changes in demographic behavior and economic activity, but over time these should even out.

Such patterns are visible in California, but often with major variations. For example, Los Angeles, the state's largest county, showed exactly this pattern from 1947 to 1971 (see Figure 3-3). Since then, however, it has seen a resurgence of growth, though never to the absolute population increments of the period from 1950 to 1975. Nonetheless, in 1988 absolute growth in the county still exceeded 100,000. Although the level of growth is now falling, the end is not in sight. San Francisco, on the other hand, is a county that is essentially built out and difficult to increase in density. As shown in Figure 3-4, the city has fluctuated from growth to decline and back again since 1947.

Every county, along with its constituent cities, has a unique situation and history, but there do appear to be some striking patterns. We may identify eight regimes of growth that reflect how counties have fared during the turbulence of the past forty years. In part, they

Figure 3-3. Annual Population Change, Los Angeles County, 1948-89

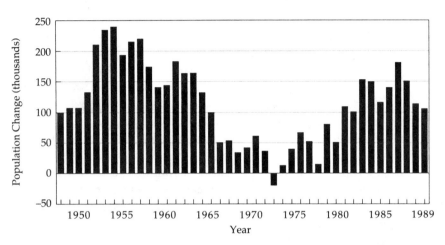

Source: California Department of Finance

Figure 3-4. Annual Population Change, San Francisco County, 1948-89

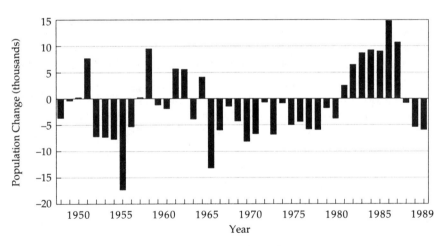

Source: California Department of Finance

reflect where counties are located in relation to outward-moving waves of growth from metropolitan centers across the state.[4]

The first group of counties are the historic cores of three major metropolitan areas, San Francisco, Los Angeles, and Sacramento (see Figures 3-3, 3-4, 3-5, and 3-6). With the exception of San Francisco, which had built out earlier, these counties all exhibit peak levels of population increase in the 1950s and 1960s, followed by sharp declines and recoveries to substantial growth levels in the 1980s. These are counties with annual population increases in excess of 20,000, and in the case of Los Angeles, ten times that amount. Although the level of increase remains high, and space still exists for new development, constraints of land availability and development regulations will place increasing obstacles to further growth. Nevertheless, their metropolitan centrality continues to make development attractive, especially for higher-density uses.

Closely associated but differing in pattern are some counties immediately adjacent to the metropolitan cores. These counties have experienced huge growth, in effect creating secondary cores. Santa Clara and Orange counties, in particular, display remarkably similar patterns, as shown in Figures 3-7 and 3-8. Growth in these counties peaked at very high levels in the 1960s, and has declined thereafter, with variations from year to year. Neither county has experienced the zero or negative growth seen in the old core counties, although Santa Clara dipped below 10,000 in 1984 for the first time since 1947. Absolute growth may be expected to continue in this group, its rate depending on economic conditions and regulatory behavior.

A third regime of growth is exhibited in counties in the first ring around the core counties, which have continued to grow in a way that fluctuates but does not show a clear trend. Examples are Contra Costa County in the Bay Area and Ventura County, adjacent to Los Angeles (see Figures 3-9 and 3-10). While they have had intermittent peaks and dips, each of these counties has sustained growth at the rate of 10,000 to 15,000 persons per year. They have additional land and may be expected to continue this pattern.

---

4. Identification of these growth regimes is based on visual comparison of patterns of growth in all fifty-eight counties. A research project funded by the California Policy Seminar is now in progress at the Institute of Urban and Regional Development at the University of California, Berkeley. It is exploring more analytic approaches to the identification and use of growth profiles for cities and counties in the state. Formal methods for comparing the shapes of such time series are somewhat limited.

Figure 3-5. Annual Population Change, Alameda County, 1948-89

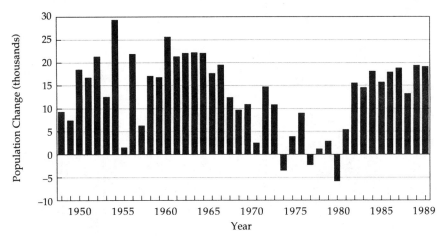

Source: California Department of Finance

Figure 3-6. Annual Population Change, Sacramento County, 1948-89

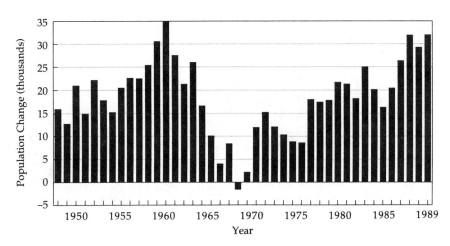

Source: California Department of Finance

Each of the first three groups has been historically close to the metropolitan centers of growth. The fourth group takes us to the peripheries of metropolitan areas, where counties exhibit recent high absolute or relative rates of growth after years of quite constant

Figure 3-7. Annual Population Change, Santa Clara County, 1948-89

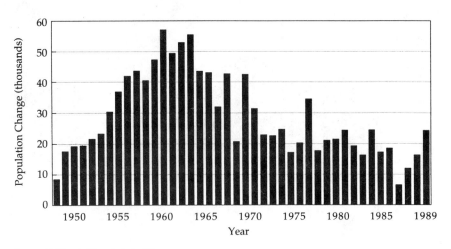

Source: California Department of Finance

Figure 3-8. Annual Population Change, Orange County, 1948-89

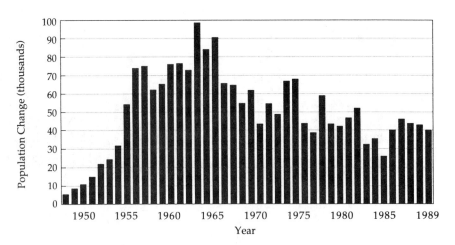

Source: California Department of Finance

levels. At high absolute levels, the best examples are Riverside and San Bernardino counties, where increases approaching 100,000 persons per year are ten times historic levels (see Figures 3-11, 3-12, and 3-13). At a lesser scale, Stanislaus County is receiving overspill from

Figure 3-9. Annual Population Change, Contra Costa County, 1948-89

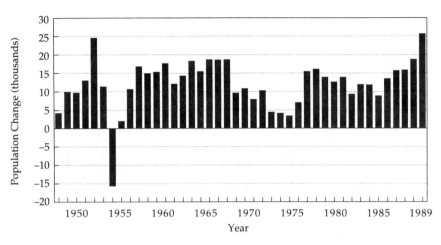

Source: California Department of Finance

Figure 3-10. Annual Population Change, Ventura County, 1948-89

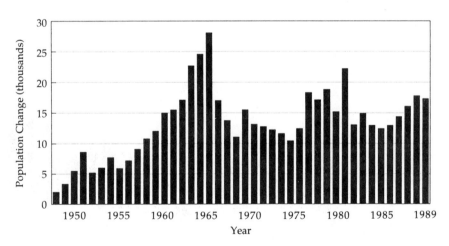

Source: California Department of Finance

the San Francisco Bay Area and has increased by up to 18,000 persons per year. Other examples from the Bay Area include Solano and Sonoma counties. A similar pattern is visible with much smaller

Figure 3-11. Annual Population Change, San Bernardino County, 1948-89

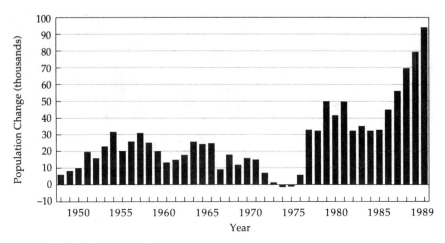

Source: California Department of Finance

Figure 3-12. Annual Population Change, Riverside County, 1948-89

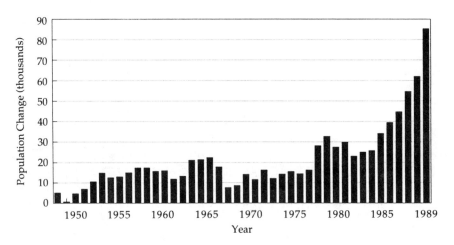

Source: California Department of Finance

magnitudes in Imperial County, relating to San Diego, and in Cala-
veras and El Dorado counties, relating to Sacramento. Each of these
counties, and others like them, are now at the outer frontier of urban
development, with all the issues and tensions that are implied. Their

Figure 3-13. Annual Population Change, Stanislaus County, 1948-89

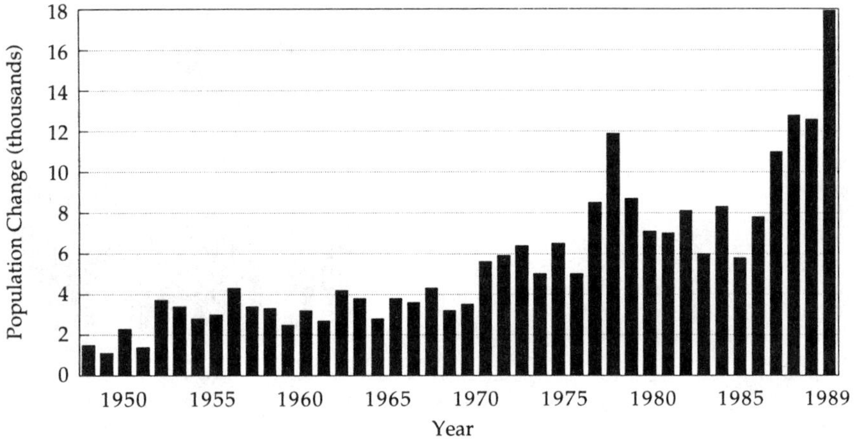

Source: California Department of Finance

percentage growth rates are very high and they are likely to be sustained.

The fifth set of counties illustrates a growth regime that differs from the previous four both in its temporal pattern and in its relation to the metropolitan centers. Many Central Valley counties show a growth pattern that is characterized by years of relatively stable but low growth in the 1950s and 1960s, very low or negative growth in the late 1960s and early 1970s, and much higher sustained growth in the late 1970s and 1980s. Among those with this regime are San Joaquin, Tulare, Madera, and Kern (see Figure 3-14, 3-15, and 3-16). Less clear but similar are Fresno, Merced, and Butte counties. Exactly why growth has occurred in this pattern is not immediately apparent, but it reflects the fact that these Central Valley counties did not fully participate in the pre-1970 round of urban growth in the state. That has evidently changed in the 1980s, even in such relatively isolated areas as Tulare County. The implications of this change may be momentous for the state's urban structure.

The next two growth regimes reflect special circumstances. Humboldt and Del Norte counties have grown in a way that is almost the reverse of the state (Figure 3-17 and 3-18). Both increased quite strongly in relation to their size in the 1950s. With the decline of the

Figure 3-14. Annual Population Change, Madera County, 1948-89

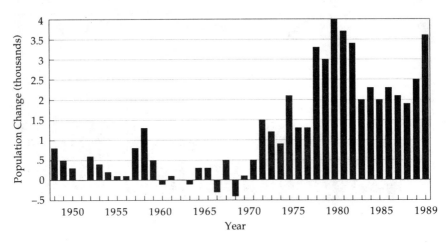

Source: California Department of Finance

Figure 3-15. Annual Population Change, Tulare County, 1948-89

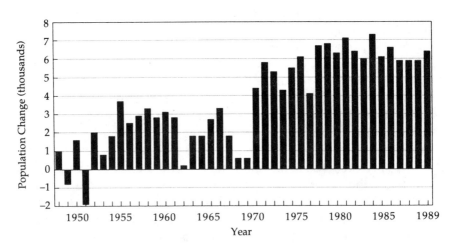

Source: California Department of Finance

lumber industry, both saw absolute population declines and severe economic distress from the 1960s onward, and both are showing some indications of modest recovery in the late 1980s. These are

Figure 3-16. Annual Population Change, San Joaquin County, 1948-89

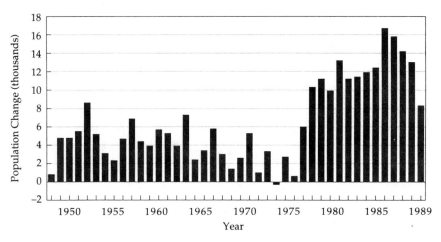

Source: California Department of Finance

Figure 3-17. Annual Population Change, Humboldt County, 1948-89

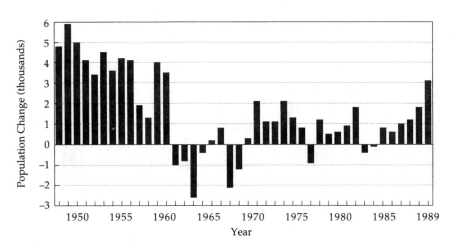

Source: California Department of Finance

isolated counties and are unlikely to be centers of substantial growth unless access is improved.

Similar in form but very different in cause are the patterns of high growth followed by low growth shown by San Mateo, Marin, and

Figure 3-18. Annual Population Change, Del Norte County, 1948-89

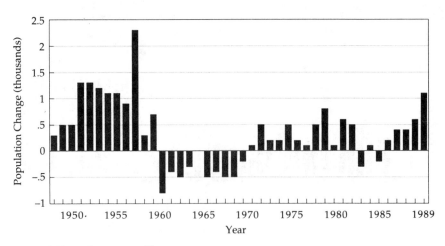

Source: California Department of Finance

Figure 3-19. Annual Population Change, San Mateo County, 1948-89

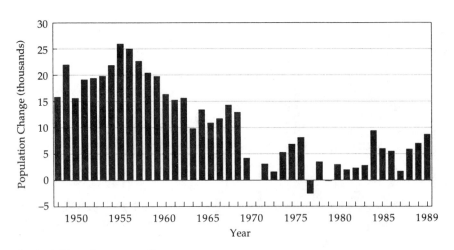

Source: California Department of Finance

Santa Barbara counties, as seen in Figures 3-19, 3-20, and 3-21. In these cases the cause is regulation rather than economic decline. The pattern is especially marked in San Mateo and Marin counties, each of which is adjacent to a metropolitan core county and might have

Figure 3-20. Annual Population Change, Marin County, 1948-89

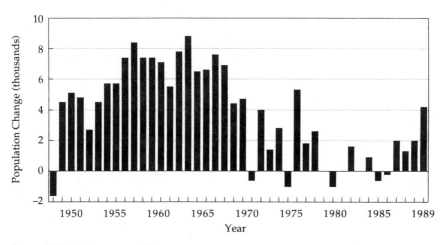

Source: California Department of Finance

Figure 3-21. Annual Population Change, Santa Barbara County, 1948-89

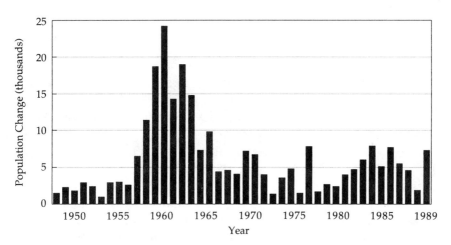

Source: California Department of Finance

been expected to grow in a pattern not similar to those of Contra Costa or Ventura in the second growth regime discussed above. Although Marin is far better known as a center of concern for environmental quality and political response, the pattern of growth in the two counties is virtually identical. In each, the expected growth path has been truncated to permit a relatively low and fluctuating rate of increase since about 1970. Despite the strong pressures for development that might be expected given their locations, each of these counties has succeeded in controlling development. However, the larger picture suggests that the growth expected in these counties has not been eliminated, but rather appears to have been displaced further out in their respective regions.

The eighth growth regime is no growth at all or modest growth with no trend. Mountain counties, peripheral to the state, such as Alpine, Modoc, and Sierra have very small populations and virtually no growth. These counties are among the most inaccessible in the state and have much public land, in contrast to counties, such as Placer, that are in the Sierra Nevada but have grown dramatically as result of their access. Similarly trendless, but showing some growth are rural counties such as Monterey and Sutter. In these cases, and many others such as Mendocino, a complex set of influences, including local regulation, may be operating to sustain the status quo.

Future Growth Areas

Not all counties in the state fit into these eight growth regimes. Nonetheless, they do bring out some important characteristics of population growth at this scale. If we want to understand how growth manifests itself in the state, we must look at the geographic pattern of pressures for development and at the local responses, both of which vary greatly. It seems clear that the critical points are now in the counties at the frontier of urban development and in those that lie just beyond them. Where metropolitan areas meet, as between San Francisco Bay and Sacramento, the urban edge becomes hard to define.

One clear lesson of this analysis is that attempts to regulate growth can be successful, but that the result may be to spur development beyond the bounds of regulation. How far it is possible to go is determined by the economics of development—how much people will pay, where they will work, and how far they will drive. But as the economy becomes increasingly dependent on services, the geographic bounds seem to be relaxing, and once development is established, it is now more than ever able to build on itself, becoming a self-generating process. Because the locations in which development is financially feasible are limited at any particular time, intense growth tends to occur in relatively limited areas. Thus, we need to go beyond the county level to consider the specific locations of development pressure.

There is no single source of information on development that is comparable to the county population data. In consequence, an attempt to identify the areas of major development pressure in the state requires the careful and laborious assembly of information from many local sources. Such an effort is in progress, but is not yet complete. An alternative is to utilize diverse public sources and judgment to identify such areas. The following discussion is based on this approach, and should be regarded as a point of departure for further analysis rather than a definitive assessment.

The principal points of development pressure are clearly related to metropolitan growth, but they are on the peripheries of the state's metropolitan areas, and in some instances beyond them. In northern California, the growth of the Bay Area westward and northwestward is creating two zones of intense development pressure toward the Central Valley. It is a feature of recent commentary on growth that it is increasingly described in terms of corridors, associated primarily with major freeways. In this instance, the corridors are on I-80 through Fairfield and on towards Davis, and on I-580 as it extends west beyond I-680, toward Stockton. The I-680 north-south corridor has itself been the location of some of the most intense development in the past decade. The I-80 corridor accounts for the growth in Solano County and is beginning to interact with development in Sacramento. The I-580 and I-680 corridors have accounted for most of the high growth in Alameda County, and in part, in San Joaquin and Stanislaus counties. Although it is not fully documented, there is a strong perception that this development is driven primarily by the emergence of a major employment center in the I-680 corridor, as well as some commuting further into Alameda County and even to Silicon Valley. It can therefore be regarded as an expansion of the Bay Area metropolis beyond the coast ranges and into the Central Valley.

Complicating the picture of growth in northern California is the emergence of Sacramento as a center of rapid growth in its own right, together with other cities further south in the Central Valley.

Although observers have documented this growth, there has been little study of its significance. Very large developments have occurred and more are planned, both north and south of Sacramento. As we have seen from the county growth regimes, the counties to the south have experienced a pattern of consistently high growth since the late 1970s. No single corridor or zone of growth stands out in this pattern of development. Rather, we may be seeing the simultaneous development of the existing string of centers in the San Joaquin Valley, historically located on U.S. 99. However, also existing in the valley is I-5, which is carrying high traffic volumes and should increasingly influence this development, especially toward Sacramento.

What kind of urban and metropolitan structure is implied by this pattern of development in the Central Valley? We may be witnessing an historic shift toward the development of a multi-nucleated linear metropolis. On the other hand, this growth might also be viewed as no more than long-distance spillover from the two major metropolitan centers, the San Francisco Bay Area and Los Angeles. At this time, there is no evidence of an emerging dynamic sector that will drive growth in the way that high technology drove Orange County or Silicon Valley. However, if these cities become the target for migration of populations moving away from the existing metropolitan areas, then there is potential for very large growth over the next twenty years. There is no effort being undertaken to look at the area in a coherent way. If growth does continue, the resulting metropolitan structure may be seriously flawed, causing environmental problems on a large scale and the loss of unique resources of agricultural land.

The specific growth areas of southern California exhibit similarities to those in the north. The most intense development in recent years has occurred along freeway corridors, especially I-10, extending eastward from Los Angeles to San Bernardino and Riverside. The rate of increase in development in this area is as fast as anywhere in the state, despite environmental problems. In the northern part of Los Angeles County, development has spilled over also into the Palmdale-Lancaster area, and there has been a surge of growth in the Simi Valley. This is not to deny the high levels of growth in other areas of the Los Angeles-Orange County area. Rather, these locations have emerged as newer points of growth, accelerating rapidly from a low base, and exhibiting the typical pattern of peripheral metropolitan development that has become so prevalent in the state. There is no immediately comparable focus of development in the southern Central Valley to compare with Sacramento. Nonetheless, Bakersfield has shown a rapid acceleration of development in recent years. Since its growth is propelled by many of the same spill-out forces that are at work further north, this growth may be expected to continue.

State Growth and Development Policy

California's high rates of growth have produced powerful impacts, in the form of development pressures, local land use conflicts, traffic congestion, air pollution, and fiscal problems. These, in turn, have led to a widespread perception of deteriorating environmental conditions and quality of life.[5] Local and regional political efforts to create regional or subregional organizations to address growth issues are one response. Examples include Bay Vision 2020 in the nine-county Bay Area region and the 2000 Partnership in the Los Angeles area. The state legislature has also begun to respond to growth issues in a variety of ways, including reports, hearings, and legislative proposals. These are important moves, but they reflect a deep uncertainty about how to deal with growth. There is no broad consensus about appropriate policies for the state or its regions to address growth and environment in the twenty-first century.

The Pro-Growth Era

Such uncertainty was not always the case. It can be argued that there was indeed a state policy toward growth and development during the decades between 1945 and 1970. Under a succession of administrations, both Republican and Democratic, a political consensus existed that saw growth and development as positive forces. As a result, the state enacted a series of measures that both accommodated and facilitated growth as it occurred. These measures created a physical and social infrastructure of unequaled quality in the U.S.

---

5. The indicators of such a perception are numerous and varied, including local growth moratoria, opposition to specific developments of all kinds, the growth of local and regional organizations dedicated to environmental preservation, and pressure on legislatures and courts.

·Most important among them were the creation of a statewide water system, modernization of the highway system, and the development of a complex, multi-layered system of higher education.[6]

This consensus was flawed in many respects. Some groups were effectively excluded from full political participation; others had enormous influence politically. The distribution of benefits was certainly not equitable. As is generally the case in politics dominated by pro-growth coalitions, development interests gained proportionally more than others.[7] Nonetheless, the large majority of the population felt sufficiently benefited by change to find it politically acceptable. Thus, there was no politically effective challenge to the idea of supporting growth.

In part this was due to the broader conditions of the time. The development of infrastructure was strongly shaped by national policy and funding, especially for water and highways, through the Central Valley Project and the interstate highway system. The Cold War and its hot interludes in Korea and Vietnam generated defense industry investment, to both service the Pacific and capture government procurements in the emerging technologically advanced industries. After the extraordinary effort of World War II, this was a period in which the sensation of economic and military power still mingled with the memories of economic disaster and tragedy in the Depression. With migration to the state at unprecedented levels, jobs being created in huge numbers, incomes rising faster than the national rate, and housing demand seemingly unending, it is scarcely surprising that business and labor regarded growth in a positive light.

What is perhaps more surprising is that the state was able to conceive and execute visionary ideas on a extraordinary scale. California established the models for infrastructure and education that the rest of the country and much of the world would follow in later

6. The creation of these systems took place over many years and with a large number of legislative acts and popular votes. Often these were controversial, as illustrated in the case of water by Marc Reisner's *Cadillac Desert* (New York, Penguin Books, 1987). Nonetheless, broad support was necessary for the large bond issues involved, and the necessary referenda did pass.

7. The concept of the pro-growth coalition has been developed by John Mollenkopf in *The Congested City* (Princeton, NJ, Princeton University Press, 1983). He argues that city politics in the U.S. traditionally have been dominated by a coalition of business and labor interests that favored development. Certainly this seems to have been the case in California during the post-war decades.

decades. These were not simply physical systems; they required the creation of complex organizations of high technical quality. Through public action, California created the basis for efficient production and an educated labor force that resulted in increasing productivity and income, which in turn propelled the state's rise from a peripheral to a central position in the U.S. economy. California's political leaders during this time made many mistakes, but they were able to recognize the nature of the forces at work, and they succeeded in making decisions that served the state well in the years that followed. However, they could not construct a consensus that was lasting.

Collapse of the Pro-Growth Consensus

During the 1970s the state's policies toward growth and development shifted dramatically. Both Republican and Democratic administrations rejected the policies of the earlier period, although their expressed objectives differed. The Reagan governorship sought to reduce taxes and public expenditures, targeting higher education especially. The Brown administration sought to reduce infrastructure expenditures, rejecting highways and large water projects as socially undesirable. Why did the consensus on growth, development, and public investment break down, even though population growth continued, albeit at a somewhat reduced level? No simple explanation is sufficient.

We may see the end of the pro-growth consensus as reflecting both external and internal shifts. The world changed in profound ways in the 1970s. Most visible was the rapid increase in oil prices in the early and late years of the decade, which created international chaos and recession. California, as an oil-dependent state, was seriously affected by the price increases and forced to adjust. The dominance of the automobile as a mode of transportation was called into question, together with the lavish use of energy to which the state's economy had become accustomed. Policies that relied on these means to accommodate growth began to be widely criticized.

Painful and politically costly as those events were, they were less important than the deeper shifts occurring in the competitive position of U.S. industrial production in relation to the rest of the world. Despite the remarkable rise of the electronics industry in Silicon Valley and the Los Angeles region, U.S. productivity ceased to grow at its former pace, and virtually all manufacturing sectors found themselves increasingly at a competitive disadvantage in world trade. Since the U.S. was a free-trade economy to a large degree, this meant that the domestic market also was opened to fierce competition, which was reinforced by the high value of the dollar against other currencies. Thanks to two decades of enormous growth, by 1970 California had become a major industrial power in virtually all sectors except basic steel. By 1985, following the worst recession since the 1930s, California had lost proportionally more of its industrial production and employment than had the more visibly impacted northeastern and midwestern states.[8] The state's economy was saved by the dynamism of the growing high-technology sectors, the huge defense build-up in the early 1980s, and the long-term shift from manufacturing to service-sector production and employment, which was much less affected by external competition.

State population growth faltered in the mid-1970s and again in the early 1980s, but it did not decline, even in the face of high unemployment. Nonetheless, the impacts of industrial contraction and slowing productivity were felt in incomes and translated into a growing reluctance to absorb rising tax burdens. The "growth dividend" of the post-war period was a product of increasing productivity. With rising incomes, people were less likely to question increasing taxes for public investments and services. But as gains in productivity and real incomes slowed, this willingness declined. Governor Reagan reflected this in his fiscal austerity at the beginning of the decade; by 1978 it exploded into the taxpayer revolt that produced Proposition 13 and later the Gann amendment to the state constitution. In the struggle for resources that ensued, new large-scale investments in water development or transportation became impossible to support politically, and education no longer commanded wide public support.

Other changes acted in concert with the disappearance of the growth dividend. Rising environmental awareness, on both a world and a local scale, led to questions about the impact of development on environmental quality. People in California had become accustomed to environmental amenities, which they sought to protect by

<hr>

8. See Michael B. Teitz and Philip Shapira, "Growth and Turbulence in the California Economy," in Lloyd Rodwing and Hidehiko Sazanami (eds.), *Deindustrialization and Regional Economic Transformation*, Boston, Unwin Hyman, 1989.

contesting large investments in freeways and water systems. The Peripheral Canal is a good example of a major project that, while it might have attracted opposition, would not have been defeated two decades earlier. Ironically, however, Californians had also become accustomed to high levels of service, especially in highway transportation. This was due in large part to the excess capacity created during the pro-growth years that allowed people to drive in urban areas at speeds unequaled virtually anywhere else in the world. It was not until that excess capacity became used up, first in Los Angeles, and later in most urban areas, that congestion and declining service levels were fully experienced. By then, unfortunately, Californians had become accustomed both to low taxes and to easy automobile transportation, a combination that could not be sustained.

Similarly incompatible priorities for taxation, public investment, and environmental quality are found in the case of housing. During the pro-growth period, housing development in the state was remarkably rapid, with supply generally meeting demand and prices stable. Despite the extraordinary increase in demand, California housing prices did not grow faster than those in the nation as a whole. This development was sustained by a system for constructing the necessary urban infrastructure, especially access highways, water, sewers, and schools, that spread its cost over the larger population. It was paid for either by the national government or through bonded indebtedness and general fund tax revenues. The result was cheap suburban housing, built at low densities with publicly funded facilities, extending outwards from the principal metropolitan cores in the state.

This model of development produced affordable new housing for middle-income people, enabling them to enter into home ownership. It was not equitable, in the sense that the costs of infrastructure were not fully borne by the immediate recipients, although in the long term mobility would allow a large proportion of the population to participate if they bought newer homes. The poor and non-homeowning groups paid for new infrastructure, but gained only through the filtering down of better housing released by movers, and through the absence of competition for older housing, which was not attractive in comparison with relatively inexpensive, new, and accessible suburban homes.

Such a model of development could not withstand the stresses of the 1970s. As a way of producing inexpensive housing, it collapsed in the face of the forces described above, together with the changing structure of households in the state. The new urban areas were partially planned, but often lacked amenities, such as parks, and relied almost entirely upon automobile transportation. Such areas were especially vulnerable to rising oil prices and declining environmental quality as the fragments coalesced into the enormous masses of urban development exemplified by Los Angeles, with its rapidly growing numbers of vehicles, miles driven, and increasing air pollution. Inflation during the 1970s, brought on in part by the rising cost of energy, created direct pressures on housing. Within urban areas, rising energy and transportation costs refocused attention on existing housing, especially in more accessible and environmentally desirable locations, creating competition and sharply rising prices.

These impacts were reinforced by shifts on both the supply and demand sides of the housing market. The recession of 1973-74 sharply reduced housing production. During the subsequent recovery and inflation, house prices rose rapidly. With real interest rates lagging behind inflation, housing became the most effective form of inflation hedge and source of capital gain open to the average household. That household was becoming younger, smaller, and much more numerous as the baby boom generation entered the market. Furthermore, even in the face of recessions at the beginning of the 1980s, migration to California continued, its sources shifting to Asia and Latin America rather than elsewhere in the U.S. However, this surge in demand occurred precisely at the time when resistance to tax increases and support for environmental regulation were coming into full flower. Tax limitation laws and federal cutbacks were ending much of the public financing of local development infrastructure, which therefore had to be financed from the development itself, through fiscal zoning of various kinds. Meanwhile, environmental opposition was pushing developers toward larger and more expensive houses. Serviced land in the major metropolitan areas became a very scarce commodity, pushing up housing prices even further.

The net result was much higher housing costs. From being a state with relatively inexpensive new housing, California was transformed into one with the most expensive new and existing housing in the U.S. Only on the distant edges of metropolitan areas and in the

Central Valley could moderately priced new housing be produced, and even there prices rose substantially as the 1980s drew to a close. Californians had realized their objectives of low property taxation and tighter control of development. But these goals were achieved only at the cost of much higher priced housing and a rising proportion of income spent on housing by all except those homeowners who did not move. In particular, the housing situation of the poor became increasingly difficult as older, low-cost housing at the cores of the metropolitan areas was demolished to make way for central city redevelopment, even as the demand for older urban housing by smaller affluent households increased. Although homelessness cannot be attributed entirely to the loss of affordable housing stock, that loss has certainly increased the numbers of people affected.

The collapse of the pro-growth consensus has affected many other areas of California's development, most notably education. Yet, for all its wide-reaching effects, the building of a new coalition and policy framework to deal with growth has been slow and hesitant. It is worth noting that the fundamental changes that have shaped the shift in California development policy—declining productivity, industrial restructuring and global competition, rising tax resistance, growing environmental awareness—generally began during the 1970s or earlier. Their consequences were fully felt only in the 1980s, in part because overcapacity in major infrastructure systems allowed absorption of continuing growth, and in part because of the reluctance of the legislature, the development industry, and the public to recognize the extent of the change. Various measures have been invented and used to deal with problems as they arose. The next section examines some of these efforts.

Responses to Growth

As growth has continued and problems have emerged, the absence of a broad consensus has not prevented responses to those problems. On the contrary, a rising level of public concern has been reflected in an array of attempts to deal with the consequences of development. However, these efforts, in contrast with those of the earlier period, have been for the most part reactive and limited in character. Where political constituencies could be assembled, action has occurred, but important areas of policy have been neglected.

Only recently have more comprehensive measures been seriously proposed.

The number and variety of attempts to deal with growth are too great to be fully described here. However, they may be summarized in two broad groups, both of which reflect the creation of political constituencies responding to specific problems. For purposes of this discussion, they will be identified as functional responses and jurisdictional responses. Functional responses deal with growth by addressing its symptoms by broad legislation, while jurisdictional responses deal with growth by controlling or managing development within specific locations.

Functional responses to growth comprise measures at the national, state, or local levels that attempt to deal with problems of a particular type, for example, air quality, traffic congestion, or toxic pollution. Laws dealing with such functional problems have been enacted in response to widespread perceptions of declining standards of performance in clearly identifiable and specific domains that are often associated with particular technical or scientific expertise. They represent, as it were, a symptomatic response to growth.

Legislation designed to deal with functional problems of growth is often complex. In the case of air quality, the debates at the national and state levels have been going on for two decades and involve major differences among interest groups and competing theories of response. Conflicts abound over the sources of air pollution, especially static versus mobile sources, each with its interest groups. Similarly, the types of pollutants and the risks associated with them are debated, with more complexity added recently by the concern over carbon dioxide and its role in global warming. Cutting across these distinctions are arguments about appropriate responses that range from direct regulation, which is in effect quantity rationing, to market and price rationing, as means to affect individual and group behavior. The result has been a complex web of laws and organizations that are largely uncoordinated and sometimes work at cross-purposes. Nonetheless, these efforts comprise the most important element of public policy influencing growth at this time.

In contrast with functional responses, we may point to those reactions to growth that seek to deal with development at the local level. In California, especially, the tradition of home rule—the ability of local governments to deal with their problems as they see them—

is very powerful. It encourages communities to deal with problems such as those produced by growth within the boundaries of their own local governments. The most evident form of this response is local growth control or growth management. Such efforts typically do not rely on the impetus of legislation at a larger geographic scale. Rather, they seek to preserve the qualities of lifestyle and environment that are valued by local constituencies by directly addressing growth itself.

Like functional responses, local growth controls reflect conflicts among constituencies, especially between existing residents and development interests. Specific functional problems, notably traffic, often are seen as the motivating force, but at heart the model of intervention is to regulate development directly by moratoria on construction, limits on the level of permissible development, or the creation of urban limit lines and greenbelts. The domain of such controls is limited by the jurisdiction within which constituencies are able to work effectively, and therefore they tend to be local in scale. Although some other states have implemented attempts at growth management, in California the only statewide effort of this type was the attempt to control development on the coast. The Coastal Act resulted from a legislative initiative that was similar in many respects to other initiatives at much smaller scales, especially in its origins in grassroots organizations. Its subsequent history has shown the difficulty of such an effort at the statewide level.

There are conflicting views as to the most important motivating factors in local growth regulation. Some commentators believe that one impetus for local ballot initiatives for growth management actually may be the desire of developers for a stable and predictable environment for development. However, such a desire would not exist without the possibility of regulation of development. The motivation of existing residents who support growth controls is primarily to maintain stability in the residential environment, which may be threatened by virtually any form of development. Hence, the common attribution of a NIMBY (Not In My Back Yard) motive to such efforts.

Whatever the motivation, the form and impact of local growth regulations tend to be adverse to development. However, because such efforts are almost entirely conducted at the local level, their impacts may do more to shift the location of development than to impede it as a whole. In vigorous markets, the net result is likely to be lower density and more dispersed development, which paradoxically may add to traffic congestion and air pollution at a regional scale. Where commuting to central locations is a major factor in traffic generation, this impact is likely to have serious consequences.

These two groups of growth responses are not mutually exclusive. Rather, they intersect in a variety of ways. For example, functional problems inevitably have spatial manifestations. Thus these responses need an areal as well as a functional domain. However, the areas involved do not necessarily reflect community boundaries or governmental jurisdictions. Air or water quality management, for example, require the capacity to respond in terms of natural air basins or watersheds. As a result, there is a tendency for these functional efforts to result in the creation of special purpose governmental entities that have an ambiguous position in relation to local governments. In California, air quality management districts or regional transportation commissions have jurisdictions that overlap with those of local governments. The potential for conflict, or at least unclear responsibility, is always present, and it may be enhanced by the way in which local governments influence the governance of the functional agencies.

Even more important is the growing perception that functional or symptomatic responses to growth, such as air pollution control, involve sequences of causation that go far beyond their original realm of concern. The recognition that automobile pollution is affected not only by the numbers of cars and their pollution control equipment but also by commute patterns, which in turn depend on location of employment and housing, has shifted the basic assumptions under which air pollution control agencies are working. As agencies such as the Southern California Air Quality Management District move toward this stance, their focus shifts from air pollution to land use regulation. In this mode, such agencies come more and more to resemble local growth management entities, but operating at a regional rather than a local scale. However, in most instances, they do not have the legitimacy of local governments as elected bodies, nor do they have a general mandate for planning. The result may be the subordination of land use planning to a single functional concern, which is generally regarded as an undesirable way in which to handle this complex area. Combined with the absence of elective legitimacy, the status and public acceptance of such agencies may be questionable.

The recognition that growth impacts are complex, extending across functional realms and jurisdictions, has given rise recently to a renewal of interest in planning for growth at a larger scale. In some respects, these proposals resemble expanded versions of older functionally directed legislation. For example, Proposition 111, passed in June 1990, raises the gasoline tax, earmarks funds for transportation, and relaxes the Gann limit on state expenditure. This initiative also calls for transportation systems management in the form of congestion management plans at the county level, opening a wide avenue for growth management.

An even more recent effort, the Brown bill, AB 242, would establish regional development and infrastructure agencies to prepare regional general plans covering air and water quality, transportation, housing, spheres of influence, and capital facilities. Local land use plans would be required to be consistent with the regional plans. Such an agency would succeed existing regional agencies, and local governments would be required to participate. If passed, this bill would mark a major change in attitude on the part of the state toward regional planning. In one sense, it is the latest in a long line of attempts to create a regional level of planning in the state. Up to now, they have all failed, but that does not mean that state legislation is impossible in the new conditions that now exist.

Even at the local level, recognition of interdependency and the intransigence of problems has occurred to a significant degree. Both in the San Francisco Bay Area and in southern California, attempts are in process to create regional organizations to deal with the complexity of growth and development. BayVision 2020 is a regional commission intended to create a blueprint for solutions to regional problems. The commission has substantial support among influential groups, including some favoring and some opposing further growth. Its impact is uncertain at this time, since it has not yet reported any conclusions. Furthermore, the absence on the commission of any local elected officials may leave it open to easy criticism. Nonetheless, its formation represents an important stage in recognition of the regional nature of growth and its consequences.

Positive as many of these diverse responses are, they do not add up to a coherent policy for addressing growth in California, nor do they reflect the full range of policy tools that might be utilized. It is to these questions that we now turn.

A Growth Policy for Caliornia

The extraordinary level of interest in growth management, and the spate of activity now occurring suggests that there would be real benefit from a review of the key goals and constraints that a policy for growth in California should address. Added to this, there is need for debate about the range of policy options that it might utilize. The aim of this section is to explore these two topics. Before doing so, we need to ask why the state should have any explicit policy toward development.

The Case for State Growth Policy

Should the state have a growth policy? Certainly, there is no evident agreement among public officials or the public on the need for such a policy. Few would question the desirability of economic growth and higher incomes for the state's population, but equating that goal with concrete actions to deal with population growth and urban development is far less likely. Despite the breakdown of consensus on growth, the state has done quite well in the past two decades, managing to absorb large numbers of migrants, yet sustaining its position within the U.S. as a dynamic center of economic development. Nonetheless, there is good evidence that the future may not be simply a continuation of the past. Within the state, the character of growth and its consequences are changing as environmental concerns increasingly shape people's perceptions. At the same time, California faces a more difficult competitive environment in the larger world, an environment in which good policy choices may be the key to economic success. Countries such as Japan, Taiwan, and Singapore have shown that managed development is not a pipe dream; rather, it is a source of great competitive advantage if it is done well.

More specifically, there are a number of reasons why growth and development choices made now are likely to be critical. At the broadest level, the state needs to be able to sustain economic growth and productivity in order to accommodate the transformation in the population that is now occurring. The changing population of California over the next twenty years, as the white population ages and relatively decreases in comparison to minorities, will require growth in order to maintain social stability and opportunity. If in-migration continues at its recent, historically high rates, the pressure for development will be immense. Even if in-migration declines, the upwardly mobile, younger population will demand housing and urban amenities comparable to those of the majority.

In the face of restrictive behavior in established urban and metropolitan areas, these populations will face two choices. Either they will vote for increased density in the areas that they control politically, or they will move to areas in the state where development is still encouraged. The first outcome is not likely, given shifting patterns of preference within existing urban areas and recent experience in Los Angeles and San Francisco, where popular pressure has consistently reduced densities. The second outcome is likely to mean a continuation of current forms of development, in which fiscal pressures favor low-density, automobile-oriented development on distant urban fringes. In the absence of major technological innovations, this pattern of development is unlikely to be able to meet environmental standards, especially for air quality. Furthermore, it threatens unique and major resources of environmental quality and agricultural lands in the state.

The case of the Central Valley is central to this scenario, although a similar pattern also exists in the coastal counties and in southern California. The next twenty years will almost certainly see the full force of development of a Central Valley metropolis. As discussed above, the pace of growth has already accelerated to a remarkable degree, and it shows no sign of slackening. These will be the critical years for development, when irreversible decisions are made that will shape the welfare of millions of people. And yet, unlike the other metropolitan areas in the state, there is no dominant governmental entity in the area, no Los Angeles, San Francisco, or San Diego. Despite the mistakes that were made, those governmental entities could and did make important collective decisions on development.

In contrast, the Central Valley area has a moderately strong focus in Sacramento, and an array of counties and cities strung out in linear fashion along U.S. 99 and I-5. This is a recipe for potential disaster in several respects. Los Angeles has demonstrated the inadequacy of auto-oriented urban development on the densest freeway grid yet constructed. The traffic and air pollution problems to be anticipated in a linear city are even worse. The prospect now is for a metropolis created by the coalescence of many independent entities, each acting in its own interest. Given their fiscal structure, collective development decisions will not be made at all, or will reflect local bargaining. Locating important metropolitan facilities will be difficult, and it is likely to result in inefficient solutions. This fragmentation of development planning almost certainly also threatens the most productive agricultural area in the world. Although farmland should not be slavishly preserved, the loss of a unique resource due to inefficient development would be poor long-term policy.

It might be argued that this form of urban development, which reproduces suburban growth without an urban organizing framework, provides for social choice among alternative environments, amenities, public expenditures, and cost levels. That may be true at the level of the individual household, but the urban structure that emerges is likely to be inefficient in terms of travel patterns and will generate air pollution, while not providing a full range of residential choice. Rather than having to absorb draconian changes in the future as pollution levels and energy costs rise, a more effective solution should consider the structural efficiency of the urban system in these terms first, and then find a way to realize the benefits of a disaggregated system of local governance.

Although the Central Valley is probably the most critical area in terms of urban structure and investment decisions, other regions in the state have similar problems. For San Bernardino and Riverside counties, like their counterparts on the fringes of the Bay Area, the costs of growth in the present pattern are likely to prove very high in the coming decades. And yet, in the absence of either regulation or incentives to produce growth in other forms and areas, there is little likelihood of change.

If, indeed, it makes sense to think seriously about policy intervention in California's growth and development, two sorts of questions need to be addressed. First, we need to clarify goals or objectives and the variables in which they are expressed. One of the key benefits of public intervention is that it makes possible a response to objectives that would not automatically be served by individual or group choices, but which are nonetheless important to the public welfare. The problem, of course, is that such objectives are not universally subscribed to and that public priorities must be established through political processes. Second, we must understand the full range of policy instruments and the associated variables that affect realization of goals. These instrumental concerns are often technical in character, but they are not purely so. Ideology, belief, values, interests, and prejudices are also entwined with the perceptions of instruments as they are with objectives.

Growth Policy Goals and Constraints

Goals for development policy at the state level will inevitably reflect the clash of interests, but an argument may also be made for recognition of benefits that are achievable only through public action. Thus, in states that have adopted development policies there tend to be broad goals reflecting widely held desires for economic growth, balanced development, environmental quality, and individual opportunity. Another level of goals reflects more specific areas of public discontent, for example, traffic congestion, air quality, housing costs, open space, and fiscal problems. In thinking about goals for state action, it is appropriate to consider both of these levels in the context of what the state can do best in comparison with other levels of government.

Given the tradition of home rule in California and the high level of disagreement about public policy and governmental roles that has existed for the past two decades, it seems as though the state's goals should be carefully demarcated. This does not imply that their scope should be narrow. On the contrary, the state is the logical level at which to view California's development from a broad perspective, establishing the framework within which other levels of government and communities pursue their own objectives. In this context, it is appropriate to ask what is missing in those local and regional perspectives.

Perhaps the most striking gap is the absence of a view of the state as an evolving and dynamic set of regions. Neither within the existing metropolitan regions themselves, nor at the state level, is there a voice for a vision of California as a place made up of places. Urban and regional development is a complex process that cannot be centrally planned. That is evident from the experience of countries that have attempted it. However, development also occurs within an economic, social, and political context that is established by public action, with its web of laws, expectations, and customs. That context can be more or less consciously shaped. As the world and its processes grow more complex, it is becoming evident that formation of the framework within which development occurs solely by the aggregation of narrow choices is insufficient. Such a process may ignore structural requirements that are critical to a larger settlement pattern that works.

At the level of the state, then, what is necessary is an overview of development that regards regional and metropolitan growth at the most general level, and asks whether that growth is creating a structure of settlement that will be effective in the long term. In this, development policy should match economic policy, which asks whether the state's economy is heading in a productive direction; whether the framework of laws enhances the creation of a viable economy. The goals implicit in such a view of development policy are neither to prevent growth nor to enhance it at any cost. Rather, they should reflect an aspiration for a workable urban and regional structure in the state, together with its associated infrastructure and services, that can meet the needs of the future population. How large that population will be cannot be determined, although it surely will be substantially larger than it is at present. What is necessary now is to ensure that the irreversible decisions about development are made in a way that enhances the likelihood of a good and productive environment for the state over the foreseeable future.

In California there has been little real debate about these questions. Yet the process of development each day is inexorably answering them in detail. As we have seen from the experience of the past forty years, the results of such a process are too often unsatisfactory in the aggregate. Few people want another Los Angeles, but the system of development that we have will almost certainly produce one. If the state is to avoid either a continuation of its present problems in new locations, or simplistic "solutions" imposed by the initiative process, it must find a way to establish a broad vision of how its urban structure will evolve in the future.

Of course, such a vision is difficult to articulate and realize. It implies the establishment of priorities for location of development and of key infrastructure facilities, both of which have been extraordinarily difficult in recent decades. It suggests consideration of new forms of transportation technology that will be costly and difficult to finance. New forms of housing and settlement patterns are likely to be necessary, with all the problems of introduction that such changes imply. And it will generate inevitable opposition both from those likely to be impacted by development and from those who resist any constraints. Nonetheless, the larger goals of a productive economy, a high-quality environment, and a society of opportunity will be increasingly difficult to realize without such a vision in a world and a state that both have more people and are more interdependent than ever before.

Choice of Policy Instruments

The problem of appropriate policy instruments and the way in which they might be used is still open, even if the need for some form of policy intervention is accepted. At present, there are two major theoretical perspectives about policy instruments for addressing the problems of growth. Conventionally, such instruments and policies are distinguished as utilizing direct regulation on the one hand, or pricing and market-like mechanisms on the other. However, many possibilities cut across these distinctions, often in subtle ways. Simple ideological selection of instruments is rarely ideal, though it is often the starting point for debate. Furthermore, we may conceive of a policy framework that employs these mechanisms at different levels of scale, from statewide to regional to local. Depending on how sensitive behaviors and outcomes are to local conditions, alternative instruments and scales may be appropriate. To add even further to this complexity, the question of what type of organization is most appropriate for achieving public objectives with different instruments at differing scales has scarcely been addressed. Given the vast range of public, quasi-public, and private organizations engaged in growth issues, this is not a trivial concern. Thus, in thinking about growth policy, we need to address at least these three dimensions—instrumental theory, scale of application, and form of organization for implementation.

If we follow this schema, what can be said about the responses to growth up to this time? First, the dominant instrumental theory that has been used is regulation. Direct control is appealing for its concreteness and apparent direct connection between objectives and means. Thus, most recent efforts to shape growth and its consequences have been regulatory in character, from zoning to emissions control. This contrasts both with the use of infrastructure investment as an instrument for shaping development in the earlier period, and with proposals for using pricing or other market mechanisms to achieve social objectives that have been advanced more recently by economists.

Although it is unlikely that regulation could ever be replaced entirely by such mechanisms in development policy, there is a good case to be made that it has been overused and that the results are at least inefficient. In environmental policy at the national level, there is increasing interest in using pricing to reflect the full costs of resource use, and in California a water market is slowly emerging from years of debate. In transportation there is a growing recognition that no amount of freeway capacity can satisfy traffic demands in the absence of pricing, rationing, or congestion. If congestion is unacceptable on the grounds of time loss and air pollution, then pricing or rationing of some kind will occur. Similarly, the substitution of cash payments for free parking, together with substantial parking charges, is gaining favor as a means of encouraging alternative modes of transportation.

For development, such mechanisms need to be explored much further. For the most part, they have been used primarily for revenue raising in order to offset the tax limitations imposed in the late 1970s. As such, their effects have often been to encourage lower-density and higher-cost housing, or to divert development to more peripheral locations. Thinking about ways to utilize market-based mechanisms to encourage development that enhances urban structure should be an important project for the next decade.

Shaping urban growth will also require the use of infrastructure investment, especially highway and transit funding. As California increases in population density, the viability of alternative forms of transportation will increase. In Europe the process of creating a single economy is already taking advantage of the development of high-speed ground transportation systems, such as MAGLEV, to shape a new pattern of urbanization. National governments and cities are competing to secure their place in the European urban system by virtue of their location on the emerging network. In many respects, California offers an excellent opportunity to explore a similar development in the U.S. Now is the time to begin serious consideration of such a system for the state. That consideration should take explicitly into account the impact of such a system on urbanization and regional development in California. Implementation of a system should not simply serve existing patterns of urbanization, but also shape the urban system itself.

The second aspect of policy design and implementation set out above concerns the level at which it is directed. From the state perspective, the most important elements here are, first, an effort at the state level to monitor and influence development at the broadest scale and, second, the creation of effective policy direction at the regional level.

The need for a state perspective on growth has already been discussed. How that perspective can be achieved is no simple matter. State policy will always be developed between the governor and the legislature. No other institution can take over that function. What can be done is to improve the visibility of development issues and the quality of information upon which judgments can be based. Such a function should include monitoring of development, research on its nature and the forces driving it, and the ability to answer the governor's or legislators' questions about development and its impacts. This would be an intelligence function, capable both of gathering information and of interpreting it with a high degree of sophistication. As the eighth largest economy in the world, California has remarkably poor information about itself. The legacy of an earlier era, one of small state government and limited access, which worked during the years of growth consensus, no longer functions in a time of much greater complexity. This function would enhance the intuitive understanding of the state by its political decision makers, an understanding that is now inadequate despite the efforts of state staff under conditions of limited budgets. It is time for California to develop the capability to understand and manage its own growth that is appropriate to a rich and populous state.

At the regional level the state's principal task is to ensure that the regions have the political and organizational structure to make good collective decisions about those aspects of development that are their concern. Avoidance of central direction means that this includes most decisions. Effective implementation means that the power to make difficult decisions should not be diluted by local vetoes over regional issues. Such a structure need not be a single form for all regions, but each will require a state mandate.

If those mandates can be developed in cooperation with regional initiatives, so much the better. In fact, they are unlikely to be achieved in any other way. Nonetheless, local officials and constituencies ultimately must embrace regional decisionmaking powers to solve their most important problems. If there is one lesson from the existing councils of governments, it is that voluntary federations are too weak to do the job of supporting metropolitan development. And special-purpose agencies inevitably are distorted by their single functional nature. How powers ultimately are allocated will depend on political processes, but if there is no commitment at the state level to regional decisionmaking power, then creation of effective regional organizations is unlikely. If there are no effective regional organizations for development, then the outlook for California's environment will be bleak as the state's population continues to grow, which it surely will.

The author is indebted to many people for discussion and ideas. Foremost among them are John Landis, Al Lipson, Lance Barnett, Elizabeth Deakin, Peter Hall, John Kirlin, and the participants in a California Economic Development Corporation workshop on growth in California.

MANAGING CALIFORNIA-
MEXICO RELATIONS

Katrina Burgess and Abraham Lowenthal

4

A dramatic increase in the two-way flow of goods, capital, technology, people, and
cultural influences has brought Mexico and California closer together today than at
any time since the state gained independence from Mexico in 1848. The strong ties
between the two countries present unprecedented opportunities for mutual gain,
but also create economic and social problems that must be dealt with jointly if
benefits are to be realized.

Policy challenges involve the promotion of closer economic ties; minimizing the
negative effects of illegal flows of people, goods, and services; managing the pace of
border development to ease pressures on infrastructure and the environment; and
enhancing opportunities for Mexican immigrants in California, whose presence in
ever growing numbers may well hold the key to the state's economic future.

Many of the important policy choices facing state and local officials
in California during the 1990s and into the twenty-first century will
be shaped by the state's contiguity with Mexico. It is time for California's leaders to focus on how best to meet the challenges and opportunities presented by Mexico's proximity.

A single political entity until 1848, Mexico and California were
divided by nineteenth-century wars and intrigues into what was to
become the most populous, diverse, and highly industrialized of the
United States of America to the north and a larger, relatively poor,
and unevenly developing country to the south. For many decades,
Mexico and California followed very different patterns of development, becoming more unlike each other with every successive
generation.

In recent years, however, the two societies have begun to converge. The entire region from Cancun to Eureka is more closely
intertwined at the end of the twentieth century than at any time
since Mexico lost control over its rich northernmost territory. It is
increasingly hard to define the dividing line between Mexico and
California. The border is crossed more than sixty million times each

year, and goods and capital travel between the two regions with rising frequency. Decisions and actions taken in Mexico have major consequences for California, and those taken in California strongly affect Mexico.

This chapter maps the impact of Mexico's proximity upon California, and upon policy choices facing the state's public officials. Its aim is to help California officials improve the chances that Mexico's net effect on California will be consistently positive in the years ahead and mitigate the adverse consequences for the state of sharing a 200-mile border with a developing country undergoing disruptive change.

Changing California-Mexico Relations

In the last twenty years relations between Mexico and California have been transformed by what Clark Reynolds has dubbed "silent integration."[1] A dramatic increase in the two-way flow of goods, capital, technology, information, people, and cultural influences has created a complex web of relationships between the two regions. Although they continue to be separate politically, California and Mexico are becoming linked in transnational labor and capital markets, which in turn facilitate closer social and cultural ties. The border that formally divides them is increasingly less meaningful than the economic and demographic changes that are pulling them together.

The silent integration between California and Mexico reflects broader trends in the global economy. Technological advances, particularly in transportation and communications, have made it much easier for both capital and labor to cross national frontiers in search of economic opportunity. As firms move through the product cycle, they develop multiple centers of production to provide the combination of low-skill labor and advanced technology necessary to remain competitive. Entire villages in the developing world are becoming linked through migration to labor markets in the industrialized countries. Trade flows, in turn, are bolstered by intra-firm transactions and by the increased purchasing power of less developed communities integrated into migratory networks.

---

1. Clark Reynolds, "Mexican-U.S. Interdependence: Economic and Social Perspectives," in Clark W. Reynolds and Carlos Tello (eds.), *U.S.-Mexican Relations: Economic and Social Aspects*, Palo Alto, Stanford University Press, 1983, p. 21.

Economic globalization has contributed to a highly asymmetrical interdependence between Mexico and California. Mexico has come to rely heavily on California for capital, technology, markets, and jobs. Mexico shipped over $3 billion worth of goods to the state in 1988, and machinery and electrical equipment account for more than one-third of the goods sold to Mexico by California firms. The most dynamic sector of the Mexican economy is the *maquiladora* industry,[2] which has become Mexico's second largest source of foreign exchange and is rapidly transforming southern California and northern Mexico into an integrated region of production. California also hosts an estimated 300,000 cyclical workers from Mexico and at least two million permanent immigrants.

Mexico's dependence on California has been deepened by the ambitious program of economic liberalization launched by the Mexican government since the mid-1980s. In an effort to strengthen its ties to the global marketplace, Mexico has joined the General Agreement on Tariffs and Trade, eliminated most import permits, slashed tariffs, adopted a more market-based exchange rate, sold off or reorganized more than 700 state-owned enterprises, liberalized its foreign investment regulations, and taken steps to re-privatize its banking sector. In early 1990 Mexican officials began consultations with the United States over the possibility of negotiating a free trade agreement. All these reforms have linked Mexico's development prospects even more closely to the global economy, particularly to dynamic regions such as California.

Changes in the international environment have likewise increased California's dependence on Mexico. Faced with competition from abroad, the state is being forced to increase productivity, reduce costs, and rely more heavily on exports to fuel economic growth. Mexico, which is California's third largest export market and a major supplier of low-cost labor to California firms on both sides of the border, is playing a key role in helping the state to meet these challenges.

---

2. *Maquiladoras,* or in-bond plants, were established under Mexico's 1965 Border Industrialization Program. They operate under special tariff and investment rules that enable them to be 100 percent foreign-owned and to import all raw materials, parts and equipment, and machinery duty-free. The program is supported by U.S. trade law, which allows U.S.-based companies to reexport the final products into the United States, paying duty only on the value added in Mexico.

Interdependence is only part of silent integration, however. California's domestic landscape is being transformed by the presence of Mexicans in California and by the shared challenges of border development. Not only is the state tied to Mexico through trade, investment, and finance, but it is evolving into an increasingly transnational economy and society. As a result, even quintessentially domestic issues such as education, social services, and housing are affected by Mexico's proximity.

Silent integration raises important policy choices for California public officials. Some of the linkages between the two regions are mutually beneficial and should be encouraged. Others threaten to become serious problems if not managed effectively. Although California officials cannot control the process of silent integration, they can enhance the prospects that Mexico's proximity will have a net positive impact.

Contributions to the California Economy

Over the past two decades, and particularly in the last few years, Mexico has become an important player in California's economic development. Although restructuring in both regions is likely to change Mexico's role in the California economy—increasing California's demand for workers in the service and trade sectors and heightening Mexico's importance as a supplier of goods, services, and markets—the two economies will continue to be highly complementary. As Reynolds has observed, "if the United States is to preserve its economic power and social progress in an increasingly interdependent world, it must be prepared to exchange goods and services, labor, capital, and technology with Mexico on a scale unprecedented outside its own borders."[3] This is especially true for California.

Immigrant Labor

Immigration is at the heart of silent integration. Drawn by favorable job prospects and economic prosperity, an unprecedented number of Mexicans are coming to California to live and work. Latinos, mostly of Mexican origin, comprise nearly 25 percent of the state's thirty million residents, compared to 12 percent in 1970; their share

---

3. *Supra* note 1, p. 45.

of the state's population is projected to reach 30 percent by the year 2000. Only Mexico City has more Mexican residents than Los Angeles.

For most of the twentieth century, between half and two-thirds of California's new residents were accounted for by migration from other parts of the United States. Since the 1980s, however, the largest single contributor to California's population growth has been foreign immigration. Nearly one in two new California residents is a recent immigrant, and more than half of the 250,000 foreign immigrants who come to the state each year are from Mexico.[4] The vast majority of Mexican immigrants in California live in urban areas and are employed in low-skill jobs in services, retail, construction, and light manufacturing.[5] These urban immigrants have played a crucial role in allowing California to resist the deindustrialization of its economy. During the 1970s California experienced an increase in blue-collar jobs at twice the national rate and an expansion in manufacturing employment at nearly four times the national rate.[6] Although the state lost ground in traditional industries such as steel, rubber, and autos, it has continued to enjoy rapid growth in high-tech sectors such as aerospace, communications, and electronics and in labor-intensive sectors such as textiles, apparel, and furniture.

California's competitive edge in manufacturing is closely related to its access to low-cost Mexican labor. An Urban Institute study suggests that 53,000 manufacturing jobs and 37,000 jobs related to manufacturing would have been lost in California if no Mexican immigration had taken place between 1970 and 1985.[7] Mexican labor has been especially vital to the garment, electronics, furniture, rubber products, and food processing industries. Faced with intense foreign competition, these industries have come to depend heavily on the low-cost immigrant labor provided by small, non-unionized

---

4. *California Population Statistics*, Palo Alto, Center for the Continuing Study of the California Economy, 1988, p. 51.
5. Although only 10 to 15 percent of the state's Mexican immigrants work in the fields, California agriculture continues to rely heavily on Mexican workers, who represent nearly three-quarters of its labor force.
6. Thomas Muller and Thomas J. Espenshade, *The Fourth Wave: California's Newest Immigrants*, Washington, D.C., Urban Institute Press, 1985, p. 54.
7. *Ibid.*, pp. 149-50.

firms operating as subcontractors.[8] Despite popular perceptions that Mexican immigration has hurt the California economy, most Californians have realized net gains from immigrant labor. Mexican immigrants do not typically compete with native U.S. workers for the same jobs, and the economic expansion that has accompanied immigrant labor has kept earning levels in California competitive with those elsewhere in the United States. Except for Latinos, whose wages are close to the national average, workers in California have substantially higher earnings than their counterparts nationwide.[9]

The underlying cause of the wage declines and job losses that have occurred in California since the early 1980s has not been immigration but economic globalization. Unless firms can cut costs at home, they are likely to move their operations abroad or to go out of business. By enabling California to adjust more slowly to increased foreign competition and maintain its economic dynamism at a time when other parts of the United States have been in decline, immigrant labor has served as a buffer against the dislocating changes taking place in the global economy.[10]

The Maquiladora Industry

The maquiladora industry is a second key component of silent integration. With the collapse of oil prices and the sharp devaluation of the peso in the early 1980s, Mexican wages became among the lowest in the semi-industrialized world. The combination of low labor costs and proximity to the U.S. market generated a dramatic surge of interest in the maquiladoras. Today, nearly 1,800 plants export more than $6 billion worth of goods to the United States each year, mostly in electronics, automotive parts, and textiles. Nearly half of all maquiladoras in Mexico are located along the California-Mexico border, and the majority of these are owned by California-based corporations. In 1987 plants located in Tijuana exported an estimated $1.2 billion in goods to southern California.[11]

8. Wayne Cornelius, "The Persistence of Immigrant-Dominated Firms and Industries in the United States: the Case of California," paper presented at the Second Franco-American Conference on Comparative Migration Studies, Paris, France, June 20-23, 1988.
9. *Supra* note 6, p. 93.
10. *Supra* note 8.
11. Larry Rohter, "Bustling Tijuana Lives Down Hooch and Honky Tonk Past," *New York Times*, August 2, 1989.

Maquiladoras have enabled California manufacturers to compete in world markets without severing ties with the rest of the California economy. Rather than establishing offshore facilities thousands of miles away, these companies have kept their labor-intensive operations close to home. As a result, other sectors of the California economy have shared the benefits of the maquiladora boom. In San Diego the demand for U.S. inputs and maquiladora-related services has contributed to rapid population growth and an unemployment rate of only 3 percent. According to the U.S. International Trade Commission, the maquila payroll generates between $73 million and $95 million each year for the economy of southern California.[12]

In addition to easing the export of jobs by California manufacturers, the maquiladora industry is attracting significant investment to the border region from abroad. A growing number of Asian firms are setting up shop in northern Mexico, particularly in Tijuana. The number of Japanese-owned maquiladoras quadrupled between 1986 and 1989, and Japanese firms now employ 10 percent of the Tijuana work force. Taiwan and South Korea are also establishing a presence in the industry, in an attempt to compete more effectively with Japan and to make up for their recent loss of special tariff breaks under the U.S. System of Generalized Preferences. In order to avoid U.S. duties on reexports, these firms often supply their Mexican plants from California-based subsidiaries, which employ local workers, use local services, and bring trade-related jobs to the state.

Trade

Trade is another aspect of silent integration. Mexico has become California's third largest export market, after Japan and Canada. In 1988 over $6 billion worth of goods passed to and from Mexico through the state's customs districts, representing nearly one-seventh of Mexico's total trade with the United States. An estimated 92,500 California jobs are directly or indirectly tied to exports to Mexico.[13]

Mexico's outward-looking development strategy has enhanced its potential as a market for California products. Exports by California

---

12. Bruce Stokes, "Boom at the Border," *National Journal*, July 29, 1989, p. 1924.
13. The jobs figure is derived from a multiplier developed by the U.S. Department of Commerce, which estimates that every $40,000 of exports translates into one direct or indirect job.

firms to Mexico jumped from $1.9 billion in 1986 to $3.7 billion in 1989. Although some of this growth can be explained by a fall in the U.S. dollar, Mexico's shift from fourth to third place among California's export markets is largely a result of Mexico's economic reforms. Not only have these reforms lowered trade barriers to California goods, but they have attracted the attention of California exporters by generating favorable coverage of Mexico in the U.S. press.

In addition to opening up new markets, Mexico's economic policies are creating a demand for products in which California has a comparative advantage. Recent steps to liberalize Mexico's computer trade, combined with tax incentives for domestic producers, could help boost the Mexican computer market to $3 billion by 1993, or three times its current value. Proposed modifications of Mexico's laws governing intellectual property rights should give high-tech companies an added incentive to establish facilities in Mexico, generating intra-firm transfers across the border. California firms are ideally equipped to benefit from these changes and to supply Mexico with the high-tech goods and services it needs to achieve international competitiveness.

Increased trade with Mexico is currently welcomed by most sectors of the California economy. Exporters are discovering new markets, and consumers enjoy access to low-cost Mexican goods. Even import-sensitive industries such as electronics and textiles have not complained loudly about Mexican competition, perhaps because they are able to compete through the use of low-cost Mexican labor on both sides of the border. Trade relations between the two regions are not friction-free, to be sure. California's agricultural interests have raised strong objections to import competition from Mexico, and labor unions have long been opposed to granting Mexico special U.S. trade preferences. If other sectors in California begin to lose their competitive edge, they may join the efforts of these groups to restrict trade with Mexico.

Finance

Financial capital flows are a fourth component of silent integration. During the late 1970s and early 1980s banks based in California loaned Mexico many billions of dollars. With the onset of Mexico's economic crisis in 1981, the direction of these capital flows shifted, and vast sums flowed from Mexico into California in the form of interest payments and capital flight. Despite the costs of Mexico's economic crisis for its foreign creditors, most major banks in California probably emerged from the period having realized net gains. When Mexico nearly defaulted on its foreign loans in August 1982, California-based banks such as Security Pacific, Bank of America, First Interstate, and Wells Fargo were among Mexico's largest creditors and were highly exposed. Most of them weathered the crisis, however, by resisting requests for new lending, creating loan loss reserves, and selling off part of their Mexican debt on the secondary market. In the meantime, they continued to collect hefty interest payments from the Mexican government.

The main benefit of increased integration for California banks during the last decade has been the billions of dollars deposited in U.S. bank accounts by Mexican nationals. Since the onset of Mexico's economic crisis, capital flight to the United States has been staggering. It is estimated that more than $30 billion left Mexico between 1981 and 1986, and that private deposits by Mexican citizens in U.S. banks grew an average of 26 percent each year between 1981 and 1985. The total value of Mexican assets in the United States is estimated to be $55 billion, more than Mexico's total commercial bank debt.[14]

Significant amounts of Mexican flight capital have come to California. According to local banking officials in San Diego, Mexican exiles brought at least $3 billion to the city between 1976 and 1985. Mexicans are said to hold a total of $250 million in cash deposits and other liquid instruments just in the La Jolla and Pacific Beach branches of the Bank of America.[15] Much larger sums of money from Mexico are no doubt deposited in the major banks in Los Angeles and San Francisco.

Capital flight from Mexico to California is one example of how increased integration can be beneficial for one side of the border but harmful for the other. Although individual Mexicans have profited from capital flight, the Mexican economy has been drained of massive financial resources. California and Mexico will continue to have

---

14. Valdemar de Murguia, *Capital Flight and Economic Crisis: Mexican Post-devaluation Exiles in a California Community,"* Research Report Series 44, La Jolla, University of California, San Diego, 1986, pp. 6-7.
15. *Ibid.*, p. 24.

close financial ties, but whether they will be mutually beneficial depends largely on the health of the Mexican economy. Economic stagnation or decline is likely to increase capital flight, whereas a restoration of Mexico's position in international financial markets would benefit California banks while contributing to productive investment in Mexico.

The Costs of Contiguity

The growing links between Mexico and California offer substantial benefits to California, but they also pose some rising costs. The same porous border that facilitates trade and investment opens channels for illegal exchange. Economic growth along the border brings with it infrastructure and environmental pressures that do not respect national boundaries. Although immigration provides a valuable source of low-cost labor to California employers, it also places new demands on the state's health and human services. Without effective management by California public officials, these difficult aspects of silent integration threaten to undermine the potential benefits of Mexico's proximity.

Illegal Flows

Silent integration between Mexico and California is not limited to closer links in the production and marketing of legal goods and services. Transnational networks have also emerged to promote the illicit transfer of narcotics, undocumented workers, and toxic waste. Facilitated by advances in communications and transportation, and often spurred by the combination of poverty in Mexico and prosperity in California, these illegal flows have increased dramatically in the last twenty years.

The narcotics trade is the most glaring example of the underside of increased integration. California has become a focal point for the narcotics trade between Mexico and the United States. Centered in Los Angeles, the California market looms larger than that of any other state. Los Angeles was recently targeted by the federal government as one of the country's major illegal drug centers.

California's involvement in the drug trade has been exacerbated by a shift in cocaine supply routes and in money laundering operations.

The massive U.S. interdiction program in the Caribbean during the 1980s pushed cocaine traffickers away from their traditional routes into southern Florida and toward new routes through Mexico and into southern California. Los Angeles has also overtaken Miami as the money laundering capital of the country. The cash surplus in the city's Federal Reserve Bank—the best indicator of money laundering—surged from $166 million in 1985 to $3.8 billion in 1988.[16]

The drug trade between California and Mexico has significant implications for the state. In addition to fueling the incidence of drug-related violence along the border and in the city streets, it threatens to lead to increased militarization of the border, which could have harmful consequences for human rights. It is also involving California lawyers, judges, and law enforcement officials in the prosecution of drug-related crimes that have taken place in Mexico. Finally, it reinforces negative stereotypes about Mexico, which could reduce the willingness of entrepreneurs, investors, and tourists in California to take advantage of opportunities south of the border.

Another major illegal flow across the California-Mexico border is undocumented immigration. California is the destination of roughly half of all illegal Mexican immigrants to the United States. During the 1980s an average of more than one million undocumented workers were apprehended each year along the U.S.-Mexican border, many of them at crossing points just south of San Diego. Even recent federal legislation placing greater restrictions on illegal immigration has been unable to stem the flow of undocumented Mexican workers into California.

The illegality of this immigrant flow has created problems similar to those posed by drug trafficking. Unquestionably, it has given rise to violence, corruption, and human rights abuses along the border and has fueled negative stereotypes about Mexicans in California. But the flow has also brought significant benefits to the state. The fiscal burden imposed by Mexican immigrants is probably outweighed by their contribution to job growth and to slower increases in prices and the overall cost of living. Moreover, as a result of their lack of eligibility for many programs and their desire to avoid deportation, illegal immigrants tend to place fewer demands on public

---

16. Jonathan Beatty and Richard Hornick, "A Torrent of Dirty Dollars," *Time*, December 18, 1989, p. 55.

services than other Californians with the same socioeconomic profile.[17]

A third illicit activity along the border is the illegal dumping of toxic waste in Mexico by California firms. In response to the escalating costs of complying with environmental controls in California, a growing number of the state's 50,000 generators of hazardous waste are illegally shipping their waste south of the border.[18] In addition to creating resentment in Mexico, this trend threatens to worsen environmental problems in California as these toxic substances seep into the water and air in Mexico, and then flow across the border into California.

Rapid Border Development

Development along the California-Mexico border has taken off in the last decade, largely as a result of the maquiladora boom. Tijuana has been transformed from a dusty border town of 340,000 in 1970 to a bustling metropolis of more than one million people. Unlike the rest of Mexico, which has experienced little job growth in recent years, Tijuana has an annual employment growth rate of 7 percent. The San Diego/Tijuana metropolitan area now has a combined population of 3.5 million people.

This astounding growth is putting serious strains on the region's infrastructure and environment. According to a recent report issued by border governors from Mexico and the United States, more than $5 billion in new infrastructure spending is required to sustain border growth. The U.S. Embassy in Mexico recently estimated that it would cost $9 billion to clean up the border environment. Without such spending, the maquiladora boom may be suffocated by rising transaction costs and a deteriorating quality of life.

The region's infrastructure faces four major challenges. First, the growing volume of border traffic is creating serious bottlenecks. A lack of sufficient customs facilities and personnel is subjecting the tourists, employees, and business people who cross the California-Mexico border each day to frustrating and expensive delays. Similar

17. For analysis of the costs and benefits for California of Mexican immigration, see McCarthy and Burciaga Valdez, *Current and Future Effects of Mexican Immigration on California*, Santa Monica, The Rand Corporation, 1985; and *supra* note 6.
18. Maura Dolan and Larry B. Stammer, "Clandestine Toxic Waste Exports to Mexico on Rise," *Los Angeles Times*, May 9, 1990.

difficulties are faced by passengers at the San Diego and Tijuana airports as a result of major increases in air traffic. Although funds have been appropriated by the U.S. Congress for a second border crossing at Otay Mesa, local leaders are pushing for another crossing near Calexico and for expanded airport facilities.

A second serious problem is the shortage of housing in Tijuana. The city has not been able to build enough new units to accommodate its mushrooming population. In addition to the health problems associated with inadequate housing, the shortage is having a deleterious effect on the stability of the Tijuana work force. Steps by U.S. companies to build employee units or provide transportation for workers to and from their plants are making only a small dent in the problem.

Third, both sides of the border lack sufficient quantities of potable water. Fewer than half the households in Tijuana have running water; if they did, indeed, the water supply would have fallen more than 40 percent short of need during the mid-1980s. In the Los Angeles area, the Metropolitan Water District expects at least a 10 percent deficit in water supplies in 1990, and San Diego's demand for water is projected to increase by one-third by 2010. Since both sides of the border rely on the same water sources, they have little choice but to engage in joint management of their water resources.

Finally, communities along the California-Mexico border are generating growing quantities of sewage. In the next decade combined raw sewage output in San Diego and Tijuana is expected to increase by up to 140 million gallons per day, overwhelming facilities that are already severely inadequate. Whole sections of Tijuana are without access to sewage lines, and the waste water discharged in these areas runs downhill across the border into the Tia Juana River Valley and then into the Pacific Ocean.

The border region's infrastructure crisis is contributing to serious environmental problems. Border traffic is damaging the region's air quality, and high levels of salinity threaten scarce water supplies. Untreated sewage poses major health risks on both sides of the border and has led to the closure of U.S. beaches on several occasions. One public health expert warns that "if sewage spills continue, we may have a serious health problem by the year 2020 or 2050."[19]

Additional threats to the environment are posed by the maquiladoras themselves, for they generate very high levels of toxic waste. Despite hazardous waste regulations that closely parallel those of the United States, the Mexican government lacks adequate resources for enforcement and is forced to rely largely on voluntary compliance. Large companies often find it in their long-term interests to comply with the regulations, but many smaller firms are pressed to forego the prohibitive costs of proper waste management. In high-emission industries such as painting, furniture, and plating, many California companies are participating in the maquiladora program as a way to avoid the high costs of complying with strict air quality standards north of the border.

The border may enable California companies to avoid complying with U.S. regulations, but it cannot shield the state's residents from the effects of environmental deterioration in Mexico. The New River, which flows north from the industrial border town of Mexicali, registers high levels of dangerous industrial pollutants such as polychlorinated biphenyls (PCBs), DDT, toxaphene, benzene, and trichloroethane; the Salton Sea contains at least one hundred industrial chemicals traceable to factories in Mexico. Toxins emitted into the air in Tijuana blow into California each night, just as Los Angeles smog heads toward Mexico in the morning.

Significant progress has been made toward addressing some of the problems associated with rapid border development. In 1983 the United States and Mexico signed a path-breaking agreement to establish a framework for developing joint approaches to environmental regulation. This agreement has since been strengthened by four annexes, one of which addresses sanitation problems in the San Diego/Tijuana area and another of which regulates transboundary shipment of toxic waste. In 1990 the United States and Mexico signed a binational accord allowing for the construction of an international sewage treatment plant in San Diego. The accord signals a major breakthrough in binational cooperation and, if adequately funded,

19. John Conway, "Sewage and Public Health: the San Diego-Tijuana Region," in Lawrence A. Herzog (ed.), *Planning the International Border Metropolis*, La Jolla, Center for U.S.-Mexican Studies, University of California, San Diego, 1986, pp. 28-9.

will be a major step toward meeting the sewage treatment needs of the region.

These accomplishments are not sufficient, however, to sustain balanced growth along the California-Mexico border. The little infrastructure development that has taken place has been ad hoc and inadequately funded. Although many of the administrative obstacles to environmental protection have been overcome, the environment is likely to get worse without greater resources for treatment and enforcement.

Health and Human Services

The growing population of Mexican immigrants in California is placing new demands on health and human services. Although Mexican immigrants have relatively low crime rates and do not typically rely on public welfare, their other needs are straining the state's social service system. In the last few years an increasing share of these immigrants have been women and children, many of whom are likely to become permanent residents. This new population will put growing pressure on services such as maternal and child care, housing, and education.

Several studies show that Latinos have a better health profile than other disadvantaged groups, but recent Mexican immigrants have special needs that do not correspond to those of the state's aging Anglo residents. As a young and fertile population, they have extensive need for maternal and emergency care. Fertility rates are particularly high among the foreign-born, who tend to suffer from the health problems associated with inadequate nutrition, sanitation, and general health care in Mexico. Recent Mexican immigrants have limited access to health insurance and are able to expend only 80 percent as much on health care as the rest of the under-64 population.[20]

The arrival of hundreds of poor Mexican families is also straining the state's already inadequate low-income housing market. Nearly one-fifth of all Latino families in Los Angeles County live at or below the poverty line; many are in households of three or more persons. Public housing officials estimate that illegal immigrants may be

20. David Hayes Bautista *et al., The Burden of Support: Young Latinos in an Aging Society,* Palo Alto, Stanford University Press, 1988, p. 113.

occupying more than 30 percent of southern California's 500,000 public units. Many other Mexican immigrants are living in illegal, substandard dwellings and increasing numbers are homeless.[21]

Crisis in Immigrant Education

Mexican immigration to California is having its greatest impact on public education. Between 1967 and 1982 the number of Latino students in the Los Angeles public schools more than doubled, and the overwhelming majority of these were children of recent Mexican immigrants. According to one study, "no other school system in the United States has ever experienced such a concentrated influx of students from a single foreign country."[22] Today, Latino children make up 62 percent of the students in the Los Angeles Unified School District.[23] Forty percent of all Latino students in California drop out before graduating from high school.

Mexican immigrants often arrive in California at an educational disadvantage. Although schooling in Mexico is compulsory and free through age 15, more than 35 percent of all Mexican adults have not finished primary school, and illiteracy rates are estimated to be about 15 percent in the cities and 30 percent in rural areas.[24] These low educational levels put many Mexican students several grade levels behind their peers and often limit the extent to which their parents can participate in their education.

Many Mexican students also have little or no command of the English language. Few California schools are prepared to accommodate the state's growing population of limited English proficient (LEP) students, over 70 percent of whom speak only Spanish. In addition to facing a serious shortage of trained bilingual staff, the state's educators are paralyzed by a pedagogical debate over how best to provide LEP students with the skills they need to be academically successful.

The obstacles to educational achievement among Mexican students are exacerbated by larger challenges facing California's public schools. Severe overcrowding in the inner cities is forcing school districts to bus record numbers of poor, immigrant students to

21. *Ibid.*, pp. 126-7.
22. *Supra* note 6, p. 80.
23. *Ethnic Survey Report,* Los Angeles, Los Angeles Unified School District, 1989, p. 358.
24. *Supra* note 20, p. 84.

suburban campuses ill-equipped to meet their needs. Meanwhile, the problem of "white flight" is draining the vital element of parental support, involvement, and resources from the schools that need it the most. These problems are magnified by the tax-cutting initiatives passed by California voters during the 1970s, which have left the state's public schools without sufficient resources to serve their increasingly diverse student population.

The crisis in immigrant education has two disturbing implications for California. First, Mexican immigrants and their children are in danger of becoming trapped at the bottom of the economic ladder. In recent years there has been a significant decline in the well-paying, unionized manufacturing jobs that have traditionally provided Latinos with upward mobility. If no alternative is provided to the next generation of young Mexicans, they run the risk of becoming part of a permanent underclass, with serious implications for health and human services. In addition to relying more heavily on public welfare and crime to survive, they will be less able (and willing) to fund the retirement and health needs of the state's growing elderly population.[25]

A second, and related, outcome of failing to educate young Mexican immigrants is a potential mismatch between labor force skills and job requirements. Although job growth over the next decade is projected to support 275,000 new residents, the majority of the state's new jobs will be in the white-collar and skilled service sectors and are likely to require good technical and communication skills. Latinos, who could make up as much as 35 percent of California's labor force by the year 2030, will be ill-equipped to perform these new jobs without at least a high school education. According to one study, "unless major upward mobility occurs in the occupational structure of California's minority groups, and recent immigrants in particular, the occupational requirements of a growing and changing state economy in the next decade may not be met."[26]

---

25. For full development of this argument, see *supra* note 20.
26. *California Population Statistics*, Palo Alto, Center for the Continuing Study of the California Economy, 1989, p. 41. There is some evidence, however, that this potential mismatch may not be as severe at the national level as is commonly believed. See Louis Uchitelle, "Surplus of College Graduates Dims Job Outlook for Others," *New York Times*, June 13, 1990.

Policy Challenges

The extent to which California continues to reap the economic benefits of increased integration with Mexico will depend largely on how
well state and local officials manage the challenges posed by Mexico's proximity. These officials should continue to promote the beneficial aspects of close ties with Mexico, but they must also focus on
minimizing the potential costs.

Official action is needed at several jurisdictional levels. Many of
the issues raised by Mexico's proximity—including immigration
reform, narcotics control, trade policy, and environmental regulation—fall under the rubric of foreign policy and must be handled in
close cooperation with Washington. Other issues can be handled
largely at the state and local levels. Here, the challenge is to keep
open the lines of communication between Sacramento, local communities in California, and public and private actors in Mexico. This
process has been facilitated by the establishment of an Office of
California-Mexico Affairs in the governor's office, the creation of
offices of border affairs by the city and county of San Diego, and
joint meetings by the San Diego and Tijuana city councils to discuss
cross-border affairs.

Yet another set of issues, usually involving the impact of Mexican
immigration on local communities, demands unilateral action
within California by state and local officials. Often, these issues are
seen by policy makers as larger social questions in which Mexican
immigrants play a part.

Taking into account these overlapping jurisdictions, the newly
elected governor of California should take the lead in facing the
challenges posed by Mexico's proximity, sending a signal that action
in this area will be rewarded with attention and resources. Under the
governor's leadership, California officials and legislators should
emphasize four lines of action: encouraging closer economic ties
with Mexico; minimizing the negative effects of illegal flows of
people, goods, and services across the border; devising mechanisms
to manage rapid border development; and providing young Mexican
immigrants with the tools they need to contribute more fully to the
state's changing economy.

Promoting Economic Ties

California officials have already begun to promote closer economic ties with Mexico, particularly since relaxation of trade and investment barriers in Mexico. The California World Trade Commission holds regular trade shows south of the border, and the Office of California-Mexico Affairs recently issued a promotional brochure on the maquiladora industry. In February 1989 California opened an Office of Trade and Investment in Mexico City. During its first eight months in operation, the office handled over 1,500 trade inquiries, assisted in the negotiation of fourteen business transactions between Mexican and California companies, and facilitated the direct deposit of $500,000 by Mexican investors in California banks.

These agencies, together with the state legislature, need to build on existing activities by developing projections about the likely impact of regional and global trends on California-Mexico economic relations. One trend that deserves further analysis is the liberalization of Mexico's foreign investment regulations, which could bring significant benefits to California. In tourism, for example, the Mexican government is encouraging private investors to inject as much as $10 billion into Mexican resorts over the next six years, and President Salinas aims to attract ten million tourists a year to Mexico by 1992, twice the current number. Two areas targeted for development are Baja California and Mexico's Pacific Coast, both of which offer attractive locations for California investors. Also worth examining are the prospects for investment in infrastructure development and technology transfer, which are likely to utilize the strengths of California firms while promoting economic development in Mexico.

California officials should also look more closely at emerging trade and investment relations among California, Mexico, and Asia and devise more effective strategies for enhancing the benefits and minimizing the costs of Asia's presence along the border. These strategies should fit into California's overall policies toward the Pacific Rim, including efforts to move U.S. trade policy in a direction that serves California's interests.

Finally, California officials should thoroughly investigate the likely impact on California of a possible free trade agreement between Mexico and the United States. Such an agreement, if reached, would have far-reaching implications for California, which has closer trading ties with Mexico than any U.S. state except Texas. California officials need to understand these complex issues so that they can respond to the demands of competing interest groups in California and make the state's case in Washington once negotiations are under way.

Containing Illegal Flows

Although California officials should cooperate with federal agencies in attempting to stop the illegal flow of people, goods, and capital across the border, they are likely to have only limited success. They should concentrate their main efforts, therefore, on containing the negative effects of these flows.

California officials need to maintain an active lobbying presence in Washington on narcotics control and immigration. The supply-oriented policies currently in effect threaten to militarize the U.S.-Mexican border and to increase anti-Mexican stereotyping. State officials should advocate policies that focus more attention on the U.S. side of the problem. In the case of narcotics, this means much more money for demand reduction through education and treatment. In the case of immigration, California officials should push for increased allocation of federal funds to provide immigrant services within California and explore ways to diminish the abuses that often accompany illegal immigration.

As a way to take the illegality out of these immigrant flows, California officials should consider supporting a temporary worker program for urban immigrants. Such a program would perpetuate the economic benefits of access to Mexican labor, reduce the incidence of violence and corruption along the border, and complement an existing program for temporary agricultural workers. The program should be carefully designed, however, to meet real labor shortages and to give Mexican workers strong incentives to return eventually to Mexico.[27]

A second, and even more difficult, challenge for California officials is to play a role in defusing the negative images of Mexico that are reinforced by illegal flows. The development of productive trade

---

27. For example, the Arizona Farm Workers Union established an innovative program whereby Mexican workers contribute a portion of their salary to an economic development fund for their home communities.

and investment relations will proceed much more smoothly in an environment of understanding. Through public affairs programs, local festivals, changes in the public school curriculum, and other innovative mechanisms, California officials should seek to enhance public awareness of the richness of Mexican society and culture and to encourage mutually respectful interaction between Mexicans and other ethnic groups in the state.

Managing Border Development

Although important steps have been taken to manage development along the border between Mexico and California, much more needs to be done to ease the growing pressures on infrastructure and the environment. Without a comprehensive strategy to address the problems associated with rapid development, the region's economic boom may come to an end.

The governor should appoint a high-level select commission to assess the region's infrastructure and environmental protection needs, develop innovative proposals, and explore viable funding mechanisms. The commission should include prominent leaders from both the public and private sectors. In addition to involving state and local actors on both sides of the border, the commission should work closely with representatives from Washington and Mexico City, given their role in approving many of the necessary measures.

Rather than supplanting existing policy mechanisms, the commission would enable federal, state, and local officials to identify linkages among border issues and to explore policy options. After a finite period—at least one and at most two years—the commission should present its recommendations to the governor and the state legislature, leaving implementation to existing agencies and officials. In this way, the commission would lend much-needed order and cohesiveness to the management of silent integration without undermining the benefits of decentralized decision making.

During its tenure the commission should consider several worthwhile proposals that have thus far been stymied by funding constraints or by the political hurdles to cross-border projects. One is the construction of a joint Tijuana/San Diego airport to handle the growing air traffic and to link border development more closely to

the global marketplace. Another is the creation of a mechanism to
finance border projects, such as a binational infrastructure bonding
authority or a border development bank based in Washington but
with strong state representation. A third worthwhile idea is the
creation of a binational housing authority to construct units on the
Mexican side of the border. Building on the progress that has already
been made in developing joint approaches to border problems, the
commission should encourage California officials to translate these
and other creative proposals into policy.

Investing in the Next Generation

Meeting the health and human service needs of Mexican immigrants in California is perhaps the greatest challenge facing state and
local officials. These immigrants and their children may well hold
the key to the state's economic future, which will depend on the
ability of a shrinking and increasingly Latino work force to support
an expanding elderly population. As David Hayes-Bautista has
argued, California needs to develop an inter-generational and inter-
ethnic compact whereby aging Anglos support programs to help
young Latinos become fully productive members of society.[28] Otherwise, the state may lose its competitive edge and face a growing
number of social problems.

An innovative proposal made at the local level by Los Angeles City
Councilmember Richard Alatorre offers an example of how such a
compact might be realized. In February 1990 Alatorre introduced
legislation to establish a children's policy for the city of Los Angeles.
The proposal covers a wide array of issues, including health, education, and housing, and requires each city department to develop a
budget and agenda to address children's issues. Although the proposal extends to children from all ethnic groups, its greatest impact
will be on the city's growing population of young Mexicans.

Officials in Sacramento should adopt a similar strategy at the state
level. A statewide children's policy would provide a politically viable
mechanism for addressing the most crucial social needs of Mexican
immigrants in California. Although officials should be careful not to
add unnecessary layers to the bureaucracy or to create another
middle-class subsidy, they should devise a strategy to compel state

---

28. *Supra* note 20.

and local agencies to give greater priority to the needs of California's children.

The policy should focus on health, education, housing, and child care, all of which have a major impact both on children and on Mexican immigrants. Through their hold on the purse strings, state legislators should push agencies to reassess current policies in terms of how well they meet children's needs and to propose new or revised programs that would assist children while remaining consistent with broader policy objectives.

Creating an Institutional Framework

To give the proposed policies the momentum and sustainability they need to be effective, the governor should create an institutional framework to manage silent integration. First, the Office of California-Mexico Affairs should be expanded. With greater staff and resources, it could become a focal point for information gathering, policy formulation, informal coordination among the various levels of government and society, and lobbying efforts in Washington. The governor may also want to establish an interagency cabinet committee on California-Mexico relations to work with this office and to provide periodic feedback on how agencies are handling the issues raised by silent integration.

Second, the governor should work with public-and private-sector leaders to establish a non-profit California-Mexico Foundation. The foundation would complement the work of state and local governments by enhancing public awareness, building private- and public-sector coalitions, and mobilizing resources to fund the management of silent integration. The foundation could be particularly vital in building broad-based support for controversial initiatives such as a temporary worker program or a statewide children's policy. As an independent, private, flexible entity with the strong backing of the governor and the state legislature, such a foundation could make a real, long-term difference in the quality of relations between California and Mexico.

Third, the governor should consider expanding the proposed commission on border development into a blue-ribbon commission that could review the entire range of issues affected by Mexico's proximity. Such a commission would help to ensure the involvement of key private- and public-sector leaders and would lend a greater cohesiveness to the management of silent integration.

Looking Ahead

With their combination of human, financial, and natural resources, California and Mexico are poised to become partners in one of the great success stories of the twenty-first century. California has an enormous market, expanding job opportunities, abundant capital, and advanced technology, while Mexico offers a growing pool of cost-efficient labor, rich natural resources, and a vast potential market. These complementarities present the two regions with valuable economic opportunities.

Whether California and Mexico can fully realize their shared potential for growth depends partly on Mexico's next phase of development. The sweeping economic reforms now taking place in Mexico could spur high annual growth rates in the next decade and generate trade and investment. But if the economic liberalization fails or is not accompanied by meaningful political reforms, Mexico could revert to the stagnation of the 1980s—or, worse yet, face economic deterioration and political turbulence.

A great deal depends, as well, on the ability of California's public officials to manage silent integration. With the necessary leadership, California can realize significant gains from Mexico's proximity, particularly if Mexico's recovery strengthens. But if state and local officials fail to meet the challenges posed by silent integration, California could experience unprecedented strains on its social, economic, and political fabric. Silent integration will continue one way or another, but its impact will be shaped by how well state and local officials respond to this complex and changing relationship.

Ms. Burgess did most of the research and much of the writing for this chapter; Dr. Lowenthal provided conceptual guidance, made extensive editorial comments, and drafted some sections. The authors thank Renee Stasio for research assistance, and Steven Erie, Agustin Escobar, Mercedes Gonzales de la Rocha, Robin Kramer, Richard Maullin, Richard Rothstein, Elsa Saxod, Gabriel Szekely, and Fernando Torres-Gil for commenting on drafts. They have also drawn on previous work at USC by Denise Dresser, Carlos Gonzales Gutierrez, and the students in Dr. Lowenthal's spring 1989 seminar.

LONG-TERM CARE

Fernando M. Torres-Gil and Linda A. Wray

5

The aging of the population in the United States and in California, along with other demographic changes that limit the availability of family members for home care of the elderly and disabled, suggests that the need for long-term care services will become urgent and widespread by the end of this century. The state and the nation, preoccupied with budget constraints and competing social problems, are not moving quickly enough to prepare for what soon will be recognized as a health care crisis. This chapter provides an overview of the structure of long-term care services in California and the policy issues that must be resolved if a long-term care crisis is to be avoided.

Long-term care means many things to many people. Older people with chronic illnesses and younger people with disabilities perceive it as a health care issue. Family members who are placing a parent in a nursing home see it as an intensely emotional personal crisis. Providers of long-term care services and products regard it as a burgeoning industry. And state and local governments perceive it as a worrisome budget problem. Regardless of one's point of view, long-term care is a public policy concern that will have major impacts on the short-and long-term fiscal health of California.

Throughout the 1970s and 1980s California and the nation have grappled with how best to meet the needs of frail and older people and those with disabilities. Federal and state responses to date have been tentative and uneven, due largely to budget deficits and the cost of providing such services, but decisive action in this area will become urgent by the turn of the century.

The growth of populations of older people and those with disabilities, and political pressures brought by aging and disability organizations and interest groups, ensure that California will be forced to make important and often controversial choices in the area of long-term care. The state should use the 1990s to plan for expansion and reform of its long-term care system before such pressures force hasty and potentially imprudent decisions.

Building Blocks of Long-Term Care

Long-term care is defined as "a set of health, personal care, and social services delivered over a sustained period of time to persons who have lost or never acquired some degree of functional capacity."[1] The ability to perform activities of daily living such as walking, dressing, and bathing is central to its definition. Long-term care can also refer to the place in which a service is given (e.g., nursing home, board and care facility) or the program that provides the service.[2]

Ideally, long-term care consists of a mix of services—diagnostic, preventive, therapeutic, rehabilitative, supportive, and maintenance—that provide a continuum of care, enabling an individual to stay at home, remain in the community, or when necessary, find affordable, high-quality institutional care.

The National Picture

The availability of long-term care services in the future will be driven in large part by demographics. The aging of the U.S. population, especially the dramatic increase in the numbers of people over 85 years of age, is a large part of the demographic imperative. The proportion of people over 65 will jump from 13 percent to 20 percent of the population by the year 2030,[3] although that population is generally healthier today than previous cohorts of the elderly. The population 85 years of age and over is the fastest growing age group in the country, and it is expected to quadruple between 1980 and 2030.[4] Within that group, health concerns and the need for long-term care are significant.

While most older people with disabilities—approximately 75 percent—are cared for at home,[5] recent trends in family patterns and dependency ratios suggest that fewer caretakers will be available in the home in future years, even though the need for care will be greater. Most older men remain married until they die, and their wives, who have longer life expectancies, generally take care of them

---

1. Rosalie Kane and Robert Kane, *Long-Term Care: Principles, Programs and Policies*, New York, Springer, 1987.
2. *Ibid.*
3. U.S. Senate, *Aging America: Trends and Projections*, 1987-88 ed., Washington, D.C., Department of Health and Human Services, 1988.
4. *Ibid.*
5. *Supra* note 1.

when the need arises. The majority of elderly women, on the other hand, live alone, and thus are more likely to require institutional and community-based long-term care. The declining size of the American family, estimated to be less than two children per child-bearing woman in 1990, and the greater numbers of women in the labor force, indicate that there may be fewer adult children to care for elderly parents.[6] With older people today more likely to relocate in their retirement, geographic mobility will also affect the numbers of older people without family and social supports available nearby.

About 21 percent of Americans over 65 needed long-term care services in 1988; by the year 2024, this number will increase almost threefold.[7] Barring dramatic medical advances, the need for long-term care among older people will continue to grow.

The California Picture

The growing need for long-term care services in the national population is mirrored in California. In 1985, 11 percent of the state's population were at least 65 years old. By 2020 that population will double in size, representing nearly 16 percent of the total population and 65 percent of the long-term care population. Between 1985 and 2020 the population of Californians 85 and above will increase by 145 percent.[8]

In 1985 more than one million Californians, or about 4 percent of the U.S. population, were estimated to need some type of formal long-term care service. That number is projected to double by 2020.[9] Between 1980 and 2020 the long-term care population is expected to increase at twice the rates of growth in the total population.

The changing racial and ethnic makeup of the California population may also affect future needs for long-term care services. Early in the twenty-first century, California's demographics will shift, and whites will make up less than 50 percent of the population. The

6. U.S. Bureau of the Census, Current Population Reports, Series P-25, No. 1018, *Projections of the Population of the United States by Age, Sex and Race: 1988 to 2080,* by Gregory Spencer, Washington, D.C., U.S. Government Printing Office, 1989.
7. American Society on Aging, "Long-Term Care: Who's Responsible?" in *Critical Debates in an Aging Society,* Report No. 2, San Francisco, 1988.
8. California Health and Welfare Agency, *A Study of California's Publicly Funded Long-Term Care Programs,* Sacramento, 1988.
9. University of California, San Francisco, Institute for Health and Aging, *Long-Term Care Public Policy Agenda for California,* Pub. No. 89-W-1, San Francisco, 1989.

groups that have traditionally been considered minorities—blacks, Hispanics, Asians, Pacific Islanders, and Native Americans—are among the most rapidly growing segments of the population. In California their numbers are projected to increase to at least 40 percent of the elderly population by the year 2020, two and one-half times the 1980 level. As with the total population, the growth of ethnic minorities in the older population will be driven largely by changes in the Hispanic and Asian populations.[10] Given the current lower usage of health care services by ethnic minority groups, and their often greater health care needs, the extent of their impact on future services is uncertain.

The Nation: a Tentative Response

Currently, there is no national system of publicly funded long-term care services. Instead, there are separate and costly programs that provide a variety of services and benefits. The two largest are Medicare and Medicaid, and each has major gaps and weaknesses.

Medicare, the major source of health insurance for the elderly, primarily covers hospital and physician-based services. While Medicare does reimburse clients for limited home health care and nursing home care (when related to prior hospitalization and certified by a doctor), the program was designed to provide acute care rather than longer-term non-institutional services.

Medicaid is the major funding source for nursing home care. In 1987 this program covered 44 percent of total nursing home costs (Medicare and private insurance covered less than 2 percent), while personal out-of-pocket expenditures absorbed the remainder.[11] Unlike Medicare, Medicaid (known as Medi-Cal in California) is a state-administered program that receives matching federal funds. Medicaid is also means-tested, requiring applicants to meet poverty guidelines in order to qualify for services. Despite the program's institutional bias, states may apply for federal waivers to use Medi-

10. Fernando Torres-Gil and Jeffrey C. Hyde, "The Impact of Minorities on Long-Term Care Policy in California," in Liebig and Lammers (eds.), *California Policy Choices for Long-Term Care,* Los Angeles, University of Southern California, 1990.
11. Library of Congress, Congressional Research Service, *CRS Issue Brief: Long-Term Care for the Elderly,* Pub. No. IB88098, Washington, D.C.

caid funds for case management and home- and community-based services.[12]

More than eighty other national programs provide long-term care benefits through cash assistance, in-kind transfers, and direct social and health services. Table 5-1 demonstrates the tremendous variation in the major national funding sources and services. Each has its own eligibility criteria, oversight agencies, administrative procedures, and requirements.

Despite the existence of these national programs, the major long-term care funding sources for most families are personal expenditures and private long-term care insurance. Family members (usually women) and friends provide between 75 and 85 percent of direct or indirect long-term care costs. While at least 118 private-sector insurance companies in 1989 offered some form of long-term care insurance in more than 1.5 million policies,[13] private-sector insurance pays less than 3 percent of the total cost of long-term care services.[14]

On the national level then, there are a series of large-scale programs, biased toward acute medical care, that provide limited supportive services. The United States Congress has proceeded cautiously in expanding community-based chronic care services, which are likely to be costly. Recently enacted legislation on nationally funded long-term care coverage has imposed cost-containment measures on Medicare and Medicaid and, where possible, the reduction of coverage and benefits.[15]

California: Restrained Innovation

California has been a pioneer in implementing innovative long-term care services since the early 1970s. Yet the state's attempts to expand and coordinate long-term care funding and services have been restrained by political realities: budget bills require a two-thirds majority for passage in the legislature, and no recent state administration has ever promoted long-term care as a priority issue.

---

12. Legislation directing the application of waivers for that purpose was introduced in 1990 by Assemblyman Burt Margolin (D-Los Angeles).
13. *Supra* note 11.
14. *Supra* note 9.
15. For example, a prospective payment system was established in 1983 and a relative value scale was added in 1990, both introduced to control expenditures in the Medicare program.

Table 5-1. Federal Funding Sources for Service Needs of the Chronically Impaired Elderly

Service	Funding Source						
	Medicaid	Medicare	Social Services	SSI[a]	Aging Admin.[b]	VA[c]	HUD[d]
Medical	*	*				*	
Home nursing	*	*					
Home health aide	*	*	*		*	*	
Homemaker			*		*		
Personal care	*		*			*	
Chores/home repair			*		*		
Home-delivered meals			*		*		
Shopping assistance			*		*		
Transportation			*		*		
Adult day care			*				
Housing assistance						*	
Congregate housing; domiciliary homes; adult foster care			*	*		*	*
Respite care			*				
Congregate meals			*		*		
Adult day health care	*		*				
Social/recreational					*		
Legal/financial counseling			*		*		
Mental health		*	*				
Information and referral		*			*	*	*

Source: Adapted from Meyer Katzper, "Modeling of Long Term Care," in *Long Term Care: Who's Responsible?* Critical Debates in an Aging Society, Report No. 2, San Francisco, American Society on Aging, 1988.

a. Supplemental Security Income
b. Administration on Aging
c. Veterans Administration
d. Housing and Urban Development

In the 1970s legislation was enacted to strengthen nursing home inspection procedures; to fund the On Lok Senior Health Services program in San Francisco as an alternative to institutional care; and to authorize adult day health care pilot projects funded by Medi-Cal and waivers from national program requirements to establish the case management Multi-Purpose Senior Services Program. In the 1980s the Older Californians Act was enacted, comprehensive Independent Living Centers were initiated, Adult Day Health Care centers became permanent programs, and legislation was enacted to improve the quality of care in nursing homes and allow for second-unit and shared housing.

The proliferation of national and state-funded programs led to an attempt in the early 1980s to reform California's fragmented long-term care system. During that time the United States Health Care Financing Administration provided a systems development grant to the state to create a plan for a coordinated system of care for impaired Californians. In 1981 the first legislative attempt to develop such a coordinated system was introduced—AB 2860, the Torres-Felando Long-Term Care Reform Act. This bill conferred on the California Department of Aging responsibility for long-term care planning and coordination and directed the administration to develop a proposal for implementing its provisions.

However, the incoming administration did not share in the long-term care philosophy of AB 2860, calling its provisions unworkable and prohibitively costly. The refusal of that administration to move forward with the comprehensive statewide coordination called for in AB 2860 led to the introduction by Assemblyman Gerald Felando (R-Torrance) of substitute measure AB 2226. With the support of the administration, AB 2226 passed in 1984, consigning the Department of Aging with "the incremental development of a community based long-term care system that provides the social and health support necessary to enable frail elderly and functionally impaired adults to remain in their homes."[16]

Today, AB 2226[17] remains the basis for many of the state's long-term care demonstration programs. These programs include Linkages, a program that establishes regional sites for coordinating services useful in assisting functionally impaired adults to remain in their own homes; the "SErvice enrichED" (SEED) community long-term care project, which evaluates different approaches to service integration; and nursing home pre-admission screening programs.

16. California Department of Aging, "Request for Proposals for Linkages Sites in Accordance with AB 2226," Sacramento, 1985.
17. Welfare and Institutions Code, Chapter 1637, 1984 Statutes, Division 8.5, Section 9390.

During the 1989-90 legislative session additional incremental changes in long-term care policy were advanced. Licensure was required for home health agencies that provide skilled nursing services; respiratory therapy in nursing facilities was added to the services covered by Medi-Cal; Medigap insurance consumer protections and standards were implemented; protections were augmented for the elderly in residential care facilities and consumers buying long-term care insurance; and several demonstration programs, including Linkages, the Multipurpose Senior Services Program, and On Lok, were authorized as permanent programs. Additionally, Assemblyman Lloyd Connelly (D-Sacramento) proposed that the state either pass legislation or qualify a ballot initiative establishing a private/public sector program to subsidize the cost of long-term care insurance. Program services, to be financed by a one-half cent sales tax, included home and alternative care as well as nursing home care. The Connelly initiative was eventually withdrawn due to a lack of support by the state administration and insufficient resources for the signature drive. During the same session both senate and assembly members introduced several bills relating to the growing population of medically uninsured, access to affordable long-term care coverage, and health care cost containment.[18]

This two-decade history of long-term care activities in California reveals that the state legislature has attempted to be innovative—and has sometimes succeeded—in developing services, programs, and coordinating mechanisms that use national and state funds more efficiently. The availability of community- and home-based services has moved California closer than the federal government to a balanced continuum of services. However, services have not kept pace with the increasing numbers of Californians who may need long-term care. Each time the legislature has initiated comprehensive reforms, it has been checked by uncertain support or recalcitrance on the part of the administration and held hostage by its two-thirds majority rule on budget bills. Despite the intentions of AB 2226, the

---

18. The major health insurance bills were introduced by Assembly Speaker Willie Brown (D-San Francisco), Assembly Members William Baker (R-Walnut Creek), Bruce Bronzan (D-Fresno), Dan Hauser (D-Eureka), and Burt Margolin (D-Los Angeles), and Senators Ken Maddy (R-Fresno) and Nicholas Petris (D-Oakland).

state today has a fragmented and uncoordinated array of programs and policies.

California's Fragmented System

The structure and delivery of long-term care services in California reflects the fragmentation of state policy in this area. Figure 5-1 illustrates the six major agencies under the umbrella of the Health and Welfare Agency that administer the state's thirty-six publicly funded long-term care programs.[19] Those agencies include:

- *California Department of Aging (CDA):* provides supportive services (e.g., nutrition programs, information and referral, an ombudsman, multi-purpose senior centers, Meals-On-Wheels) funded primarily by the Older Americans Act; has major responsibility for long-term care policy and planning;
- *Department of Developmental Services (DDS):* administers care, treatment, and training to children and adults with developmental disabilities;
- *Department of Health Services (DHS):* provides medical assistance, including nursing home coverage, to low-income people through the Medi-Cal program;
- *Department of Mental Health (DMH):* provides direct and indirect services to the mentally ill;
- *Department of Rehabilitation (DOR):* assists people with disabilities through vocational rehabilitation and training programs;
- *Department of Social Services (DSS):* manages income maintenance and social service programs, including in-home support services (IHSS) and food stamps; evaluates disability status for SSI/SSP, Medicare, and Medi-Cal.

The Health and Welfare Agency classifies long-term care programs as either community-based or institutional care.[20] Examples of long-term care programs (and the agencies that sponsor them) include:

- *Community-based services:* case management (CDA), Linkages program (CDA), Multipurpose Senior Services Programs (CDA), Regional DDS centers, Adult Day Health Care (DSS), Alzheimer's Day Care Resource Centers (CDA); Alzheimer's Dis-

---

19. *Supra* note 8.
20. *Ibid.*

Figure 5-1. Organization of State-Level Long-Term Care Services

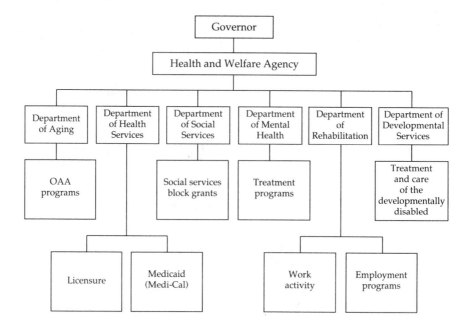

ease Diagnostic and Treatment Centers (CDA), Brain Damaged Adults Program (DMH), Adult Protective Services (DSS), Independent Living Centers (DOR), Congregate Meals (CDA), Respite Care (CDA), In-Home Supportive Services (DSS), Long-Term Care Ombudsman Program (CDA), Residential Care Services (DMH), Home-Delivered Meals (CDA);

- *Institutional care programs:* skilled nursing facilities (DHS), institutions for mental diseases (DMH), state hospitals for the mentally disordered (DMH), developmental centers for the developmentally disabled (DDS).

Additional programs and services integral to the long-term care system in California include:[21]

- *Office of Statewide Health Planning and Development:* develops state health policy and plans and conducts surveys of long-term care health facilities' operations and costs;
- *California Medical Assistance Commission:* negotiates Medi-Cal contracts;

21. *Ibid.*

- *Community Care Licensing (DSS):* regulates community care facilities;
- *Adult Day Care and Social Day Care (DSS):* provides non-medical care on a less-than-24-hour basis;
- *Licensing and Certification (DHS):* regulates licensed public and private health facilities, including acute care, skilled nursing facilities, home health agencies, and facilities participating in the Medicare and Medi-Cal programs;
- *Area Agencies on Aging (CDA):* coordinates Older Americans Act services in thirty-three planning and service areas.

Together these programs accounted for approximately $3 billion of national and state public funds in fiscal year 1987-88. California's share was approximately 40 percent. The five largest programs (Medi-Cal, In-Home Supportive Services, Developmental Centers for the Developmentally Disabled, Regional Department of Developmental Services Centers, Non-Medi-Cal Board and Care) represented 86 percent of the state's total. Approximately 33 percent of total national and state funding went to the Medi-Cal skilled nursing facility program, compared with 16 percent for the in-home supportive services program.

Despite the substantial public funds expended for this vast array of services, benefits, and oversight activities, California's system has been criticized as a non-system of institutionally biased programs.[22] For example, Medi-Cal consumes the largest source of funds for nursing home care, with the remaining funds divided among thirty-five other programs. The large number of separate agencies involved in designing, regulating, and delivering services has hampered efforts to coordinate that system.

Further, the locus of responsibility for long-term care programs is unbalanced. The Department of Aging, charged with coordinating and overseeing state efforts, consumed just over 5 percent of the long-term care budget in fiscal 1986-87, compared with nearly 35 percent for the Department of Health Services and 27 percent for the Department of Social Services.[23] In addition, relatively few people are served by these programs, despite the state's expenditures in the

---

22. Assembly Office of Research, "The Graying of California: the Third Shock Wave," in *California 2000: a People in Transition*, Sacramento, 1986.
23. *Supra* note 8.

long-term care arena. For example, the more than $4 million in fiscal year 1986-87 for the Linkages program served only 3,000 clients.

Policy Dilemmas

The legislative and executive branches in California have responded unevenly to the growing need for long-term care. Despite knowledge of the problems of design and delivery of long-term care services, the national and state governments and interest groups have approached comprehensive solutions to financing and expanding long-term care with strategies ranging from bold and costly to timid half-steps taken with considerable trepidation.

These responses to the growing needs for long-term care services have been tempered by competing social problems; controversies over eligibility and types of service; interest group politics; financing issues; and questions about service delivery.

Competing Priorities

While the needs both of people with disabilities and of frail older people are critical, long-term care competes with other priorities that may be more urgent in the short term. Homelessness, the medically uninsured, AIDS, deteriorating public education, drugs, and crime command immediate attention in many communities. Physical infrastructures of highways, bridges, and sewer systems are deteriorating. Immigrant and refugee groups have pressing needs as well.

To many policy makers long-term care is a luxury affecting a small number of people rather than a widespread social problem, yet it is likely to evolve into a crisis that affects a large proportion of California's and the nation's citizenry. Policy makers need to understand that greater costs will be incurred by postponing action until the year 2020, when the long-term care population will surge.

Long-term care is subsumed today within the context of national and state health care coverage. With thirty-seven million Americans (and nearly 20 percent of all Californians) without health insurance, many labor groups, businesses, and consumers are demanding public redress of the health care crisis. The United States Congress and many state legislatures, including California's, are currently weighing bills requiring or encouraging businesses to provide health care coverage to their employees. However, few of the recent national and state proposals to provide health care coverage to the uninsured also cover home- and community-based services. One exception in California is SB 2868, introduced in 1990 by Senator Nicholas Petris (D-Oakland). His comprehensive universal health care insurance proposal includes long-term care services focused on non-institutional and case-managed care. Most other California health care bills limit long-term care coverage to nursing facility care.

Since long-term care issues have traditionally operated on separate advocacy and political tracks from the broader concerns of the uninsured, the absence of coverage today is not surprising. The challenge for long-term care advocates, and in particular the aging network, is twofold: they must broaden their efforts in publicizing long-term care as a problem that affects the non-elderly; and they must develop alliances with other groups (e.g., the disabled, working uninsured, ethnic minorities, county hospitals) to ensure that health care solutions incorporate some form of long-term care.

Eligibility and Service Requirements

The development of comprehensive long-term care policy is complicated and politically volatile, especially around issues of eligibility and types of services. For example, most researchers and policy makers agree that an ideal long-term care system permits people to choose between home or community and medically based services. Yet federal policies currently constrain the states' flexibility in promoting social and health services as equal partners.

National studies consistently suggest that people who are older or disabled prefer to reside in their own homes and communities, yet several factors limit the availability of non-institutional services. First, many people do not qualify for In-Home Supportive Services, California's largest publicly funded social service program, and thus must absorb the costs of private home health and case management services. Second, non-institutional services may not be less expensive than institutional services; in fact, they may be more costly because they lack the economies of scale of hospitals or nursing homes. Third, the dominant role of physicians in dictating types and duration of treatment often skews services toward medical and hospital-based care.

Determining eligibility for long-term care programs often creates controversy among older and disabled constituencies. Today, most policy analysts and advocates endorse a system that bases eligibility for both programs on limited functional ability (e.g., the inability to perform two or more Activities of Daily Living). While most advocates oppose income- or means-testing for services because it engenders images of a welfare program, most policy makers and budget analysts foresee little choice if costs are to be controlled.

In addition to resolving eligibility and type of service issues, policy makers must decide whether the goals of a long-term care system are to promote independence and functional ability or to stabilize chronic or acute illness.[24] People with disabilities generally prefer the former approach, while older people tend toward the latter. The issue of where to focus expanded services—on the individual, the family, or the community—also needs resolution. What mix of services and service providers will qualify for participation and reimbursement, and who will maintain control over the disbursement of treatments and services?

A separate and increasingly visible set of issues involves the impact on long-term care funding for health care needs of AIDS patients. Should policy makers authorize disease-specific health care programs, or should they expand existing programs to accommodate unforeseen levels of health care needs? During the 101st Congress, legislators considered the allocation of earmarked monies to cities and states and to the Medicaid program for AIDS-related health care. Given current budget constraints, some members were concerned that AIDS care receives a disproportionate share of national health dollars, limiting monies available for all other institutional and non-institutional care. In addition, some federal policy makers and advocates worried about equity in Medicaid program service delivery should special coverage be permitted for people who are both poor and AIDS-infected.[25]

All of these issues represent difficult policy decisions, involving different constituencies, each with a stake in expanding and reshaping a long-term care service system. An ideal scenario for those needing services, of course, would be a universal entitlement program, qualifying all people, regardless of income, age, or disability,

24. *Supra* note 1.
25. Julie Kosterlitz, "Is Support for AIDS Slipping?" *National Journal*, June 2, 1990, p. 1351.

for non-institutional, case-managed, and institutional care, and all providers and programs for reimbursement. That scenario, financed in part through payroll taxes and co-payments, is currently embedded in SB 2868 introduced in 1990 by California Senator Petris. Because of its sweeping changes and costs, the future of SB 2868 in the legislature is uncertain. However, anything less than a universal program will require hard choices and tradeoffs.

Interest Group Politics

Who will influence the development of long-term care policy in California and in the nation? Who will address technical and administrative issues in service delivery? Decisions on need, priorities, and types of services require that the relative political influence of various political constituencies be confronted.

Senior citizens. Older people and the organizations that represent them are often powerful forces on national, state, and local levels. Their power was evidenced most recently by the rapid formation of a grassroots movement that forced Congress to repeal the Medicare Catastrophic Coverage Act of 1988, which would have expanded Medicare and Medicaid benefits.[26] That event demonstrated a political truism that, while senior citizens may not be able to promote legislative funding or expansion, they can halt the implementation of unpopular legislation and proposals.[27]

Similarly, in California, policy makers take seriously the concerns of senior citizens, who register and vote at higher rates than do other segments of the voting age public. Key groups advocating on behalf of older Californians include the umbrella Senior Coalition, the California Rural Legal Assistance Foundation—Senior Program, the Congress of California Seniors, the American Association of Retired Persons, and the Gray Panthers. In addition, the California Commission on Aging affords senior citizens access to the governor. The California Senior Legislature also focuses on influencing the state legislature.

---

26. Fernando Torres-Gil, "The Politics of Catastrophic and Long-Term Care Coverage," *Journal of Aging and Social Policy*, (1):61-86, 1990.
27. Robert Binstock, Martin A. Levin, and Richard Weatherley, "Political Dilemmas of Social Intervention," in Binstock and Shanas (eds.), *The Handbook of Aging and the Social Sciences*, New York, Van Nostrand Reinhold, 1985. See also William Browne and Laura K. Olsen, *Aging and Public Policy*, Westport, CT, Greenwood Press, 1983.

People with disabilities. People with disabilities in California have an equal interest in the politics of long-term care. The population at least 16 years of age with disabilities is estimated at nearly 11 percent of the total state population; about 75 percent of these people can be classified as severely disabled.[28] Both overall disabling conditions and those that are severe are more prevalent among women and minorities than among men and non-minorities.

Although the elderly and disability communities share preferences for independent living, home-delivered services, and comprehensive health care coverage, the specific interests of the two groups have not always coincided. The disability community also has a system of programs separate from those of the aging. Because these programs focus on rehabilitation rather than on receiving care, people with disabilities and advocacy groups representing them may prefer that long-term care services for the elderly and those for the disabled remain separate. Earlier California proposals to merge program funding within the state Departments of Aging and Rehabilitation caused consternation among both senior citizen and disability groups.[29] If developing a cost-effective system requires merging long-term care programs, the preferences and system investments of the disability and aging communities will remain major issues in the debates. Clearly, in order to minimize interest group struggles, both groups must be involved in each phase of policy formulation.

Other players. Interest by other groups in the politics of long-term care has increased in recent years. The personal nature of long-term care, the issues associated with financing services, and the diverse community of advocacy and professional groups affected by long-term care ensure that other players will continue to be concerned with long-term care policy.

While many national and state minority organizations consider long-term care a priority issue, sources of public funding have been limited for long-term care programs specific to the needs of ethnic minorities. Given the growing numbers of minority elderly, their greater likelihood of facing chronic illness, and their preference for

---

28. California Department of Rehabilitation, *Executive Summary for the California Disability Survey,* by J.M. Shanks and H.E. Freeman, Sacramento, 1980.
29. Fernando Torres-Gil and Jon Pynoos, Long-Term Care Policy and Interest Group Struggles," *The Gerontologist,* 26(5): 488-95.

home and community services, long-term care is certain to become more critical to them in the future.

Decision makers. Long-term care policy will not be decided by interest groups, academicians, legislative staff, elected officials, or civil servants alone, although many are delegated with varying authority for policy formulation and implementation.

At the national level the agency charged with Medicare and Medicaid oversight and regulations is the Health Care Financing Administration (HCFA); HCFA's director reports to the Secretary of Health and Human Services. Legislative jurisdiction over long-term care policy matters is shared among Senate and House of Representatives committees, as illustrated in Figure 5-2; California currently has several members of Congress on these committees.

At the state level, there is no single agency analogous to HCFA, in which regulatory, financing, and oversight actions are lodged. Instead, the Office of Statewide Health Planning and Development is charged with developing state health policies and surveying long-term care facilities. The Department of Aging is the lead agency for coordinating long-term care services, which are limited primarily to Older Americans Act services, demonstration projects, and waivers. The Department of Health oversees nursing homes funded by Medi-Cal, and the Department of Social Services has responsibility for the large In-Home Supportive Services Program.

Historically, the executive branch has provided little leadership on aging or long-term care service issues. Although Governor Deukmejian supported some initiatives aimed at coordinating long-term care programs, his office did not advance the issues in the long-term care debates. And while staffs of gubernatorial campaigns were briefed on long-term care issues by assembly staff in 1990, no candidates from either party elevated the issues to priority status.

In recent years, while the legislature attempted to pursue long-term care legislation, it has been successful in maintaining bipartisan support only on small, incremental changes. Few comprehensive bills have been enacted due to the lack of support from the executive branch and the two-thirds approval rule on budget matters. Aside from the initiatives introduced by Lloyd Connelly (D-Sacramento), chair of the Assembly Committee on Aging and Long-Term Care, few members of committees with jurisdiction over long-term care matters (e.g., Senate Subcommittee on Aging and Long-

Figure 5-2. Representation of California Congressional Delegation on Committees with Jurisdiction over Long-Term Care Issues

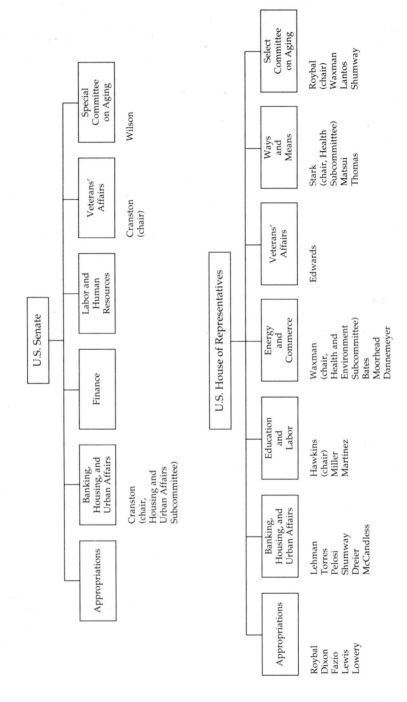

Term Care, Senate and Assembly Committees on Health, and Committees on Appropriations) were visible in the long-term care policy debates on comprehensive long-term care services until 1990. During that year Assemblyman John Vasconcellos (D-San Jose) of the Committee on Aging and Long-Term Care and Bruce Bronzan (D-Fresno), chair of the Assembly Committee on Health, introduced legislation related to long-term care.

Given the historically disjointed attention to long-term care in California government, who is responding today to the growing pressures associated with providing and financing services? Because of budget constraints, the national government has moved cautiously. Congress, the Department of Health and Human Services, and affected interest groups continue to engage in extended debate about solutions to the long-term care dilemma.

Reacting to the slow progress at the national level, several states, including California, run consumer education and counseling programs to provide information on public and private long-term care programs and insurance policies. Eight states, including California, are pressuring Congress for waivers to combine Medicaid coverage with private insurance against the costs of long-term care. In general, these public-private partnerships would encourage the growth of the private insurance market according to state standards, and encourage consumers to buy private insurance. For both insurer and consumer, Medicaid would serve as a safety net—if consumers exhaust their benefits, they would qualify for Medicaid without "spending down" to poverty; thus, insurers know that Medicaid would ultimately bear the costs of their more expensive cases.

Waiver legislation passed the U.S. Senate in 1989, but is still pending in the House. Representative Henry Waxman (D-CA), the powerful chair of the House subcommittee that oversees Medicaid, and other members are said to be concerned about the role of Medicaid as a potential safety net for the middle class, taking Medicaid funds away from low-income people, and the possible costs of the programs.[30] Again, hovering over long-term care service definitions and politics is the prickly and paramount issue of service financing.

---

30. Julie Rovner, "No Help From Congress on a Near-Term Solution for Long-Term Care," *Governing*, June 1990.

Paying for Long-Term Care

Costs of long-term care in California are projected to continue spiral-
ing upward. Assuming constant 1986-87 dollars and a base model
projection, the state Department of Health and Welfare estimates
that costs will nearly double by 2020. If those projections accounted
for the large numbers of persons not already served by the state's
long-term care programs, the costs would be even higher.[31]

Figure 5-3, developed by the Institute for Health and Aging at the
University of California at San Francisco, presents alternate public
and private options for financing projected long-term care costs.
Public financing options include incremental expansions of public
programs, voluntary public insurance, and mandatory public insurance. Private financing options focus on private long-term care
insurance.

The national government has inclined toward a combination of
public and private financing: augmenting Medicare and social services to expand respite and nursing home days and home care under
the OAA; using Medicare and Medi-Cal waivers for case management and community-based services; and proposing Medicaid buy-
in programs, in which individuals purchase private insurance with
assurances of qualifying for Medicaid when private coverage
expires. Potential funding sources include payroll taxes, general
revenues, value-added taxes, selected excise taxes (e.g., on alcohol
and tobacco purchases), income tax surcharges, and liens on estates.
The option advanced most often (included in the Pepper/Roybal
home care bill that was defeated in 1988) would lift the cap on the
payroll tax wage base (currently set at $51,000), which would provide
an estimated $6 billion per year for health care.

With a larger elderly population that is, on average, more affluent
and healthier today than in the past, private long-term care insurance is perceived as an important option. However, private insurance is not widely available today, and generally has other
shortcomings: adverse selection, limitations in care and coverage,
and high monthly premiums. In addition, even under the most
favorable economic circumstances, the Brookings Institution estimates that in 2020 only 26 to 45 percent of older Americans would be
able to afford private coverage against the catastrophic costs of an

---

31. *Supra* note 8.

Figure 5-3. Public Policy Options for Long-Term Care in California

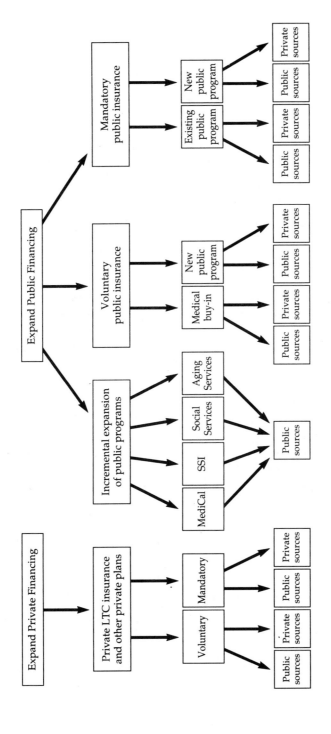

Source: University of California, San Francisco, "Long-Term Care Public Policy Agenda for California," Institute for Health and Aging Publication No. 89-2-1, 1989.

extended disability.[32] Recently enacted legislation in California was aimed at moderating these shortcomings. Introduced by Senators Henry Mello (D-Santa Cruz) and Alan Robbins (D-Van Nuys) and Assemblymember Lloyd Connelly (D-Sacramento), these bills include prohibitions against clauses requiring three days of hospitalization prior to payment of benefits and against policy cancellations based on age or health condition, as well as Medigap-like consumer protections for long-term care insurance marketing.

Given the strengths and weaknesses of both public and private options, public-private cooperation is a feasible alternative, and one that is currently being pursued by a number of states. For example, public funds might subsidize the voluntary purchase of private insurance premiums. States might mandate the expansion of private long-term care policies or the addition of long-term care services in existing medical insurance policies, or provide incentives to purchase private long-term care insurance that meets state standards.[33] The national government's examination of private long-term care insurance policies and the use of medical individual retirement accounts and home equity conversions, delegate to individuals and their families a larger share of the responsibility for financing long-term care needs.

Clearly, these developments suggest that financing long-term care services may be costly. Proposed financing options will be directly affected by the perception of long-term care as a priority social need and by the political actions of interest groups, decision makers, and the public. Recent state and national opinion polls indicate that strong public support exists for public funding of long-term care. A recent Gallup poll on California health care indicated that 65 percent of Californians believe that government is spending too little for the care of senior citizens, and 73 percent would pay additional taxes to support the health care of those in need.[34] Whether these findings

---

32. Alice Rivlin and Joshua Wiener, "Who Should Pay for Long-Term Care for the Elderly?" *The Brookings Review,* 6(3): 3-9.

33. Alaska, Ohio, and South Carolina currently offer long-term care insurance to their state employees and retirees, with the enrollees paying the full premium costs. Unlike other long-term care proposals described earlier, federal waivers are not required in order to provide coverage to state employees.

34. University of California, San Francisco, Institute for Health and Aging, *Long-Term Care Public Policy Agenda for California,* Research Brief No. 7, San Francisco, 1989.

translate into political support for increased taxes for long-term care services remains an open question.

Service Delivery

An additional issue concerns the structure of long-term care service delivery systems at the local level. Expansions of existing services will directly affect the city, county, and state agencies that provide the services.

The complex and fragmented laws, regulations, and financing sources administered by multiple agencies of the federal and state governments result in equally complex, fragmented, and often inaccessible services in the community. For example, in general, county departments of health oversee nursing homes, while county departments of social services have jurisdiction over the IHSS programs, and city and county area agencies on aging coordinate other long-term care services. In addition, private, for-profit home care programs proliferate in more affluent areas. Only recently did the state impose operations standards for board and care facilities that provide housing for individuals who might otherwise be institutionalized.

This array of programmatically unconnected services heightens the critical importance of effective case management, information and referral services, and written understandings among state, county, and city agencies. In response to that need, some localities (e.g., Los Angeles County) have promoted cooperation across the city, county, and private sectors through long-term care task forces.

Major expansions of long-term care services will impel fundamental reforms in service delivery and a major restructuring of existing programs. Like financing reforms, reforms in service delivery are likely to be difficult. For instance, legislation in the early 1980s proposing the coordination of services through a state long-term care corporation or through area agencies on aging generated significant and intense interagency disputes.

Other service delivery issues include the availability and specialized training of health and long-term care personnel. By 2000, approximately 50 percent more physicians, nurses, occupational and physical therapists, geriatric social workers, case managers, gerontologists, and mental health workers will be needed than are available today in order to fully staff all forms of health and long-term care services for the elderly.[35] While geriatricians are in short supply today, the granting of board certification and the presence of geriatric medical programs (e.g., at the University of California, San Francisco, the University of California, Los Angeles, the University of Southern California, and Stanford University) may ameliorate that situation in the future.

Service Needs of Minorities

Finally, several present and potential characteristics of minority elderly populations have major implications for long-term care policy in California. First, because of lower income levels, the capacity of today's elderly minorities to pay for health and long-term care is limited. For example, Mexican-Americans, the predominant Hispanic group in California, have the highest proportion of medically uninsured persons in the United States (30 percent, compared with 9 percent for white non-Hispanics).[36] Without improvements in present income patterns, significant portions of California's minority population will confront serious problems in assisting their elderly parents and financing their own long-term care needs. Second, minority elderly are more likely to need long-term care because of greater tendencies toward chronic illnesses at earlier ages than in the white population.

Strong family and informal support networks are common among minorities,[37] and minority elderly are less likely to reside in long-term care facilities than are non-minority elderly. However, it is uncertain whether these patterns will continue in the future, given trends toward assimilation, upward mobility, and geographic dispersion.

35. California Employment Development Department, *California Projections of Employment by Industry and Occupation: 1987-2000,* Sacramento, 1990.
36. F.M. Trevino and A.J. Moss, "Health Insurance Coverage and Physician Visits among Hispanic and Non-Hispanic People," in U.S. Public Health Service, National Center for Health Statistics, *Health, United States, 1983,* DHHS Pub. No. (PHS) 84-1232, Washington, D.C., U.S. Government Printing Office, 1983.
37. R.J. Taylor, "Aging and Supportive Relationships among Black Americans," in Jackson (ed.), *The Black Elderly: Research on Physical and Psychosocial Health,* New York, Springer, 1988. See also M. Sotomayor and A. Curiel (eds.), *Hispanic Elderly: a Cultural Signature,* Edinburg, TX, Pan American University Press, 1988; Louise Kamikawa, "Expanding Perceptions of Aging: the Pacific Asian Elderly," *Generations,* 6(3): 26-27, 1982; Carmela G. Lacayo, *A National Study to Assess the Service Needs of the Hispanic Elderly: Final Report,"* Los Angeles, Asociacion Naciional Pro Personas Mayores, 1980.

Politics of Long-Term Care

Current long-term care policy dilemmas point out the inherently political nature of long-term care and the difficult choices that lie ahead. Both the national and state governments will wrestle with the complexities of the financing and delivery of long-term care services in the next few decades.

Repeal of the Medicare Catastrophic Act of 1988 appears to have stymied the movement toward development of a comprehensive national long-term care system in the near future. In fact, one of the key factors leading to the grassroots opposition to the legislation was its exclusion of long-term care insurance coverage. After the repeal, national policy makers shifted their attention to other policy issues, citing the federal deficit, the need to contain escalating health care costs, and concern for the uninsured as obstacles to consideration of costly expansions of Medicare and Medicaid long-term care. At the state level, budget deficits have encouraged efforts to contain costs by reducing services.

Nonetheless, long-term care issues remain on the public agenda at both national and state levels. Many of the health care bills introduced in the 101st Congress provide for additional funding for home- and community-based care.[38] The Elder-Care Long-Term Care Assistance Act (HR 3140), introduced in 1989 by Representative Henry Waxman (D-CA), proposes in-home long-term care services and nursing facility care under Medicare. Senator Edward Kennedy (D-MA) introduced a Lifecare bill (S 2163) in 1990 that would provide home care to elderly people, disabled children, and adults with disabilities under age 65 who are eligible for Medicare. Both bills would finance the programs by eliminating the Medicare payroll tax wage cap. The Medicare Benefit Improvements Act (HR 3880), introduced in 1990 by Representative Fortney (Pete) Stark (D-CA), would re-authorize the expanded mammography, home health care screening, respite, and hospice benefits lost in the repeal of the Medicare Catastrophic Act. These benefits would be fully financed by a modest increase in the Medicare Part B premiums.

In California, the passage of Proposition 111 in June 1990, loosening the Gann spending level constraints, will allow California more flexibility in spending for health and aging services. However, that

---

38. *Supra* note 11.

flexibility will result in intense competition among advocates for long-term care and those seeking coverage for other health and social needs.

Short-Run Prognosis

The prospects for short-run resolutions are limited. The executive and legislative branches on both national and state levels are preoccupied with the politically popular health care issues of the medically uninsured and national health insurance, which are generally considered separate from long-term care. Congress is likely to consider, but unlikely to adopt, proposals to improve the quality and financing of nursing home care and to develop publicly funded community- and home-based services. Policy makers will continue to debate whether a universal national health care system can afford to include long-term care services. Thus, long-term care likely will remain a secondary issue in the foreseeable future.

The repeal of the Medicare Catastrophic Act of 1988 illustrates the impasse. To some, the repeal fueled a growing backlash against older people, and the share of the federal budget devoted to programs for them, and a shifting allegiance toward children and the poor. To others, it was a temporary setback that will be forgotten by the 1992 congressional and presidential elections, during which the electoral power of older people will recast long-term care into an important political issue. More likely, unless a dramatic political event elevates long-term care to primary status, we will see continued incremental expansion of publicly funded long-term care.

Long-Run Prognosis

The long-run outlook is more promising for a comprehensive long-term care service system. Demographic pressures, increasing numbers of people with disabling conditions (particularly among women and ethnic minority populations), the aging of the baby boomers, the escalating electoral clout of those groups, increased geographic mobility, and changes in living arrangements will command the attention of governments and propel the development of a comprehensive long-term care service system.

Within ten years we can expect public funding of coverage for a continuum of home- and community-based services for younger and older people with at least two or three functional disabilities. Such a system will include means-testing and cost-sharing provisions for low- and middle-income groups and cost-containment mechanisms. Private medical insurance, governed by strict state standards, will be expanded to include a range of long-term care services; public funds will subsidize the purchase of such policies on a sliding income scale. In addition, tax incentives will encourage private-sector businesses to provide expanded dependent care benefits for caretaking of both children and disabled parents.

Strategies

Because of California's special demographic circumstances, the state may not have the luxury of waiting for federal action on long-term care. It must proceed soon with a structural strategy as well as incremental reforms, despite the inherently politicized nature of long-term care. The new governor's office and the legislature should work closely with the powerful California congressional delegation to shape joint federal-state strategies, ensuring that federal proposals meet California's needs.

The framework for a coordinated system was authorized in AB 2860, and recent legislative activity in the areas of health insurance and long-term care suggests an atmosphere of greater awareness, discussion, and urgency. The new administration is in an enviable position to court an increasingly large electorate — the diverse population of baby boomers and their families — by taking a leadership role on the long-term care issue.

Interest groups and others concerned with health and long-term care should continue to negotiate the basic features of a statewide long-term care system. Task forces, universities, and advocacy groups should convene long-term care "summits" and come to agreement on recommendations for policy changes. Some of the issues to be considered have been proposed by the National Council on Aging: shared responsibility between the national and state governments; universal eligibility, signifying a multi-generational approach to long-term care service; a social insurance approach to financing; and inclusion of housing, social services, and rehabilitation as integral services.

The long-term care service system must build upon and coordinate existing services, setting minimum standards for those services. Area agencies on aging are logical candidates for coordinating the services in the community, while the state Department of Aging has greater latitude and administrative authority to plan and oversee state-level programs. Culturally sensitive programs and successful projects such as On Lok, the Multipurpose Senior Services Program projects, and Linkages should be continued and expanded. With political pressures building in support of long-term care, California universities must produce the personnel needed to staff long-term care programs.

In addition, California must educate the public about the implications of increased life expectancies and the very real possibility that all people will someday need long-term care. In order to moderate needs and costs, the state must also encourage consumer education on financing long-term care and preventive health care practices; gerontology instruction in high schools and colleges; and congregate-care facilities and other alternative living arrangements for older people.

California policy makers and advocates must use the 1990s as a decade of opportunity to prepare for the next century's long-term care needs. Electoral support for expanding the long-term care service system will emerge in the near future. In California that support may manifest itself in a long-term care services initiative by 1992. The nation and the state will be forced to confront the needs of expanding numbers of older people and people with disabilities, the political interests of baby boomers and their elected officials, and the complex dilemmas associated with coordinating and financing a continuum of long-term care services.

The authors thank Tom Porter, principal consultant for the Assembly Committee on Aging and Long-Term Care, for his insights and invaluable comments and Jeff Hyde, doctoral student at the University of Southern California, for assistance with this chapter's graphics.

REFOCUSING CALIFORNIA CORRECTIONS

Chester A. Newland

6

California's reliance on a dichotomous system of correctional extremes—incarceration or minimally supervised probation—leaves the state with few options for dealing cost-effectively with growing numbers of offenders. Despite a massive infusion of monies into facility construction, correctional institutions remain overcrowded and probation caseloads are so high that supervision is difficult or nearly impossible. Professional thinking now supports the expanded use of intermediate community-based correctional sanctions, with incarceration reserved for those offenders who require long-term isolation from society. Related recommendations, outlined in this chapter, include adoption of a community corrections act, development of sentencing guidelines, streamlining of court procedures, and an automated corrections management information system to serve all components of California's criminal justice system.

A strategic shift is needed in California's corrections policy, which currently relies largely on a dichotomous system of costly incarceration and minimally supervised probation. Jails, prisons, and youth facilities are generally well managed from a security perspective, but, due to chronic overcrowding and rapid movement of offenders in, out, and about, they have become nightmares of expensive logistical management. With high returns of parole violators, California's prisons are threatening to become perpetual motion machines. On the opposite side of this binary system, probation is often so minimally supervised that control is a myth.

Experience of other states—and creative experimentation by California corrections officials—has demonstrated a constructive strategy for improvement. Such a strategy calls for a corrections policy based on balanced use of prisons and jails, fines and victim restitution, programs for substance abusers, and work furloughs and electronic surveillance in a matrix with other intermediate sanctions. A major focus of this strategy is on community-based corrections.

Enhanced public safety, improved correction of offender behaviors, and long-term cost control are the objectives.

Four system changes warrant priority action to make the needed strategic shift in California corrections policy:

- adoption of a California Community Corrections Act;
- creation of a system of structured sentencing guidelines that encompasses a matrix of graded corrections options and establishment of a mechanism for ongoing monitoring and updating of that system;
- reform of court operations to reduce delays and enhance justice;
- development of an automated corrections management information system to serve all components of California's criminal justice system.

These strategies are strongly recommended in the January 1990 report[1] of the California Blue Ribbon Commission on Inmate Population Management, which was mandated by SB 279 (Presley) in 1987. As have most such studies nationwide, that report concluded that the complexities of crime and public safety today are beyond easy prescriptions for solution, but that dominant problems are easily identified and that their urgency makes action to ameliorate them imperative. This chapter, which outlines these recommended actions, begins with a discussion of the major corrections problems that account for their urgency—institutional crowding and rapid turnover, high costs, drugs, and the discontinuity caused by short-term isolation from society followed by abrupt reentry and, for many, repeated returns.

California Corrections Today

Crowding of correctional and criminal justice systems is a major problem throughout the United States, and California is no exception.[2] Although sixteenth among the states in prison incarcerations per 100,000 population and only forty-second in the rate of imprisonment to arrests for FBI index crimes (homicide, robbery, aggravated assault, larceny, arson, motor vehicle theft), California ranks first in

1. Blue Ribbon Commission on Inmate Population Management, *Final Report,* Sacramento, January 1990.
2. The nationwide character of prison crowding is reported in James H. Burow and Carl T. Trisler, "America's Overcrowded Prisons," *The GAO Journal,* Washington, D.C., U.S. General Accounting Office, Fall 1989, pp. 22-34.

absolute numbers of felony arrests and in total number of state prison inmates.[3] That high ranking is largely a function of California's size.

In numbers, but not in percentages, the state also ranks first in prison overcrowding. California Youth Authority facilities and local jails are overburdened also. Eighteen county jails, which house 54 percent of the state's average daily jail population, had court-ordered population caps in early 1990.[4] Los Angeles County, with a cap of 21,851, was operating over that in 1989 at nearly 175 percent of its rated capacity of 15,528, and crowding was higher on weekends; total jail inmates of that one county exceeded prison totals in forty-five states. As shown in Table 6-1, prisons, jails, and youth facilities throughout California were operating at well over capacity in June 1989, and projections for all categories of institutions are for continued growth.

For index crimes the state ranked eighth among the states in 1988, behind Florida, the District of Columbia, Texas, Arizona, Washington, Oregon, and New Mexico. The state's property and violent crime rate remained stable for six years, starting in 1983, but it recently began to climb: during the first six months of 1989 reported homicides were up 11.3 percent over the same period in 1988; robbery was up 13.4 percent; and motor vehicle theft was up 13.5 percent.

While rising crime reflects the troubling extent of California's public safety problem, it does not reveal the two interrelated factors that have contributed most to soaring corrections populations: drug offenses and parole revocations. Drug arrests fell briefly following decriminalization of marijuana in California in 1976-77, but they have been on the rise ever since. Drugs accounted for one-third of all adult felony arrests in 1988, when felony drug arrests (158,510) exceeded those for property crimes (152,992). Drug abuse also is involved in a large proportion of non-drug crimes. As reported in 1988 by the National Institute of Justice, in San Diego and Los Angeles "over 70 percent of arrestees for all types of crimes tested positive for drug use (excluding marijuana)."[5] Of 29,551 new commitments to the California Department of Corrections (CDC) in

3. *Supra* note 1.
4. California Board of Corrections, County Correctional Facility Capital Expenditure Fund, *Annual Report,* Sacramento, Board of Corrections Jail Planning and Construction Division, 1990.
5. The NIJ research is cited by the Blue Ribbon Commission, *supra* note 1, p. 69, chart 5-1.

Chester Newland

Table 6-1. Inmate Population Projections and Facility Overcrowding

Facilities	Population and Capacity				Projected Increase 1989-94 (%)
	June 1989		Projected 1994		
	Capacity[a]	ADP[b]	Capacity	ADP	
Department of Corrections	49,307	82,855	73,233	136,640	65
	(overcrowding: 168%)		(overcrowding: 189%)		
Department of Youth Authority	6,057	8,523	6,956	9,478	11
	(overcrowding: 141%)		(overcrowding: 136%)		
Jails[c]	51,684	68,424	71,600	89,673	31
	(overcrowding: 132%)		(overcrowding: 125%)		
Juvenile halls, camps, ranches		8,999		10,142	13
Total		168,801		245,933	45

a. The California Department of Corrections and the California Youth Authority use "design capacity" and jails use "Board of Corrections rated capacity" to determine overcrowding.
b. Average daily population.
c. Average daily population may be artificially deflated because numbers may be expected to rise at a higher rate once new jails come on line and court-imposed population limits are eliminated.

1988, 76 percent had histories of drug abuse; and about 85 percent of California Youth Authority (CYA) wards were found to have substance abuse problems in 1989.[6] The National Academy of Sciences Working Group on Drugs and Crime has reported that violent and property offenders who abuse drugs commit twice as many offenses as all such criminals and that their offenses increase with frequency of use.[7]

Drug violations are also the primary reason for parole revocation, and parole violators now account for 16 percent of average daily prison populations. The parolee population has grown enormously, from 9,000 in 1978 to 55,000 in 1989, and more of them are being returned to prison for parole violations. In 1978 parole violators returned to prison totaled only 1,011; in 1988 that figure was 34,014 (including repeat violators). In part, returnees to prison have increased because overcrowded jails can no longer accommodate

6. California Department of Corrections, *Substance Abuse Treatment and Education Services for Inmates and Parolees: a Report to the Legislature,* Sacramento, December 1989, p. 1.
7. Norval Morris and Michael Tomy, *Between Prison and Probation,* New York, Oxford University Press, 1990, p. 191.

short-term stays by parole violators. Yet most returnees to state prisons are short term: 81 percent of parole violators remain in state prisons less than six months.

Parole violators are not the only group that contributes to the rapid movement of offenders in and out of institutions: of new commitments to CDC facilities in 1988, about 5,000 served three months or less, 8,000 served six months or less, and 18,000 served one year or less.[8] The velocity of this revolving-door movement disrupts California prisons and undermines performance of their primary function of long-term incarceration.

Probation—the other extreme of California's dichotomous corrections system—is even more overburdened than the institutions and parole. As of December 1989 probationers totaled 285,018, or 66 percent more than the number of inmates in all of California's state and local correctional institutions. Caseloads of probation officers averaged 200 in 1989, making supervision, in most cases, difficult or nearly impossible.[9] The Blue Ribbon Commission reports that today "probation supervision is largely a matter of monitoring for rearrest or compilation of presentence reports. According to informal reports from the field, probation officers in many jurisdictions carry caseloads which permit only minimal contact with the probationer."[10]

A sentence of probation also does not mean that institutional populations are unaffected: of felons convicted in 1988, only 6 percent were granted probation without jail time; for 60 percent jail was a condition of probation.

Jail crowding is affected as well by crowded court calendars and resulting delays in judicial processing. In January 1990 approximately 49 percent of California's jail population consisted of unsentenced prisoners awaiting trial. The combination of routine court delays and highly publicized exceptional cases of many years duration is undermining the justice system and public confidence in it.

Costs of Corrections

Costs of new jails completed or authorized for 1982-94 total $1.27 billion of county funding and $1.5 billion of state funding, expendi-

---

8. *Supra* note 1, p. 42.
9. Probationer statistics are from Charlotte Rhea, Bureau of Criminal Statistics, Sacramento. Caseload average is from the California Probation, Parole and Correctional Association.
10. *Supra* note 1, p. 47.

tures that are expected to bring the number of jail beds up to 71,600 by 1994. Despite these expenditures, a jail bed shortfall of 18,073 is projected; jails operating at 132 percent of capacity in 1989 are expected to be at 125 percent in 1994.

The state is involved in similarly ambitious building efforts. CDC's construction program totals $3.2 billion, for a total of 24,362 new beds already added and 12,940 more being built. Even with the new additions, however, CDC expects to be operating at 189 percent of capacity in 1994, compared to 168 percent in 1989. The CYA's building program totals $83 million for 1,116 new beds. With these additions, CYA is expected to reduce overcrowding only slightly from the 1989 level of 141 percent to a 1994 level of 136 percent.

Operating costs of new facilities will make the long-term capital and bond interest costs pale by comparison. A March 1990 study by the Board of Corrections (BOC) reported operating costs for FY 1987-88 in fifteen California counties and twenty facilities constructed and opened since 1980.[11] Not including debt financing, costs per prisoner averaged about $39 a day in high-security pretrial facilities and $28 per day in dormitory-style facilities housing mostly sentenced prisoners. In its projection of life-cycle costs, the BOC reported that "when conservatively estimated, future operating costs will constitute from 93 to 95 percent of the total county expenditures" on a jail. Among the facilities studied, the high-security facilities averaged $15.7 million in front-end (planning, design, and construction) costs and $196.9 million in thirty-year operating costs; dormitory facilities averaged $8.3 million in front-end costs and $161.1 million in operating costs. These life-cycle costs promise a particularly bleak future for California corrections.

Operating costs of local and state corrections in California increased dramatically over the last decade. In fiscal year 1977-78 annual operating costs totaled $826 million; by FY 1986-87 that total had increased to $2.7 billion, and by 1990 to $3 billion. Corrections' share of the state budget grew from about 2 percent in FY 1981-82 to over 6 percent in FY 1989-90.

Operating costs of California corrections as a percentage of overall criminal justice expenditures are shown in Table 6-2. Costs increased from 28 percent of the total in 1972-73 (and from a dip to 27 percent in

11. Board of Corrections, *The State of the Jails in California, Report No. 5: Jail Operating Costs*, Sacramento, Board of Corrections Jail Planning and Construction Division, March 1990, p. iii.

Table 6-2. California Criminal Justice Expenditures, 1972-87 ($ millions)

Component	Expenditures									
	FY 72-73		FY 77-78		FY 82-83		FY 86-87		FY 87-88	
	$	%	$	%	$	%	$	%	$	%
Law enforcement	904	56	1,578	55	2,981	56	4,243	51	4,509	50
Prosecution	58	4	149	5	281	5	415	5	453	5
Public defense	25	2	55	2	112	2	186	2	213	2
Courts[a]	160	10	279	10	516	10	826	10	898	10
Corrections	465	28	827	28	1,465	27	2,700	32	3,013	33
Jails	87		155		346		622		713[b]	
Probation	156		270		391		535		549	
Prisons	140		277		496		1,216		1,410	
CYA	82		125		232		327		340	
Total	1,612	100	2,888	100	5,355	100	8,370	100	9,087	100

Source: California Bureau of Criminal Statistics and Special Services.

a. Includes court and court-related costs
b. The FY 1987-88 jails total is $7 million below that reported in the State Controller's Transaction Report, cited in *The State of the Jails in California, Report No. 5: Jail Operating Costs,* Sacramento, Board of Corrections, March 1990, p. i.

1982-83) to 33 percent in 1987-88. Note that although probation costs increased from $156 million in 1972-73 to $549 million in 1987-88, they declined from 34 percent of corrections expenditures to only 18 percent.

Other System Problems

Crowding in all components of the corrections system, court delays, and the high costs of building and operating correctional facilities are not the only problems facing California corrections and criminal justice today. Corrections must also deal with a population that includes many individuals who are substance abusers, mentally deficient or mentally ill, or lacking in education and job skills. Gangs, AIDS,[12] and changing demographics also challenge the ability of corrections officials to manage offender populations, especially where high rates of staff turnover mean that offenders often

12. Several good publications are available on the subject of AIDS in correctional facilities and programs. See: National Institute of Justice, *AIDS in Correctional Facilities: Issues and Options,* Boulder, CO, April 1988; National Institute of Justice, *AIDS in Probation and Parole,* by Dana Esser Hunt, Boulder, CO, June 1989; California Department of Corrections, *AIDS in the Department of Corrections,* Sacramento, October 1986; California Youth and Adult Correctional Agency, *Report to the Legislature: AIDS Educational Program,* Sacramento, January 1989.

have greater experience in correctional routines (and their disruption) than those who must supervise them. Even where turnover is low, rapid expansion of staff to handle growing offender populations has resulted in more correctional personnel with limited experience at all levels.

Discontinuity and isolation of correctional facilities, combined with the short-term nature of much incarceration, also complicate efforts to deal with deficiencies offenders may have and aggravate the crime problem for communities outside. Because of their isolation, it is impossible for many institutions to link work, training, and treatment to community-based programs that might facilitate re-entry to society and reduce the likelihood of reoffending. The frenzied logistical operation that segregates offenders briefly from criminal opportunities also separates them from rehabilitative systems in the communities to which most return with few if any constructive ties.

Programs do exist in California institutions, and, to their credit, the state's correctional institutions do an impressive job of keeping order under increasingly impossible conditions. The BOC provides strategic leadership, technical assistance, training, and standards for local jails, and the CDC has a national reputation for effective security management. But the factors that account for California's well managed institutions also define limits to maintaining that record—even with all the new construction—if other changes are not made in the criminal justice apparatus. In addition to officially maintained order through generally unfailing controls, security in the state's prisons and jails has depended on the provision of humane amenities, including wholesome food, clean surroundings, exercise, and health care, as well as selective but generally available privileges and services, including work and educational opportunities. Except for adequate food, basic cleanliness, and controlled television, it is increasingly difficult to provide reasonable access to amenities and services due to crowding, rapid turnover, and lack of authority for expanded work opportunities—along with the growing intrusion of drugs and gangs.

Policy Choices
California's major policy choices in corrections today are not either to build more costly institutions or to rely more heavily on an already

overburdened probation system, as they were portrayed in the 1980s. For the foreseeable future, the state will need both to continue expansion of jails, prisons, and youth facilities and to provide intermediate sanctions for use in addition to the present-day extremes of incarceration and traditional probation. California must fashion a more comprehensive corrections system of graduated punishments and functionally differentiated correctional interventions. Such a system is needed to enhance public safety by providing a more effective network of reasonable social controls.

Intermediate sanctions were introduced in the late 1970s in other states and on a limited basis in California, with a principal purpose of reducing correctional costs. Results, however, have generally been widening nets of social control—not visible cost reductions—at least in the short run. Due to the punishment orientation that dominated the 1980s, new sanctions introduced for use in lieu of more severe ones were more commonly used in lieu of less severe sanctions, with the result that more people were exposed to higher levels of penal control.[13]

Professional thinking today supports a comprehensive system of intermediate correctional interventions, not primarily as a short-term prospect for reducing corrections costs but as a means of controlling crime and promoting public safety. The public attitude of "trail 'em, nail 'em, and jail 'em" has contributed much less than desired to the public safety goal. Where employment and services are limited, even warehousing protects people from criminals while they are locked up, and this has had considerable appeal in California. But there is much evidence to suggest that incarceration is effective in promoting public safety only when it is reasonably employed. Although some people must be locked up for life and others for long periods, short-term, revolving-door imprisonment in institutions—especially those far removed from community-linked support systems—contributes only marginally to long-term correction of criminal behaviors, and it creates costly logistical burdens that limit resources for more positive corrections efforts.

To address this dilemma the Blue Ribbon Commission on Inmate Population Management has recommended adoption of a community corrections act, with state funding to encourage local jurisdic-

---

13. *Supra* note 7.

tions to develop intermediate sanctions in addition to incarceration and traditional probation, and it has supported CDC and CYA use of similar sanctions for parole violators. A related commission recommendation urges creation of a sentencing law review commission to develop sentencing guidelines, including a matrix of intermediate sanctions in addition to incarceration and traditional probation.

Intermediate sanctions between imprisonment and minimally supervised probation are briefly described below. Financial sanctions are highlighted first to stress their distinctive importance. Although they may be considered intermediate sanctions, financial penalties can be equal to or stronger than short-term incarceration in their punitive and deterrent effects. Following discussion of financial sanctions, general policy considerations with respect to intensively supervised intermediate correctional options are discussed. Then four categories of non-financial sanctions are briefly summarized.

Financial Penalties

Financial sanctions have been widely used in the United States, but compared to western Europe this country has rarely imposed financial penalties severe enough to undermine the profitability of some crimes. With increasing commerce in illegal drugs and adverse social impacts of white-collar crimes and property offenses, more use needs to be made of financial penalties as punishments, possible deterrents, and sources of revenues.

Three forms of financial penalties are noted by the Blue Ribbon Commission: fines, including installment payments, in lieu of jail or as a condition of probation; day fines, based for equity purposes on offenders' daily earnings; and restitution/community service. Limited use of restitution in California has taken two forms: direct compensation by offenders to victims or their dependents and victim compensation from a restitution fund derived from financial penalties.

Throughout the United States, fines typically are so low that they seldom are as punitive or potentially deterring as incarceration. Exceptions are fines for federal securities violations and some other business crimes, but even there a criminal may be left with ill-gotten gains of $1 billion after a fine of $600 million—not a small profit. If a dealer in illicit drugs can sustain for long an annual income of several million dollars or even a few hundred thousand, a few years of incarceration may not seem too high a price to pay for the benefits of criminal wealth left in friendly hands or unforfeited investments. Full forfeiture of wrongfully gained wealth and of all assets connected to illegal activities merits consideration as a policy of choice in California and nationally, along with imprisonment, to deal with such crimes. Forfeiture of other holdings and of future high earnings also warrants consideration for social restitution, just as portions of lower earnings of other offenders currently are sometimes paid to victim compensation funds.

At the level of more ordinary fines as penalty assessments, in Los Angeles today—as elsewhere under conditions of jail crowding—offenders may opt for jail time instead of a fine, knowing that, because of crowding, they most likely will serve no time. Maximum limits on fines need to be modified statutorily to become part of an effective penalty system in which financial sanctions are more commensurate with incarceration. Provisions also should be made to ensure full payment of financial penalties; private collection agencies may be useful for this purpose in some cases.

Because of changes in the political economy of crime and corrections, charging offenders for corrections services, similar to levying of court costs, is becoming a practice of choice in California. As of January 1990 the Board of Corrections reported that twenty counties were charging fees for home supervision, forty-seven were charging for work furlough, forty-one were charging for work-in-lieu programs, and five were charging for county parole.[14] Charging of corrections costs can result in differential justice, which may be unfair if financial circumstances of offenders are not carefully weighed, but, as with day fines, differences can be considered to achieve fairness.

Financial sanctions beyond fees sometimes are employed for those in custody, although they are minimal. Employment in prison industries at low pay and performance of other work is related in form, but work in CYA and in restitution centers, where higher compensation from private employment is authorized, permits more meaningful imposition of sanctions by requiring payment of portions of earn-

---

14. California Board of Corrections, *Operating Cost Study,* Sacramento, January 1990.

.ings for victim compensation and correctional expenses. The Blue
Ribbon Commission recommends that CDC be granted authoriza-
tion to allow private-sector involvement in prison-based businesses,
such as the Free Venture program for youth currently operating in
CYA institutions.[15] An effort was made to do that in 1989, but it
failed. Governor Deukmejian then led an effort to qualify a prison
inmate labor initiative for the November 1990 ballot, and he
announced in May that sufficient signatures had been collected. As
Proposition 139, it won support of both 1990 gubernatorial nomi-
nees. Such authority is needed for two reasons. First, work for
inmates is consistent with the realities of today's market exchange in
crime and punishment, in which costs of crime to victims and to
society need to be paid in part by offenders. Second, the opportunity to work is consistent with the rehabilitative ideals of traditional California corrections, encouraging development among
inmates of the discipline and resources for eventual success outside.

California is slowly embracing more stringent financial sanctions,
but the movement has been largely in response to budgetary constraints as corrections costs have skyrocketed. Urgently needed are
more systematic actions to increase reliance on a full panoply of
financial sanctions in a comprehensive accountability system. Such
a system must balance the realities of the brisk exchange economy of
crime and punishment in America with the lingering rehabilitative
ideals that underlie California's use of the term corrections.

Other Intermediate Sanctions

Intermediate sanctions fit between incarceration and minimal probation, and, as a practical matter, are additions to those two extremes
in a more comprehensive armory of sanctions designed to improve
correctional outcomes. Some also may serve as cost-saving alternatives to incarceration, but that will require a period of transition to
test varied applications.

Costs of intermediate corrections interventions that require more
intensive supervision than regular probation cannot be estimated
from general probation expenditures. The latter range from $300 to
$2,000 per probationer per year, whereas the costs of intensive super-
vision, where now applied in California, range from $1,500 to

---

15. *Supra* note 1, p. 130-1.

$7,000. Annual costs per case for a few other intermediate corrections activities in California are: $3,000 to $8,000 for diversion to specialized treatment programs; $8,000 to $10,000 for "shock" (including a period of incarceration) probation; $8,000 to $12,000 for halfway house and work release programs; and $8,000 to $10,000 for county parole.

Costs of intermediate interventions clearly are higher than minimally supervised probation, but they are substantially lower than incarceration (the average cost of state incarceration in 1989 was $19,874). If the addition of such interventions would reduce the numbers of offenders sentenced to jails and prisons, then total corrections costs would be lower. But if experience from the punishment era of the past fifteen years holds, and intermediate interventions draw offenders away from regular probation rather than from high-cost incarceration, then total corrections costs would increase.

The primary purpose of intermediate sanctions, however, is not to cut costs, but to provide interventions that contribute to correction of criminal behaviors and the conditions and incentives that lead to crime. Jails and prisons will remain the most practical sanctions for many, especially violent offenders, because incarceration is the most effective means of protecting society from such people and because, for some, it satisfies public expectations for punishment. But prisons can better perform their primary function of keeping some offenders locked up for long periods and of preparing some inmates for reentry into society if those who do not require incarceration are diverted to other sanctions.

In designing a comprehensive system of sanctions, attention must be given to practical matters of purposes, costs, and implementability. Economy is essential in all correctional programs, and both costs/benefits of programs and opportunity costs of foregoing other policy choices must be considered. Current and long-term affordability, taking into account California's other priority needs, must be factored into any plan for change in the corrections and criminal justice system.

Practical manageability also is an issue. Implementation requirements are often neglected in the design of public policies. Given the complexities of crime and corrections in California, and the added complications of the judiciary and the larger criminal justice system, it is easy to understand the appeal of a dichotomous system of simple extremes. Corrections organizations have limited capacities for implementation of complex policies, as have all organizations, and this fact must be taken into account in the design of a comprehensive system of graded sanctions.

In addition to cost-effectiveness and implementability, two other characteristics are essential for workable intermediate sanctions: intensive supervision and community linkages. Close supervision is basic. Mandatory offender participation in targeted correctional programs needs to be enforced through technological and other monitoring, including face-to-face contacts, drug testing, and supervised self-disciplinary measures. To accomplish that, reasonable supervisory caseloads are necessary, along with general and specific support systems. Community linkages help to provide those supports and maintain the continuity necessary for return to productive society.

In addition to financial penalties, several categories of intermediate sanctions are recommended for consideration by the Blue Ribbon Commission: preadjudication sanctions; postadjudication noncustody sanctions; custody options; and prerelease and parole programs.

Preadjudication sanctions. Eighteen preadjudication sanctions are identified by the commission as promising. These range from police diversion, field citation and release, pretrial release by probation and other enforcement agencies, and station/jail citation to supervised release and pretrial diversion. One that should be more widely used in California is night court or use of judges on call at night and on weekends (when most felony bookings occur) to lower the number of pretrial defendants in custody. Typically, jail populations on weekends increase as much as 25 percent over average daily populations (referred to as the peaking factor) because most courts are closed. Another promising procedure, increasingly common, is the use of interviewers to collect personal information on defendants for release on their own recognizance or on bail.

Postadjudication noncustody sanctions. Aside from financial penalties, several noncustody sanctions may warrant greater application. Electronic monitoring is a recent innovation that is attracting strong support nationwide as a means of enforcing noncustody sanctions such as house arrest and curfews. Three types of electronic monitoring devices are available: active, with computerized random telephone checks; passive, with radio transmission from a wrist or ankle bracelet; and tracking to facilitate intensive monitoring.

Intensive supervision probation (ISP) is a needed sanction, but caseload sizes in California frustrate these efforts. ISP commonly involves regular and frequent contacts and structured programming. Electronic monitoring may facilitate control, permitting reduction of other types of contacts. Specialized probation caseloads may facilitate addiction treatment and other special services. For drug addicts, mandatory drug testing may provide needed discipline. Rigorous structure and strict enforcement are keys to effective ISP, whatever controls are employed.

Other noncustody sanctions include community service work, juvenile day programs, and in-home family services. The most used sanction for adult felons is jail followed by probation. While this reduces the custody burden of the state's prisons, it adds to overcrowding of jails.

Custody options. Commonly used custody options include juvenile halls, camps, farms, and educational facilities; county or state work furlough, weekend sentences, and work release; and training and work programs in prisons and youth facilities. Several recent innovations have attracted nationwide attention but only limited use as custody options. In addition to short periods of confinement preceding probation, commonly used for both adults and juveniles, are military-style boot camps (highly publicized but as yet not much used); privately operated wilderness challenge programs; and adult camps involving outdoor work, which have been sparingly but successfully used in California for some years.

Special programs within prisons and youth facilities to deal with problems associated with crime are available only to small numbers of adult inmates and juvenile wards. Most strikingly deficient are drug and alcohol abuse programs, although efforts are underway to respond to the shortage.[16] Despite the great need for such assistance, as of 1989 only 3,300 prison inmates and 1,820 CYA wards were enrolled in substance abuse programs.

There is also a need for substantially increased employment, training, and educational programs. Only 7,000 inmates were employed in prison industries in 1989, and only seventy-nine CYA

---

16. California Department of Corrections, *Substance Abuse Treatment and Education Services for Inmates and Parolees: a Report to the Legislature,* Sacramento, December 1989.

wards were employed in the Free Venture program of private-industry work training. In CDC 3,700 were assigned to camps that provided outdoor work, and 26,000 had institutional work assignments. In CYA 2,225 were involved in work experience, including 1,585 in forestry camp programs. Academic programs for youth had 6,829 participants, and vocational training 3,000. In prisons, considering total numbers of inmates, educational programs are only marginally used, with 6,250 inmates in vocational training, 5,600 in academic programs, and 250 in apprenticeships. Literacy programs are conducted by both CDC and CYA. CDC also operates psychiatric intensive treatment programs (675 served in 1989), and it provides sex offender treatment (100 participants in 1989). CYA provides both intensive psychiatric treatment (134 in 1989) and specialized counseling (135 in 1989), as well as sex offender counseling (eighty in 1989). Community-based treatments for mental illness and support systems for the deficiently skilled could both be better accessed, with reduced disruptions to much needed continuity, if community corrections and treatment options were more available.

Prerelease and parole. Against the odds of numbers and geographical isolation, transitions from incarceration back into communities are supported by limited reentry services. CDC has few drug treatment programs for parolees, but varied initiatives are being attempted.[17] A pilot Substance Abuse Revocation Diversion program is designed to provide intensive supervision and support in nine communities throughout the state. In the Fresno area the Substance Abuse Treatment Unit provides a ninety-day program. Halfway houses offer support, including help with drug and alcohol problems.

There are also promising but still limited programs that assist parolees in finding and keeping employment. CDC has supported four Jobs Plus programs through contracts with community-based organizations, but funding has been provided to serve only 500 parolees. Intensive supervision parole is commonly provided for CYA wards, and similar interventions are needed for CDC and county parolees.

---

17. *Ibid.*

Intermediate Sanctions and the Community Corrections Act

Intermediate interventions involving community-based programs are designed to protect the public by monitoring and controlling offender behavior, reduce the likelihood of future crime by providing treatment and services that address crime-related problems such as deficient education, unemployment, addiction, and mental illness, and avoid the discontinuity associated with short periods of isolation followed by abrupt reentry to society. At the same time, by slowing the velocity of offender movement in and out of institutions and reserving correctional facilities for the smaller numbers of offenders who need to be confined, a policy of expanding intermediate sanctions gives those institutions the opportunity to perform the functions for which they are best suited.

The Blue Ribbon Commission on Inmate Population Management, recognizing the costs of expanding community-based corrections programs, has recommended the adoption of a California Community Corrections Act (CCCA). Under the act a state and local government partnership would be created. Target populations would be nonviolent property offenders, including drug abusers, eligible for commitment to the CDC or CYA as well as jail commitments and presentence detainees. The CDC and CYA would contract for slots in local community corrections programs approved by them for these functions: community detention, victim restitution, community service, mother/child programs, electronic surveillance, house arrest, intensive probation and parole supervision, specialized probation and parole, work furlough, residential and nonresidential substance abuse treatment, and others to be identified.

State financing would provide strong incentives for sustained participation by counties, including:
- start-up grants to counties for front-end planning, development, and implementation at 90 percent of costs the first year, 75 percent the second year, and 50 percent the third year;
- construction funding at a rate no higher than 75 percent of the cost to the state to construct a minimum-security bed ($50,000 in 1989);
- payment for contracted slots at a rate of 85 percent of the average cost of state incarceration ($19,874 in 1989—reduced from higher projections by marginal savings from overcrowding).

Incarceration would remain as an option for offenders who fail in community corrections programs, and 20 percent of community corrections facilities would be used for local commitments.

The proposed CCCA includes proven measures to safeguard public safety as a first consideration. It provides for a selective range of intermediate sanctions, all tested in practice and found to be implementable. Flexibility is possible in local corrections plans, which would be approved by the state.

Justice System Reforms

To facilitate reforms called for in the proposed California Community Corrections Act, changes are required in three fundamental subsystems of the criminal justice apparatus. First, sentencing structure needs modification to establish a matrix of sentencing guidelines and to allow for coordinated monitoring. Second, courts must be made more efficient and effective, with processes reformed to promote timely handling of cases. And third, a state-of-the-art information system is needed to enhance corrections management, including tracking of offender status.

Sentencing Structure

Two requirements must be met in reform of California's sentencing system. First, a system of sentencing guidelines should be established to provide a matrix of graded and interchangeable corrections options—imprisonment, jail, financial penalties, and community corrections programs ranging from minimal to intensive supervision. Second, ongoing monitoring is needed to evaluate sentencing outcomes and to advise on needed changes. The Blue Ribbon Commission recommends creation of a Sentencing Law Review Commission to make recommendations on these and related requirements.

A comprehensive sentencing system would be based on a uniform matrix of graded categories and interchangeable options to serve as authoritative guidelines in all sentencing decisions. In essence, it would constitute a grid of presumptive sentences based on offenses and offender characteristics. Appellate review would be provided for when sentencing guidelines are not followed. This system would counteract the complexity that has resulted from the piecemeal proliferation of sentencing provisions in California. That complexity has contributed to justice system delays and to overcrowded jails and prisons.

Ongoing monitoring—the sort of facilitative coordination now provided by the California Board of Corrections to serve other system needs—is required to assess sentencing outputs, longer term outcomes, and needed changes. Minnesota first adopted such an oversight mechanism in 1978, and it has been credited with reducing institutional crowding while encouraging use of more effective correctional options. There, and in other jurisdictions that make use of this system, a permanent commission establishes, monitors, and modifies the guidelines and provides guidance to courts on implementation.

Reform of Court Operations

Reasonable time standards and streamlining mechanisms are needed for judicial processing of cases. In January 1990 almost half of California's jail population was comprised of pretrial detainees. Because of lengthening court delays, presentence confinement time in jails increased from four months in 1978 to almost eight months in 1988.

The Board of Corrections has identified several streamlining processes now employed on a limited basis that merit greatly increased use. These include night court, bail schedules, telephone bail, early case screening by prosecutors, preferential docketing of jail cases, and voluntary control of continuances by judges. Such innovative technological options as video arraignment and electronic recording, already in limited use in California, are supported by the Blue Ribbon Commission, as is the development of formal standards to expedite decisions on pretrial detention and release.

Information Systems Reform

California currently has no automated corrections information system to facilitate statewide coordination of corrections management or to provide needed information to law enforcement officials. The Blue Ribbon Commission has recommended such a system to track offenders. It would facilitate prompt identification of arrested probationers and parolees, as well as critical behaviors of offenders.

As intermediate sanctions are added to California's correctional system, such real-time information will be needed to simplify coordination of resource use and to facilitate assignment and control of offenders. It will also be essential in monitoring and modifying a comprehensive sentencing structure. Finally, an automated corrections information system would enhance coordination among jails, prisons, and other correctional facilities and programs, enabling improved management of all components of California's corrections system.

COMMANDS OR INCENTIVES TO
IMPROVE AIR QUALITY

John J. Kirlin

7

The traditional command-and-control approach to regulation has been effective in some instances in reducing emissions affecting air quality, but much more could be accomplished if such controls were supplemented with market- or incentive-based strategies. Incentive-based regulations have been shown to be equally or more effective at less cost and more easily adapted as experience with them accumulates or conditions change. This chapter reviews the findings of recent research in this country and abroad to provide a basis for informed policy making. Because scientific data in this area is incomplete, suggestions are offered for devising good policy in a context of uncertainty and change.

Despite substantial efforts at improvement, southern California has the worst air pollution of any region in the United States, violating all national standards for air quality. The current South Coast Air Quality Management Plan (SCAQMP), adopted in 1989 by the South Coast Air Quality Management District (SCAQMD) and the Southern California Association of Governments, is the most ambitious ever adopted in the nation. That plan, however, relies largely upon the traditional command-and-control style of direct regulation to achieve its objectives of reducing emissions from stationary and mobile sources.

A substantial body of current thought supports the conclusion that command-and-control regulation (CCR) will be insufficient to meet air quality standards, and that it should be supplemented by less intrusive market-oriented or incentive-based regulation (IBR), which can be more effective at less social and economic cost. As other regions of the state and nation develop their own plans to deal with environmental pollution, they should be aware of the growing recognition of the advantages of IBR. A top official of the Environmental Protection Agency offered these observations in testimony before the House Committee on Ways and Means:

The approaches to controlling pollution that have worked well in the past may work less well in the future...Encouraging pollution prevention requires influencing an extremely diverse set of activities...less easily and effectively reached by a traditional command-and-control approach...Market-oriented approaches to control will be of great interest [as] they potentially affect activities that would be extremely intrusive to affect with traditional forms of regulation [and] can substantially reduce control costs.[1]

Within California two recent publications also reflect the growing awareness of the value of IBR. In its 1990-91 report on the budget, the Legislative Analyst's Office devotes seventeen pages to improving air quality, concluding that incentive-based regulation is preferable to command-and-control approaches and recommending, among other measures, that the legislature amend the California Clean Air Act to explicitly authorize the use of IBR policies.[2]

The Bay Area Forum, in a document that is likely to stimulate debate, also supports the use of IBR in efforts to reduce emissions both directly (e.g., charging "smog fees" based on emissions from each vehicle) and indirectly (e.g., higher gas taxes and bridge tolls, employer-sponsored incentives to affect employee travel behaviors).[3]

More reliance on incentive-based regulation is virtually certain to be required in future efforts to improve air quality. These strategies offer enhanced effectiveness in some instances, along with increased economy in the use of societal resources and wider choice on the part of individuals and businesses. In addition, they are more easily adapted to take advantage of knowledge gained over the long term. It is this adaptability that gives IBR its greatest advantage over CCR strategies under conditions of high uncertainty and complexity, conditions that unquestionably characterize the problem of improving air quality in this state and nationwide.

It should be noted at the outset that a blend of CCR and IBR approaches is undoubtedly going to be needed to improve air quality. To date substantial improvements have been achieved through CCR approaches, and more improvements are being sought. But

---

1. J. Clarence Davies, Assistant Administrator for Policy, Planning, and Evaluation, U.S. Environmental Protection Agency, "Testimony before the Committee on Ways and Means," U.S. House of Representatives, March 6, 1990, pp. 2-3.
2. Legislative Analyst's Office, *The 1990-91 Budget: Perspectives and Issues*, Sacramento, CA, 1990.
3. Bay Area Economic Forum, *Market-Based Solutions to the Transportation Crisis*, San Francisco, February 1990. The report is published in two sections, an *Executive Summary* and *The Application*. The Bay Area Economic Forum is a partnership of the Association of Bay Area Governments and the Bay Area Council.

equal, or greater, progress can be made with IBR strategies, which have been little used to date. There is inadequate scientific evidence to suggest the precise combination of IBR and CCR strategies that will be required to achieve a specified level of air quality improvement. But, even in a situation of uncertainty and complexity, policy choices must be made. There is sufficient evidence to begin the process of implementation and testing of different IBR strategies, alone and in combination with CCR approaches, and to move in an iterative fashion toward effective policy for improving air quality in California.

To provide a base of knowledge on which to build, a search of existing literature on improving air quality through "market" or incentive-based strategies was undertaken. Of special interest were mobile sources of emissions. Three methods were used to identify relevant literature: computerized searches of the holdings of the Library of Congress, Dialogue (through the state library), and Compuserve; a "snowball" search for items referenced in documents obtained; and recommendations provided by knowledgeable individuals. Over 150 items were obtained for review, including journal articles, books, monographs, reports of legislative hearings, newspaper accounts, and descriptions or studies of air quality improvement efforts in other nations.

This chapter presents a summary and analysis of findings from the literature reviewed, with special attention to the effectiveness of IBR strategies, and a discussion of policy choices for California in the context of available research. The chapter begins with a brief description of IBR and CCR strategies and the major differences between them.

Command-and-Control vs. Incentive-Based Strategies

Incentive-based regulation, also referred to as economic or market strategies, is distinguished from more traditional command-and-control regulation primarily by its operation through incentives rather than controls. In many cases incentives can be interpreted through the lenses of economics and involve market transactions, but they are effective because of their incentive effects.

CCR commonly consists of four steps: planning (which identifies strategies to meet standards); approving control technologies; permitting polluting sources (with use of approved control technologies); and monitoring and enforcement (to ensure that permit conditions are fulfilled). An example of a CCR process is found in control of automobile engine emissions. Plans are developed to meet national air quality standards by reducing emissions by so many tons, and this figure is translated into allowable emissions per automobile manufactured. Control technologies such as catalytic converters are approved. Automobile manufacturers receive "permits" to build new cars as they meet prescribed standards. Enforcement is achieved by testing vehicle performance for a sample of automobiles produced at the factory and by inspection of automobiles as a condition of license renewal.

IBR strategies rely on an entirely different approach, which begins by recognizing the social costs of private actions, including costs of damage to the environment. Society's ownership of the environment is institutionalized by shifting the burden of proof for environmental impacts to individuals and firms and creating incentives to avoid polluting the environment. Regulatory activity is redirected from planning to accomplishment, with monitoring and enforcement focused not on developing new rules but on ensuring full operation of incentives in place and improving the effectiveness of those incentives as experience accumulates.

An example of an IBR strategy to reduce automobile emissions is to increase the cost of parking, which is now often free for those who drive to work or shop. Appropriate parking fees would acknowledge the social costs of driving, establishing society's ownership of the air by charging those who pollute it. Drivers would have incentives to reduce parking expenses but wide flexibility in how they do so, whether by taking public transit, carpooling, bicycling, or walking, for example. Enforcement of required parking fees would be needed, and monitoring of driving patterns and associated emissions would provide information on the basis of which parking fees could be adjusted.

A further distinction between IBR and CCR strategies—one that has great importance for effective implementation—is that IBR requires only the specification of a goal or standard to be met, a general expectation that emitters of pollutants can meet that standard, and the capacity to monitor progress in controlling emissions and to adjust incentives over time. CCR strategies require specification of both the standard and the control technologies to be adopted to achieve it, a significantly greater burden upon the scientific underpinnings of policy making and implementation. Moreover, in specifying control technologies, both the likelihood of error and the negative consequences of error are increased. Under an IBR approach the regulatory technologies used will vary, increasing the likelihood of success by some strategies. This not only provides some level of emission reduction, but affords greater opportunities to learn which technologies are most effective.

Findings from Research

Review of available literature on IBR and CCR strategies in improving air quality yielded findings in three major areas:

Effectiveness and efficiency of IBR. A substantial body of analysis supports use of IBR as more effective and efficient than CCR, but much of the literature advocates that strategy on the basis of theory only. There is, however, enough evidence to make a strong case that IBR should be a major tool in improving air quality.

Effects of alternate IBR strategies. Little conclusive evidence is available concerning the impacts of specific IBR measures, but rough estimates of effects exist by which some measures can be ordered in terms of likely effectiveness.

Cumulative and interactive effects. No jurisdiction has implemented the broad range of IBR and CCR strategies likely to be needed to achieve air quality standards in California, and few models exist of such complex systems. As a consequence, little is known of cumulative or interactive effects.

These findings provide evidence in three progressive steps of acquiring understanding needed for effective policy making in a complex world. In the first step the question is of evidence of effectiveness and efficiency, but the measures are gross; the point is to establish that IBR has some effects. In the second step the goal is more ambitious: to establish the impacts of specific IBR strategies with sufficient precision that choices among them can be made. In the third step interdependencies and cumulative effects are confronted; here the goal is to determine the linkages to other systems, to anticipate consequences, and to understand tradeoffs among valued goals.

As will be seen, some information is available in all three areas, but the totality of understanding may still be judged inadequate to allow policy choices that will be accepted by all as supported by scientific fact. In such a situation policy choices nonetheless must be made; techniques for making the necessary choices in a situation of uncertainty and complexity are discussed in the final section of this chapter.

Effectiveness and Efficiency of IBR

Only a few references have been selected to illustrate the findings derived from this group of analyses, which is quite extensive, including much of the early work on IBR strategies. An example is seen in Anderson, *et al.*, which explores how charges for emissions can be implemented (e.g., purpose, economic basis, rate, administration, use of revenues) and describes several examples of this approach (e.g., in East Germany, Japan, and the United States).[4]

Analyses in this category written in the early 1980s show somewhat greater sophistication and more evidence is available to analyze, but the focus remains on illustrating the major impacts of an IBR strategy. For example, Liroff examines air pollution offsets,[5] Tietenberg surveys experience with transferable discharge permits for stationary source air pollution,[6] and a volume edited by Magat includes chapters on marketable pollution rights and tradable emissions permits from a 1981 conference.[7] This style of analysis, quite common in the 1970s and early 1980s, is little seen in the later 1980s, by which time more sophisticated questions and more ambitious analyses are the norm.

This body of analysis established the main claims of advantage of IBR over CCR strategies. First among these is that IBR strategies are more efficient in reaching goals, requiring less of society's resources to meet the same standard. Second, IBR strategies are asserted to be more effective in meeting environmental quality standards, ideally providing incentives to reduce emissions from a much wider set of

4. Frederick R. Anderson *et al.*, *Environmental Improvement through Economic Incentives*, Baltimore, The Johns Hopkins University Press for Resources for the Future, 1977.
5. Richard A. Liroff, *Air Pollution Offsets: Trading, Selling, and Banking*, Washington, D.C., The Conservation Foundation, 1980.
6. Thomas H. Tietenberg, "Transferable Discharge Permits and the Control of Stationary Source Air Pollution: a Survey and Synthesis," *Land Economics*, 56:4 (November 1980), 391-416.
7. Weley A. Magat (ed.), *Reform of Environmental Regulation*, Cambridge, MA, Ballinger, 1982.

sources than is possible with CCR strategies. Finally, this literature recognizes that while public revenues can be generated through IBR strategies, the case for IBR rests not on revenue generation or the use of those revenues, but rather on the incentive effects created by pricing negative externalities.

Effects of Alternative IBR Strategies

The prototypical article in this category analyzes the effects of charging fees for parking, and most focus on transportation demand management. It is in this area, particularly, that quantified measurement of effects is found. In a sophisticated analysis of several case studies and surveys, Willson and Shoup conclude that:

> ... ending employer-paid parking reduces the number of solo drivers by between 18 and 83 percent, and reduces the number of cars driven to work by between 15 and 43 percent. Estimates of the price elasticity of demand for solo driving range between -0.10 and -0.71, meaning that as the price of parking is doubled, solo driving is likely to decrease between 10 and 71 percent.[8]

However, strong effects of charging for parking and other transportation demand management techniques were not found in a small matched sample of buildings near Los Angeles International Airport. In that study nearly 90 percent of the employees drove to work alone regardless of the program of parking fees or car pool enticements used.[9] The range of impacts seen in the Willson and Shoup survey, and the contradictory evidence seen in this evaluation, suggest that caution should be exercised in using these analyses in policy making: effects are usually found and they can be major, but their magnitudes will vary.

Ridesharing programs have also been analyzed. Ferguson found that even in the presence of free parking, larger firms encouraging ridesharing could achieve some mode shift to ridesharing, at the expense of both solo driving and public transit.[10] In addition to larger firm size, a personalized ride matching service and flexible work schedules encouraged ridesharing. Manufacturing employees

8. Richard W. Willson and Donald C. Shoup, "Parking Subsidies and Travel Choices: Assessing the Evidence," presented at the Annual Meeting of the Western Regional Science Association, February 24, 1990.
9. Charles Blankson and Martin Wachs, "Preliminary Evaluation of the Coastal Transportation Corridor Ordinance," Los Angeles, University of California, August 1989.
10. Erik Ferguson, "An Evaluation of Employer Ridesharing Programs in Southern California," Atlanta, Georgia Institute of Technology, July 1989.

were less likely to rideshare than employees of service firms, and while employees of public agencies showed a higher level of public transit use than those of private businesses, they showed a lower level of ridesharing. In this study direct incentives for ridesharing were not effective. Additionally, larger firms could provide ridesharing programs at less cost than smaller firms.

Another recent survey of eleven applications of Transportation Demand Management (TDM) programs found that six achieved trip reductions of greater than 20 percent.[11] Firm size did not have an effect, but effects were found for constraints upon employee choice (such as limited parking and/or paying for parking) and positive incentives (such as subsidies for use of public transit and ridesharing).

Cumulative and Interactive Effects

Considered broadly, quite a bit is known of the cumulative and interactive effects of seeking to improve air quality. However, the knowledge is most often of the existence of interactions and cumulative effects without a lot of precision as to exact relationships involved.

Four different types of analyses are seen here. Two pieces offer broad discussions of the relationships among air quality, mobility, and growth in the California economy. Marsh has already been quoted; his strength is in showing the challenges faced by the policy and planning processes underway. An Assembly Office of Research report focuses on specific policy alternatives, including alternative fuels, reducing reliance on the private automobile, and reducing total energy use.[12]

A second type of analysis focuses on energy use and global effects. For example, a study by the American Petroleum Institute estimated that to keep U.S. energy use constant through 2000, while allowing for modest economic growth, would require increasing energy prices three-to fourfold.[13] In contrast, the American Council

---

11. J. Richard Kuzmyak and Eric N. Shreffler, "Effectiveness of Existing TDM Programs," prepared for the ITE National Meetings, September 1989.
12. Lindell Marsh, "Air Quality, Transportation and Development: a Case Study of Regional Plans in Southern California (Part I)," *Environmental and Urban Issues*, 27:2 (Winter 1990), 6-18; and Assembly Office of Research, *California 2000: Exhausting Clean Air: Major Issues in Managing Air Quality*, Sacramento, October 1989.
13. *The Oil Daily*, December 19, 1989.

for an Energy-Efficient Economy proposed ten policies to encourage energy efficiency drawn from the analyses of several groups, the best known of which is the National Resources Defense Council. They claimed that these policies could have a large, near-term effect of reducing energy use and carbon emissions (down 20 percent), while population, economic output, and living standards are increasing.[14] Included here too are analyses of the potential of alternative fuels in transportation,[15] and of shifting electricity generation to reliance on other fuel sources.[16]

Closely related is the literature that ties energy use to global economic forces and urban form. Most visible in this genre is a group working at the Lawrence Berkeley Laboratory. For example, in 1987 Rosenfeld argued that conservation had overwhelmed the OPEC oil cartel, that the United States was losing the energy efficiency race to Japan, and that public policies should seek much greater efficiencies in construction and operation of buildings, all in a short paper.[17] In other work the group has advocated planting of trees and using white paints as ways of reducing heat island effects in urban areas, thereby reducing energy use for air conditioning, which generates heat as well as emissions.[18]

The fourth type of analysis in this category is focused on vehicular use. A major thrust of this literature is to discern the interrelationships among safety, energy conservation, congestion, and air quality. Public policies exist in each area, but the interrelationships among the four are complex, and focusing on one goal can lead to lack of progress or even backsliding on another.

A comprehensive analysis of national policies focused on automobile safety, energy use, and pollution is available, for example. Crandall and associates found that the three regulatory programs

14. Howard S. Geller, "National Energy Efficiency Platform: Description and Potential Impacts," Washington, D.C., American Council for an Energy-Efficient Economy, August 1989.

15. For Example, Barry McNutt and Marianne M. Mintz, "Will Air Quality Needs Force the Development of a Market for Alternative Transportation Fuels?" prepared for the 82nd Annual Meeting of the Air and Waste Management Association, June 28, 1989.

16. For example, Independent Power Corporation, *Air Quality Improvements in the Electric Power Industry: Cost or Savings to the Ratepayers,* Oakland, CA, April 1989.

17. Arthur H. Rosenfeld, "Conservation, Competition and National Security," presented at the Hearing on Energy Security, Subcommittee on Energy and Power, U.S. House of Representatives, November 4, 1987.

18. Hashem Akbari *et al.*, "Summer Heat Islands, Urban Trees, and White Surfaces," Berkeley, Lawrence Berkeley Laboratory, 1989.

are administered by three separate regulatory agencies with little concern for the legislated goals of each other. Increasing safety adds weight, which decreases energy efficiency and increases fuel use an estimated 3.5 percent; reducing emissions is estimated to exact a 7 percent penalty in fuel use. These penalties in fuel use and increased automobile prices also encourage keeping cars longer, thereby delaying the advantages of new vehicles. Finally, the standards reduce sales of U.S.-manufactured automobiles, reducing employment in that sector.[19]

It is well documented that increasing fuel economy of automobiles can increase total emissions. While increased fuel efficiencies produce fewer emissions per mile driven, lower per-mile fuel costs encourage greater driving, an effect compounded by real prices of gasoline as low as two decades ago. Since tailpipe emissions standards are stated in grams per mile (not grams per gallon of fuel burned), total annual emissions per automobile increase.[20]

Another area where conventional public policy wisdom is not having the expected effects regards public transit systems, where increased capital investments and operating subsidies were expected to spur use, improving overall air quality. Ridership of all public transit is decreasing as a share of total trips. Especially costly per passenger mile traveled have been fixed rail systems. Projected use levels have not been achieved, and large subsidies flow to those whose commute patterns follow available rail lines or who own property near stations.[21]

Large capital grants from the national government during the 1970s financed new rail systems in Washington, D.C., Atlanta, Baltimore, Miami, Portland, Sacramento, and Buffalo, and rail systems are under construction in Los Angeles and San Jose. Major expansions of older rail systems occurred, and many systems increased the number of buses operated. These investments managed to halt the decline in absolute ridership (17.3 billion rides in 1950; 8.2 billion

---

19. Robert W. Crandall *et al.*, *Regulating the Automobile*, Washington, D.C., The Brookings Institution, 1986.

20. J. Daniel Khazzom, "The Use of Energy Conservation as a Strategy for Reducing Emissions in the Transportation Sector," testimony before the Fuel Committee, California Energy Commission, June 1989; Carmen Difiglio *et al.*, "Cost Effectiveness of Future Fuel Economy Improvements," *The Energy Journal*, January 1989.

21. Peter Gordon and Harry Richardson, "Notes from the Underground," *The Public Interest*, 94(Winter 1989), 77-86.

in 1965; 7.3 billion in 1970; and 8.3 billion in 1987), but transit ridership continued to decline as a percentage of all trips (3.6% in 1969, 3% in 1977, and 2.6% in 1983). Between 1965 and 1983, operating costs per vehicle mile of transit climbed at a rate more than twice as fast as inflation. The percentage of costs covered by fare box revenues dropped to 39 percent, while governmental subsidies covered 57 percent.[22]

Finally, there are increasingly sophisticated analyses of the operations of complex TDM systems. As one example, the OECD published an analysis of transportation policies in ten cities that provides a good description of the physical, policy, and institutional features of each. Particularly interesting are the analyses of Hong Kong and Singapore, each of which has used multiple strategies to reduce traffic congestion and to improve air quality. Included are restrictions on automobile ownership, several competing and complementary systems of public transit, and charges for access to certain areas by automobiles (Hong Kong has not continued its experiment in electronic road pricing, but Singapore continues its program in area licensing).[23]

An analysis of the trip reduction ordinance of Pleasanton, California, found that it represented an extensive use of public powers and private resources in cooperation. However, the trip reduction goals set in the ordinance project a greater use of single-occupancy automobiles than is now the case.[24] This case illustrates, again, the necessity to have a good understanding of the system a policy seeks to change.

What appears to be among the most ambitious and sophisticated modeling of Transportation Control Measures available is now underway for the Metropolitan Transportation Commission, focused on the San Francisco Bay Area. This analysis first defines eight different effects from TCM strategies: changed travel times; changed travel costs; limited travel options; expanded travel

22. Martin Wachs, "U.S. Transit Subsidy Policy: In Need of Reform," *Science*, 244(30 June 1989), 1545-9.
23. OECD, *Cities and Transport*, Paris, 1988.
24. Elizabeth A. Deakin, "The Pleasanton, California, Trip Reduction Ordinance," Berkeley, Institute of Transportation Studies, June 1986.

options; altered traveler perceptions; changed vehicle technology; relieved activity congestion; and modified land use.[25]

Five analytic tools are available to screen the effects of alternative TCMs in the Bay Area: inference based on elasticities; STEP, a model of travel choice probabilities for an actual sample of Bay Area households and workers; LOCATE, based on the STEP sample, but including models for work mode choice, auto ownership, and residential location; CHAIN, a model of sequences of trips, starting from the home; and inference based on case studies. Preliminary runs of these models to screen ten alternative TCMs project the greatest improvements in air quality by increasing fuel prices $2 per gallon, which is projected to reduce work-related vehicle miles traveled by 8.6 percent and non-work miles by 11.5 percent.[26]

Blending IBR and CCR Strategies

The case for using both IBR and CCR strategies to improve air quality in California relies on evidence that both work alone and that the two can be usefully combined.

As command-and-control approaches dominate current air quality improvement policies, it is worthwhile beginning with a brief review of suggestions for making those strategies more effective. Many of the current CCR-based policies are likely to remain, however many IBR-based policies are adopted, since they have had considerable success in reducing emissions from stationary sources and in spurring development with lower emissions.

Oates *et al.* provide a balanced analysis of the circumstances in which CCR strategies succeed and analyze costs and benefits of controlling Total Suspended Particulates (TSP) in Baltimore using CCR and IBR strategies. They find that CCR strategies achieve essentially the same levels of air quality improvements and essentially the same net benefits as IBR strategies. The primary explanation for achieving the same level of net benefits is that CCR strategies achieve "overcontrol" in some sites, as the regulations require adoption of control devices that reduce emissions below the standards. As a result the CCR strategies cost more, but also provide greater

25. Greig Harvey, "Screening of Transportation Control Measures for the San Francisco Bay Area, Part I: Methodology," Oakland, Metropolitan Transportation Commission, November 17, 1989.
26. *Ibid.*

improvements in air quality. These authors conclude that "a carefully designed and implemented [CCR] system may stack up reasonably well relative to a feasible [IBR] counterpart...Badly designed [CCR] measures...will yield bad outcomes."[27]

Thomas Schelling had made much the same point earlier, arguing that "sensible" control regulation may be as effective and efficient as "acceptable" incentive-based strategies. He argued that pricing mechanisms are a practical approach to environmental protection, but that many of the same benefits can be obtained from sensible, well designed controls. Also, the barriers to implementing effective and efficient pricing mechanisms are often the same:

> Ignorance of how damages relate to emissions, and disagreement about the severity of damages and the money value of reducing them, impose difficult or even insurmountable problems; but when the problems are insurmountable, they are for both charges and standards.[28]

Thus one argument for considering both CCR and IBR strategies is that, when well designed, one can be roughly as effective and efficient as the other and the impediments to success are shared. As Schelling suggests, difficulties in measuring environmental damages become political barriers to action because of uncertainty regarding effective policies.

Others make more positive arguments for using both CCR and IBR strategies. Hahn, a senior staff economist at the Council of Economic Advisors, argues:

> ... most low cost technology-based standards have been applied. What remains are a series of high cost options...The command-and-control approach is unlikely to make significant progress towards meeting the ozone standard in severe non-attainment areas. Thus, it is worthwhile considering new approaches which may. One possibility is the use of market-based approaches.[29]

A recent assessment of how to reduce ozone by the Office of Technology Assessment evaluated both CCR and IBR strategies to reduce emissions of volatile organic compounds (VOC) and nitrogen oxides (NO_x). Sixty control measures were evaluated, of which the most cost-effective for reduction of VOC was controlling volatile

27. Wallace E. Oates *et al.*, "The Net Benefits of Incentive-Based Regulation: a Case Study of Environmental Standard Setting," *American Economic Review*, 79:5 (December 1989), 1233-42.
28. Thomas C. Schelling, "Preface," in Thomas C. Schelling (ed.), *Incentives for Environmental Protection*, Cambridge, MA, The MIT Press, 1983.
29. Robert W. Hahn, "Innovative Approaches to Revising the Clean Air Act," *Natural Resources Journal*, 28:1 (Winter 1988), 173.

gasoline vapors during refueling of vehicles. The most cost-effective approach for reduction of NO_x was controlling emissions from electric utility boilers. Both of these are CCR strategies. But transportation control measures and taxes on gasoline to reduce use—both IBR strategies—are also found to be effective and to have large cumulative air quality impacts.[30]

It is useful to consider how CCR and IBR strategies could be used jointly to reduce vehicular emissions. Breedlove advocates marketable emission permits for both stationary and mobile sources and suggests that markets could be devised so that stationary sources could purchase mobile source emission permits and vice versa.[31] Rosenfeld *et al.* advocate using a revenue-neutral gas guzzler/gas sipper fee/rebate program, an energy-efficiency sales tax adjustment at time of purchase, or an emission-based variation in annual registration fees to encourage purchase of fuel-efficient and reduced-emission vehicles. Both Breedlove and Rosenfeld advocate measures that provide front-end incentives, at time of purchase if possible, as automobile purchasers are not as sensitive to longer term price increases such as those associated with gasoline taxes.[32]

In both these analyses, existing standards on tail pipe emissions and fuel efficiency would remain in place. The IBR measures are seen as ways to achieve levels of air quality improvement unattainable with CCR measures or, if attainable, at a much greater cost.

Ferguson argues that voluntary transportation demand management efforts, which are incentive-based, have not usually achieved significant results unless implemented within the framework of CCR regulations that set ground rules for cooperation. Simultaneously, CCR measures have greater effect if accompanied by private actions supportive of their goals. As an example of interdependence, he cites developers' resistance to reducing free parking in projects unless proven and marketable transportation alternatives are readily available.[33]

30. U.S. Congress, Office of Technology Assessment, *Catching Our Breath: Next Steps for Reducing Urban Ozone: Summary,* Washington, D.C., July 1989.
31. Buzz Breedlove, "Air Pollution: Cleaning the Air for Profit Using Marketable Permits," Sacramento, Senate Office of Research, May 1989.
32. Arthur H. Rosenfeld *et al.*, "Policies to Improve Energy Efficiency and Reduce the Impact of Global Warming," presented at the workshop on Energy Policies to Address Global Climate Change, Davis, University of California, September 6-8, 1989.
33. *Supra* note 10, p. 19.

In late 1989 UCLA Extension conducted a symposium to assess policy implications of recent behavioral research on transportation demand management. The major conclusion of symposium participants was that commuter behavior is rational in terms of the structure of transportation incentives and disincentives faced. This suggests that IBR strategies can directly affect vehicle use and can supplement, or replace, CCR strategies to improve air quality. Available behavioral research includes a few unequivocal findings, including: flat transit fares are inefficient and inequitable; increasing the cost of parking is a prerequisite for reducing single-occupant driving; no TDM program, such as ridesharing, will succeed if parking is free or heavily subsidized; and individuals place high value on predictability of travel time and on minimizing "out of vehicle" time.[34]

The need for additional research is evident too. The South Coast Air Quality Management Plan projects significant reduction in vehicle trips through improving the jobs-housing balance, but it is not at all clear how this goal can be achieved. Available research provides only a few suggestions as to how a jobs-housing balance policy can be effectively implemented. At present, this strategy is at the stage of analyses of effective measures of jobs/housing balance, identification of specific policies, and estimates of effects.[35] Implementation of this strategy under the adopted SCAQMP will be the most ambitious effort anywhere to balance jobs and housing within subregions and will test not only the ingenuity of policy design, but also the commitment of many local governments, developers, and businesses. This effort is certainly worth pursuit, even if it is novel, challenging to implement, and the evidence shows that locational decisions of households are influenced by complex factors.

The most extensive experience with blending CCR and IBR strategies is from Singapore, an urban area with about one-fifth the population of southern California. Singapore is also less economically developed and governed by less fragmented and less democratic processes than is California. Nonetheless, some insights can be gained from analysis of that case. In 1975 the government of

34. Richard Willson and Elham Shirazi, *Symposium Summary: Transportation Demand Management: Policy Implications of Recent Behavioral Research*, Los Angeles, Public Policy Program, UCLA Extension, October 12-13, 1989.

35. Bruce Lee Livingston, "Using Jobs/Housing Balance Indicators for Air Pollution Controls," Berkeley, University of California, Institute of Transportation Studies, May 1989.

Singapore adopted increased vehicle taxes, road user charges, and parking management to reduce use of single-occupant cars, especially in the central business district.[36]

The vehicle taxation system includes four elements: import duties, registration fees, additional registration fees designed to encourage scrapping older cars in favor of newer, more fuel-efficient cars, and annual road taxes based on engine capacity. For a 2000cc new car not replacing an old car, duties, taxes, and license triple the market cost of an automobile. Off-street parking fees were initially increased from $100 to $175 per space per month, depending on location, and on-street parking fees were also increased. Purchase and display of special licenses were required for car entry into the central business district. The licenses were originally priced at $6 per day or $130 per month for private cars, and the prices were subsequently increased to $11 per day and $220 per month. The special license initially was required for entrance in the central business district between the hours of 7:30 and 9:30am, but that was subsequently extended to 7:30 to 10:15am.

The main effects of these policies were reduced car use, slowed growth in car ownership, reduced congestion in the central district during the morning peak, a shift in travel mode from cars to buses and carpools, an estimated savings of $3 billion on road construction, and improved air quality. The changes in traffic volumes and modal splits are dramatic. Before adoption of the measures 75,000 cars entered the restricted district during the morning rush period, which dropped to 43,000 shortly after adoption, and had risen to only 57,000 by 1983 (against a projected level of 114,000 without the measures). Prior to these policies buses carried 33 percent of the ridership; shortly after policy implementation began their share grew to 46 percent, and it had increased to 69 percent by 1983.

Two useful lessons from this example are found in the effectiveness of strong incentive plans and in the low likelihood that policies this powerful could be adopted in California. These policies were possible in Singapore because of the relatively low rates of automobile ownership (one car per fourteen persons), a highly compact central business district, and high overall population density (4,251 persons per square kilometer, more than twice the density in the

---

36. This discussion is adapted from OECD, *Cities and Transport*, Paris, 1988, pp. 72-4.

central business district of Los Angeles). It is unlikely that any government would impose such policies in the southern California region. None has the powers to do so, opposition would be fierce, and there is insufficient capacity in alternative transportation systems to make success probable.

A third useful lesson is the necessity to revise policies as experience is accumulated. Increasing the restricted zone license fee has already been mentioned. But one component of the original plan, involving car parks outside the restricted zone from which vans would convey passengers to central business district destinations, had to be abandoned totally. Users preferred buses to the car park and van combination. The car park lands were eventually sold off for other purposes, and the vans shifted to low-intensity routes in the suburbs. Ironically, the car parks and vans were the largest public capital expenditure made in support of the plan to reduce trips.

Policy and "Science"

Efforts to improve air quality are bedeviled by incomplete scientific understanding. Increased understanding is needed in three areas: the causes of air pollution, the consequences or "costs" of air pollution, and effective strategies by which air quality can be improved. In general terms, these three types of understanding correlate with theories based in chemistry, economics (using information from life and physical sciences), and public policy design.

There is relatively good (though still improving) scientific understanding of the causes of air pollution; the current policy-critical debate here concerns relationships between carbon dioxide and other emissions and changes in global climate.[37] The scientific understanding of the consequences of air pollution is less adequate. Questions regarding how to value emissions remain unresolved, for example. Scientific understanding is weakest regarding effective strategies to improve air quality.

Policies adopted to counter global environmental change are increasingly relevant to air quality improvement efforts. This focus causes greater attention to all forms of carbon dioxide emissions, for

37. For a review of issues and evidence, summary of public testimony, and bibliography, see U.S. Department of Energy, *Interim Report: National Energy Strategy: a Compilation of Public Comments*, Washington, D.C., April 1990.

example, and generates policy proposals ranging from encouraging use of fuels with reduced CO_2 emissions to planting forests to sequester carbon from the atmosphere. Specific emissions, such as chlorofluorocarbons (CFCs), are known to have a large impact on the ozone layer; an international agreement has been reached to reduce CFC emissions. Attention to global environmental change also encourages longer time horizons and a focus on impacts such as changes in sea level or the capability to grow crops. These considerations are quite distinct from the usual shorter time horizons and human physiological measures of negative impacts seen in analyses of air quality.

Despite the growing attention to global climate changes in air quality policy debates, that topic does not receive further attention here. For purposes of examining the potential for greater use of IBR strategies to improve air quality in California, the adequacy of scientific understanding of the costs of air pollution and of effective strategies by which air quality can be improved are of more immediate importance.

Costs of Air Pollution

The consequences of air pollution are ideally assessed by determining the marginal external costs imposed by emissions upon society and the marginal costs of reducing emissions by some quantity. In practice there are four dominant approaches to valuing emissions: calculated impacts, revealed preferences, proxy, and behavioral/market evidence. Hedonic price estimation is sometimes used when prices are not visible.

Calculated impacts of emissions focus on the costs imposed by pollution or the benefits gained by pollution reduction. For example, the workdays lost to pollution in southern California have been estimated at $10 billion per year, and a survey of consumer preferences in avoiding sickness resulted in the following daily values: coughing, $1.25; eye irritation, $1.75; throat irritation, $2; and headache, $2.50. Benefits can be calculated as avoided costs, as in increased longevity, more productive crops, or less building deterioration, for example.[38]

Revealed preferences are a commonly used method in valuing emissions in regulatory rule making. In this technique, the costs of controlling an emission under rule making are taken to be the value of that control. Thus, if an air quality management district promulgates a rule that requires dry cleaning establishments to spend $15,000 per ton of reactive organic gases (ROG) eliminated, the value of reducing emissions of ROG by one ton is $15,000.

In establishing value by proxy, analysts calculate the tons of a pollutant removed by an action the cost of which is known, making that cost the value of the emission. For example, the California Energy Commission considered the value of $7 per ton for CO_2, derived from the proxy cost of sequestering a ton of carbon by planting trees.[39] This approach adds a concrete alternative action to the analysis.

The fourth approach to valuing emissions is to determine how individual and business behaviors in marketplace interactions establish prices for emissions. Directly observable prices are visible when business can buy and sell "rights" to emissions, as in the EPA offsets program. When a business wishes to begin operations with any emissions in a non-attainment area, it must purchase emission rights from existing businesses to offset the new emissions it will cause. A recent review analyzed such offsets in the South Coast Air Quality Management District for the 1983-85 period. Prices paid per ton of VOC in 1985 ranged from $850 to $3250, with an estimated mean of $2500 at the end of 1985. Prices paid for NO_x ranged from $2000 to $5500, with an estimated mean of $5000 at the end of 1985.[40]

Where prices are not visible, they can sometimes be estimated from behaviors. This is the approach used in hedonic price estimation. In a typical analysis, the selling price of a single-family house

---

38. Gayatri Schilberg *et al.*, "Valuing Reductions in Air Emissions and Incorporation into Electric Resource Planning: Theoretical and Quantitative Aspects," Sacramento, JBS Energy, Inc., Consulting Economists for Independent Energy Producers, presented to the California Energy Commission, Docket 88-ER-8, August 25, 1989.

39. Jonathan Koomey, "The Environmental Value of Reducing Green House Emissions," Berkeley, University of California, Energy and Resources Group, January 25, 1990, testimony before the California Energy Commission, Hearings on the 1990 Electricity Report, Docket 88-ER-8.

40. Robert W. Hahn and Gordon L. Hester, "Where Did All the Markets Go? An Analysis of EPA's Emissions Trading Program," *Yale Journal on Regulation*, 6:1 (Winter 1989), 121.

would be the dependent variable, and variables known to affect selling price (such as size of home) and air quality would be the independent variables whose effects upon the selling prices of homes are estimated through statistical techniques. A recent review of such analyses found a variety of technical difficulties that result in different and sometimes contradictory results. Graves *et al.* found a modest positive value for "visibility" and a modest negative value for total suspended particulates, their air quality variables, in an analysis of home sales in the four counties of the South Coast Air Quality Management District. The results, especially regarding visibility, varied as the statistical manipulations took different forms.[41]

The range of values derived with the four approaches can be quite large, and there are even substantial differences within the same approach. While use of several approaches to valuing emissions could contribute to accuracy by allowing triangulation of values from the different approaches, that may not be happening in this case. Table 7-1 reports valuations using the three approaches for which information is available for specific pollutants. While no information is available for calculated values, that category is shown to parallel this discussion. Comparison across approaches to valuing emissions is not easy. No comparisons are possible across three approaches, and only two—NO_x and PM_{10}/particulates—can be compared across two approaches. However, these two comparisons are very interesting, as the values found in market exchanges of EPA offsets are dramatically lower than those found by the revealed preferences approach. Part of the difference is probably attributable to the fact that offset prices were obtained for 1985 and the revealed preferences data for 1988 and 1989. However, the offset prices also include substantial transaction costs; each exchange must be approved by the EPA after a long, complex, and expensive review, so they may well overstate actual emission values.

One reason for the lack of convergence in values is that the approaches are not directly comparable, at least in what they value best. The direct calculation approach focuses on effects upon individuals, businesses, or the ecosystem, each complex entities in themselves, and consequently encounters difficulty in measuring impacts of discrete amounts of individual emissions. It is difficult to

---

41. Phil Graves *et al.*, "The Robustness of Hedonic Price Estimation: Urban Air Quality," *Land Economics*, 64:3 (August 1988), 220-33.

Table 7-1. Values of Emissions Estimated by Different Approaches ($ per ton).

		Approach					
		Revealed Preferences					Market
Pollutant	Calculated Impacts	CEC[a]	SCAQMD[b]	SCE[c]	IEP[d]	Proxy	Prices
NO_x	—	11,000	24,500	40,000	24,500	—	5,000
SO_x	—	11,500	18,300	—	18,300	—	—
PM_{10}	—	7,800	—	—	—	—	2,000
ROG	—	3,300	17,500	—	17,500	—	—
CO	—	—	—	—	—	—	3,000
CO_2	—	—	—	—	14.70	7	—
CH_4	—	—	—	—	375	—	—
N_2O	—	—	—	—	3,250	—	—
SO_2	—	—	—	—	—	—	3,000
VOC	—	—	—	—	—	—	2,500

Sources: Robert L. Therkelson, "Valuing Emission Reductions for Electricity Report 90," Sacramento, California Energy Commission, November 21, 1989, Staff Issue Paper No. 3R; Gayatri Schilberg, *et al.*, "Valuing Reductions in Air Emissions and Incorporation into Electric Resource Planning: Theoretical and Quantitative Aspects," Sacramento, Independent Energy Producers, August 25, 1989; Robert W. Hahn and Gordon L. Hester, "Where Did All the Markets Go? An Analysis of EPA's Emissions Trading Program," *Yale Journal of Regulation.*, 6:1 (Winter 1989), pp. 109-153.

a. California Energy Commission
b. Southern California Air Quality Management District
c. Southern California Edison
d. Independent Energy Producers

determine the impact of a marginal ton of emissions of NO_x on the health status of 1,000 people or on a forest.

Revealed preferences, in contrast, focus on specific pollutants, because the authorizing legislation is written to allow control of individual pollutants. This approach, however, has shown little capacity to value interactive effects, as when several gases contribute to changes in environmental conditions. Considering each pollutant individually could underestimate their interactive effects and could also result in policies that impose large financial burdens on society without clear indication of which pollutants should be reduced first in a given circumstance. Regarding interactive effects, oxides of nitrogen (NO_x) are a notable example, since they react with hydrocarbons to form smog, precipitate as one component of acid rain, and count as a greenhouse gas possibly contributing to global warming.

Valuation by proxy also focuses on single pollutants, so it runs equal risks of missing interactive effects and of not providing information about priorities in cases of multiple emissions.

In application, hedonic estimation techniques are limited by the lack of precise data on the pollutants impacting specific locations and individuals. Home resale prices and information about housing characteristics are available at the level of individual houses and community characteristic data are available at the census tract level, but data on pollution are rarely available at even the census tract level. In contrast, pricing information available for offset sales is specific to pollutant, time, and place. However, there are insufficient markets in many pollutants to provide good price data. As a consequence of these limitations, valuation data from both hedonic estimations and offset market transactions are currently limited to a few pollutants and a few locations.

Policy for a Context of Uncertainty and Change

Existing strategies for improving air quality in California are almost certainly inadequate to the task. At one level this is recognized in the South Coast Air Quality Management Plan, which envisions improvements being achieved in three stages, the first relying on technologies that are now available and can be applied within five years, the second relying on anticipated technologies that can be adopted over the next fifteen years, and the third relying on technologies not yet even visible. In a more important sense, however, the inadequacy is institutionalized in the planning process and is so fundamental that whatever specific plan is developed, today or twenty years from now, it will be inadequate.

The complexity of the challenge is reflected in the linking of the SCAQMP to two other plans—a Regional Mobility Plan and a Growth Management Plan—that also must be implemented if air quality targets are to be achieved. As Lindell Marsh points out, these three plans cover air quality, transportation, and growth management in a region with a population larger than that of forty-eight other states and that by the year 2010 is expected to add more people and housing than currently exist in 80 percent of the states, add more than 50 percent to its current employment base, more than double its regional gross product, and develop an area of land twice the size of the city of Los Angeles.[42]

Sweeping changes in the operations of many businesses, governments, and households are required to implement the SCAQMP. In some cases, major societal infrastructure must be expanded. For example, full implementation of the electrification strategy of the SCAQMP will require a 45 percent increase in the maximum possible 1988 energy output of the three southern California utility systems (Southern California Edison, Los Angeles Department of Water and Power, and Burbank/Glendale/Pasadena) by the year 2010. At the same time, oil is to be replaced as the fuel in generating plants, but natural gas supplies have been curtailed to utilities three times from January 1988 to mid-1989 because of supply shortages and limits on distribution capacity.[43] While technically feasible, expansion of utility generating capacity and increasing the supply of natural gas will require siting, financing, constructing, and then operating major new projects. One analysis examined the barriers to achieving the electrification goals of the SCAQMP and concluded that it was effectively engaged in electricity resource planning, a role historically reserved for the California Energy Commission and California Public Utilities Commission.[44]

Implementation of the Regional Mobility Plan (RMP) linked to the SCAQMP will require massive investments in public transit. But available funds are inadequate to maintain the existing system, let alone expand public transit capacity to achieve the RMP goal of increasing public transit use from the current 6 percent of all trips to 19 percent. Additionally, existing regional transit planning and implementation processes take too much time and are too vulnerable to challenge to achieve the increases projected even if financing were not an issue.[45] Moreover, as already noted, there is no experience in implementing the jobs-housing balance strategy important to trip reduction, a strategy that requires influencing decisions of local governments that make land use decisions, developers, finan-

42. *Supra* note 12.
43. California Energy Commission, *Electricity: 1988 Report,* Sacramento, June 1989, pp. 5/4-5/5.
44. Joint Committee on Energy Regulation and the Environment, *Electric Resources and Environmental Impacts,* Sacramento, April 1990.
45. Southern California Association of Governments, "Institutional Considerations for Implementation of the RMP Transit Element," prepared for the Transportation and Growth Management Task Force, Los Angeles, September 28, 1989.

cial institutions, businesses, and households that undertake development and occupy the resulting space, and employees/households who make decisions about distances between residence and job.

An additional important reason for institutionalized inadequacy in California air quality planning is the virtually exclusive reliance on CCR strategies. This is a flawed model. As expressed by Hahn and Hester, IBR strategies extend CCR strategies.[46] IBR strategies will not replace all CCR strategies, but the two strategies used together can be much more powerful than either alone. What is needed to more effectively improve air quality in California is a combination of changed attitudes regarding useful "science" and modified policy designs. If one expects the scientific underpinnings of public policy to be perfect, providing irrefutable evidence of the nature of a problem and of how it should be solved, then the current understanding of the causes and consequences of air pollution—most particularly of effective curative strategies—would allow no action at all.

Whole new uncertainties about air pollution and changes in the global environment recently have been raised. There is imperfect evidence of the impacts of specific pollutants upon humans or plant life, so judgmental techniques are used to value emissions. Yet accurate valuation is critical to focusing energies and resources on the most pressing pollutants. Toxicologists making risk assessments now recognize that simple linear extrapolations from animal studies, the most common technique used to identify toxins, probably underestimate the risks associated with some and overestimate risks associated with others. As a consequence, public policies allocating societies' resources are likely to mismatch resource with risk.[47]

To improve the scientific basis for air quality policy making it is important to expect less, yet demand more. This paradoxical statement suggests that instead of looking for a single scientific approach to improving air quality, it is preferable to recognize ignorance, uncertainty, and diversity of opinions, then develop and use multiple, partial sources of information to more accurately and fully understand how to proceed.

46. *Supra* note 40, p. 113.
47. Malcom Gladwell, "Risk Assessment Techniques Throw Researchers a Curve," *The Washington Post National Weekly Edition*, April 2-8, 1990, p. 39.

In this effort, some interesting tools have been suggested. For example, Akbari and colleagues at the Lawrence Berkeley Laboratory propose the use of conservation supply curves, which compare a wide variety of policy options against effectiveness (e.g., tons per day reduction) and cost. Using this tool, they conclude that their list of least cost recommendations (white surfaces, two times and three times more Rhodium in auto catalytic converters, improved exhaust gas recirculation in cars, and tree planting) would reduce NO_x 25 percent of current levels by the year 2005 at a cost of $624 per ton while reducing energy use. In contrast, the measures included in the SCAQMD plan have a median cost of $27,000 per ton, but a mean cost of $54,400, because one SCAQMD strategy (domestic solar water heater retrofits) costs $652,000 per ton.[48] This technique of analysis can be used to identify least cost alternatives for achieving other air quality improvement goals.

Another tool is seen in the summary of recent behavioral research prepared for the October 1989 UCLA Extension Symposium on TDM.[49] Bringing together several researchers and policy makers working on the same problem led to a fertile exchange. One result was to identify the few areas where there was widespread agreement on the current state of knowledge (e.g., commuter behavior is rational, reducing parking subsidies is a prerequisite for effective TDM programs). Equally important was to identify areas of significant disagreement, such as that regarding the efficacy of monetary incentives to ridesharing. More informed policy choices can be based upon such distillations of expert analyst and practitioner knowledge.

One problem is that any policy is developed in a context of differing values and objectives. This is well illustrated in the case of subsidies for employer-paid parking now found in the national tax code. Present tax law allows businesses to deduct costs of employee parking as a normal expense, but requires inclusion of any employer payment for transportation of more than $15 per month in employee income reported on W-2 forms. As seen in the discussion of TDM, available research shows that removing the parking subsidy incen-

48. Hashem Akbari *et al.* "Conservation Supply Curves for Reducing Urban Pollution," Berkeley, Lawrence Berkeley Laboratory, May 11, 1989, Figure 3; and Arthur H. Rosenfeld *et al.* "Policies to Improve Energy Efficiency and Reduce the Impact of Global Warming," Berkeley, Lawrence Berkeley Laboratory, August 9, 1989.
49. *Supra* note 34.

tive is the single most effective action needed to needed to reduce single-occupant driving. However, the U.S. Department of the Treasury opposes changes in these tax code provisions, arguing:

... change in this area would come either at the price of serious administrative difficulty if parking were made taxable, or significant budgetary cost if transit pass and vanpooling exemptions were expanded. We do not believe this kind of change is warranted on tax policy grounds at this time...the desirability of additional incentives for employer-provided commuting benefits deserves further study, particularly as to the efficiency and fairness of providing such incentives through the tax system and solely in connection with employer-sponsored programs.[50]

At least as important as new tools of analysis are new ideas regarding policy strategies. One critical element of the basic strategy here has already been mentioned several times: IBR strategies need to be combined with and extend the CCR strategies now dominant. In addition, policy makers need to respond less rigidly to uncertainty and change in scientific understanding, failures in policy making, and changing preferences. At the risk of some caricature, the current policy approach can be contrasted to a preferred approach along several dimensions, as shown in Table 7-2. The seeds of policy making using preferred strategies are already evident. For an example of how learning can occur, Hahn and Hester report that, compared to the EPA, states had approved more than twice the number of activity "bubbles" under which a firm agrees to reduce total emissions without regulation of the ways in which reductions shall be made. This was attributed largely to the fact that state review and approval processes contain fewer steps than those of EPA.[51] The EPA could increase the number of "bubbles" approved by reducing transaction costs associated with the application process.

Learning as a policy is implemented can also improve upon the performance of CCR measures. For example, it appears that Volkswagen is dramatically more successful at reducing NO_x emission from its cars, while achieving high miles per gallon fuel efficiency, than are other manufacturers. Volkswagens emit less than half the grams of NO_x per gallon of fuel burned than do Hondas of equivalent gas mileage, for example.[52] Yet the CCR strategy gives Volkswagen no incentive to maintain this contribution to air quality

---

50. Michael J. Graetz, Deputy Assistant Secretary (tax policy), statement before the U.S. House of Representatives, Committee on Ways and Means, March 6, 1990.

51. *Supra* note 40, p. 128.

52. Akbari, *supra* note 48, Figure 7.

Table 7-2. Current and Preferred Policy Strategies

Attribute	Strategy	
	Current (CCR)	Preferred (IBR within standards)
style	standards, rules	incentives in context of standards; rules where appropriate
assumptions re: science	perfect and cumulative	imperfect and disjointed
assumptions re: knowledge	high	mixed
assumptions re: ability to change behaviors	high and low cost	moderate and mixed cost
assumptions re: individuals and organizations	hostile, self-interested, ignorant	benign, self-interested, learners
focus of action	plans and rules	cutting emissions
how error and change handled	not expected; adherence to rules is defense	expected; anticipate with redundant and reversible policies; learn from errors
how policy improved	through science and technology forcing rules	through science and learning as policies implemented
who discovers improvements	scientists and rulemakers	emitters and scientists
disciplines used	engineering, law	engineering, law, economics, policy design
defining metaphors	rule maker, rule enforcer	policy maker, learning facilitator

improvement and gives other manufacturers no incentive to improve the emission performance of their vehicles beyond that required to meet CCR standards.

The incentives to improve performance over time offered by IBR strategies yield their greatest advantage. This is well recognized. For example, after arguing that CCR strategies can sometimes be as effective as IBR strategies, Oates *et al.* note:

> Over the longer haul, it is of great importance that we have a system that embodies the appropriate incentives for research and development of new abatement technologies. Incentive based approaches…have compelling advantages over typical command and control regimes on this count. Even here, however, there is some scope for designing command and control programs in ways that encourage, rather than impede, R & D efforts.[53]

Under the preferred strategy, rules requiring a specific CCR measure can still be imposed if that is found to be appropriate. But rather than the first and only strategy, those measures are generally turned to after consideration of IBR strategies.

This approach shifts most of the burden for discovering ways to reduce emissions to those who cause emissions, gives them incentives to make those discoveries and reductions, and creates a collaborative rather than hostile relationship between policy makers and those whose behaviors they seek to change.

53. *Supra* note 27, p. 142.

The Environmental Defense Fund and the Regional Institute of Southern California have joined together to analyze the potential of incentive-based strategies to contribute to cleaner air in southern California in a project entitled Cleaning Southern California's Air and Protecting its Economy (CSCAPE). This chapter is based on preliminary work undertaken for the project. Assistance was provided by Deborah Belasich, Thomas Kirlin, Jeff Chapman, and Peter Asmus. Tom Graff and Michael Cameron of the Environmental Defense Fund and Pat Russell and Marilyn Ryan of the Regional Institute of Southern California provided helpful comments and support.

BEYOND NIMBY: DEALING WITH HAZARDOUS WASTE

Peter Asmus

8

Not In My Backyard! has become a rallying cry for citizens throughout California and the United States when confronted with the prospect of locating a toxic waste treatment facility in their neighborhood. To confront this so-called NIMBY problem, an unorthodox marathon negotiating exercise between interested public and private parties in California resulted in a hazardous waste management approach that has been heralded as a national role model.

The unique county-based plan, however, quickly became embroiled in a dispute between state and local governments over final facility siting authority. By early 1990 representatives from state and local governments had begun to make some headway in narrowing their differences. This may set the stage for implementation of a sophisticated approach to hazardous waste management that has the added benefit of promoting waste reduction in addition to the siting of new treatment facilities.

Hazardous wastes are substances that are toxic, flammable, corrosive, infectious, or reactive. They are either known to cause or suspected of causing increases in mortality or serious, incapacitating illnesses.

The issue of hazardous waste management is complicated by ongoing debates over what is hazardous and what is not. California has the most inclusive definition of hazardous waste in the country, and this distinction has created some unique challenges, among them the generation of public support for siting hazardous waste treatment facilities.

California's hazardous waste problem is immense. According to the Department of Health Services (DHS), the state produced approximately 1.55 million tons of hazardous waste in 1987; the hazardous waste management industry handled well over 100 pounds of hazardous waste for every Californian.[1] Other entities,

---

1. Department of Health Services, Toxics Substances Control Program, Alternative Technology Division, "Draft Status Report on Hazardous Waste Management in California," Sacramento, September 15, 1989 (revised September 21, 1989), p. 1.

including Chemical Waste Management Inc., the largest waste handler in California, claim this figure drastically understates the scope of the problem since documentation of different kinds of wastes, and their final destinations, is so incomplete.

Placing a dollar figure on current treatment and disposal costs is difficult because of the myriad categories of wastes, some twenty-three different local, state, and federal laws relating to disposal of hazardous waste, and the variety of private and public treatment and disposal entities. State and private sources estimate that treatment of hazardous waste costs $185 per ton, for a total price tag of $300 million a year using DHS waste volume figures—a conservative figure according to most experts. Costs surely will accelerate as landfills continue to close and more expensive treatment systems become mandated by new environmental regulations. Today, approximately 200 permitted treatment facilities manage the majority of wastes shipped off-site for treatment.

A report released in 1986 notes that 60 percent of California's waste stream is produced by only 1 percent of all hazardous waste generators in the state, while 88 percent of those who generate hazardous waste each produce less than 100 tons annually.[2] This latter group, typically small to medium-sized businesses such as neighborhood dry cleaners, are becoming the focus of hazardous waste management debates because of the regulatory burdens placed on them and their lack of technical expertise and capital to identify and fund cost-effective waste reduction and treatment solutions. One study estimates that over 50 percent of small-quantity generators dispose of some of their waste illegally.[3]

The distribution of hazardous wastes throughout California is concentrated near major metropolitan centers such as Los Angeles, San Francisco, San Jose, and San Diego. According to DHS numbers for 1985, the Los Angeles Basin generated just over 50 percent of California's annual hazardous waste stream. The San Francisco Bay Area generated 29 percent, central California 10.5 percent, and the San Diego area 6.5 percent. Rural areas in northern California generated only 2.7 percent, while counties located in the Sierra contrib-

2. Governor's Task Force on Toxics, Treatment and Technology, *Final Report,* vol. 1, May 1986, p. 127.
3. Division of Environmental Studies, University of California, Davis, and Senate Office of Research, "Managing Hazardous Wastes Produced by Small Quantity Generators," 248-S, Sacramento, April 1987, pp. 15-17.

uted less than half of 1 percent of the state's hazardous waste total. Figure 8-1 displays anticipated hazardous waste generation by county for 1995.

The emergence of environmentalism as one of the public's primary concerns and the now familiar cry of Not In My Backyard! have aggravated attempts to develop solutions to the hazardous waste management crisis throughout the United States. One result has been that California exports much of its wastes to states with less stringent environmental controls, a trend that has become increasingly popular in the past few years. But along with this reaction, the NIMBY syndrome has also focused local government's attention on waste reduction, the ultimate answer to the hazardous waste management problem.

Evolution of the Tanner Process

A series of events brought the toxics crisis into focus in California at the start of the 1980s. Most of the major landfills in southern California closed within a few months of one another. Local governments, responding to constituents' concerns about the prospect of hazardous waste incinerators in their neighborhoods, rejected several proposals for local treatment centers. Finally, new regulations signed into law by Governor Jerry Brown required that the state no longer rely on landfills but instead seek better treatment options for hazardous waste. California was the first state in the country to take such an aggressive stand.

In response to this and other developments in local hazardous waste management, Assembly Bill 1543 by Los Angeles Assemblymember Sally Tanner, current chair of the Assembly Toxics and Environmental Safety Committee, was signed into law in 1982 (Chapter 89). This legislation established California's Hazardous Waste Management Council, composed of sixteen representatives from state and local government, industry, and public interest groups. The council was to study options to address the NIMBY problem, including state preemption of local land use decisions, and to recommend legislative solutions.

Among the states that rely heavily on a public policy model of state preemption are Arizona, Kansas, Maine, and New Hampshire. In New Jersey, another example of state preemption, a state-level inde-

Figure 8-1. Projected Recurrent Waste Generation by County, 1995

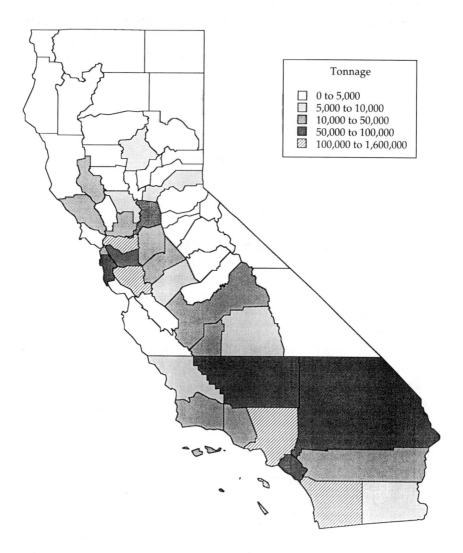

Tonnage

☐ 0 to 5,000
☐ 5,000 to 10,000
▨ 10,000 to 50,000
■ 50,000 to 100,000
▨ 100,000 to 1,600,000

pendent siting commission recently was established. The political advantage of such an approach is the co-opting of those groups traditionally opposed to the siting of facilities by holding them partially accountable for siting decisions.[4] New Jersey's independent siting commission is seen as a convenient way to bypass the traditional stumbling blocks to approving a facility. The tradeoff in accepting preemption of local land use decisions is that citizens become intimately involved with the proceedings of the siting commission.

California, however, opted not to follow New Jersey's lead and instead developed its system through the Hazardous Waste Management Council's use of a series of innovative mediation techniques. These policy sessions began to remove some of the stumbling blocks to establishing useful dialogue between traditional adversaries in the siting of waste treatment facilities.

Industry was the first to make some accommodations to local governments during these meetings, suggesting that cities and counties retain initial siting authority, but that a state council be set up as an appeals body with override authority.[5] Local governments agreed to allow the state to override local land use decisions, which formed the basis for legislation. Industry began to realize that treatment facilities would have be considered within the context of a comprehensive approach to waste management before siting decisions would be acceptable to local government officials.[6]

Last-minute amendments included in the legislation, which became known as the Tanner process, called for the phasing out of land disposal of all untreated or liquid wastes by May 1990. While the California Legislature passed the legislation in 1984, it was vetoed by Governor Deukmejian. The following year the identical legislation was again vetoed. The governor finally signed AB 2948 (Article 3.5, California Health and Safety Code Section 25135 *et seq.*, and Article 8.7, California Health and Safety Code 25199) into law in 1986. The basic provisions of the legislation are:

4. Jim Sinclair, "The NIMBY Game: Implementation of New Jersey's Hazardous Waste Disposal Facility Siting Policy," unpublished dissertation, University of Southern California, Washington Public Affairs Center, 1990, p. 4.

5. David Morell and Christopher Magorian, "Siting Hazardous Waste Facilities: Local Opposition and the Myth of Preemption," Cambridge, MA, Ballinger Publishing Co., 1982. This book includes a critique of the New Jersey preemption model and was influential in structuring California's local government approach to hazardous waste management.

6. Daniel A. Mazmanian, Michael Stanley-Jones, and Miriam J. Green, "Breaking Political Gridlock: California's Experiment in Public-Private Cooperation for Hazardous Waste Policy," Claremont, CA, Claremont Colleges California Institute of Public Affairs, 88-15342, 1988, pp. 53-63.

- It provided $10 million in state funds for counties to develop hazardous waste inventories, identify sites for specific hazardous waste treatment technologies, and produce county hazardous waste management plans to guide future policy decisions.
- The bill established a bureaucratic process for evaluating proposals for treatment facilities based on the creation of a separate Local Assessment Committee (LAC) for each proposal. This entity gives advice on the final terms of arrangements between local government and treatment facility proponents. These LACs work in conjunction with the Governor's Office of Permit Assistance.
- The bill also set forth the composition of a special state appeals board to hear appeals related to both denied and approved projects and, where necessary, to override local land use decisions. The primary basis for decisions made by this state appeals board is consistency of the proposed facility with the approved county hazardous waste management plan.

The Tanner legislation is considered a landmark because, in theory, it balances local concerns of appropriate land use with statewide priorities of securing treatment facilities to meet the needs of the entire state. Beyond the legislative delays, one of the reasons it has taken California so long to set in place a hazardous waste management strategy is California's reliance on counties to produce inventories of hazardous waste within their borders. Unexpectedly, all fifty-eight counties decided to participate. Since detailed information about sources and quantities of hazardous waste for counties often was virtually nonexistent, a tremendous education process ensued.

San Diego developed a thirty-one-member advisory committee, which included representatives from government, industry, environmentalists and citizens groups, and one member from each of the eighteen cities in San Diego County. Many counties, such as Orange, augmented allotted state grants with local funds. Orange County received $250,000 in state funds, but has spent approximately $1 million in preparing its county plan.

Despite this initial interest on the part of the counties, only thirteen California counties now have plans approved by the state (see Table 8-1), and the working relationship between state and local officials is severely strained. Fifty-two counties submitted complete

Table 8-1. Status and Funding of County Hazardous Waste Management Plans

County	Fair Share Language	Plan Status[a]	DHS Funding	(County Funding)[b]
Alameda	Yes	D	$205,029	—
Alpine	Yes	A	50,033	—
Amador	Yes	D	90,544	0
Butte	Yes	D	112,778	($25,244)
Calaveras	Yes	A	69,043	(16,000)
Colusa	Yes	D	53,043	(8,711)
Contra Costa	Yes	A	286,608	(30,000)
Del Norte	Yes	W	63,367	0
El Dorado	Yes	W	128,898	0
Fresno	Yes	D	184,799	0
Glenn	Yes	D	50,032	0
Humboldt	Yes	I	113,967	(56,033)
Imperial	No	A	136,450	—
Inyo	Yes	I	114,026	(41,000)
Kern	Yes	D	187,487	(275,000)
Kings	No	A	104,062	0
Lake	Yes	D	111,532	(25,662)
Lassen	Yes	W	53,140	(4,000)
Los Angeles	No	A	607,994	(507,000)
Madera	Yes	D	129,467	6,269
Marin	Yes	W	120,532	(18,328)
Mariposa	Yes	D	60,995	(13,000)
Mendocino	Yes	I	120,512	(46,000)
Merced	No	D	125,741	0
Modoc	Yes	W	58,645	—
Mono	Yes	D	52,282	0
Monterey	No	A	140,500	0
Napa	Yes	W	111,132	1,005
Nevada	Yes	D	95,796	0
Orange	Yes	D	252,354	(684,938)
Placer	Yes	D	91,000	(15,000)
Plumas	Yes	D	58,079	—
Riverside	Yes	A	153,300	(137,120)
Sacramento	Yes	D	213,330	(11,780)
San Benito	Yes	A	90,578	—
San Bernardino	Yes	A	254,154	(89,523)
San Diego	Yes	D	274,000	(6,400)
San Francisco	No	W	155,740	140,000
San Joaquin	No	D	105,532	(63,992)
San Luis Obispo	Yes	D	147,873	(5,693)
San Mateo	Yes	D	190,000	(122,000)
Santa Barbara	Yes	D	202,000	(198,000)
Santa Clara	Yes	D	271,550	(45,000)
Santa Cruz	Yes	D	117,832	(26,250)
Shasta	Yes	D	96,519	(18,500)
Sierra	Yes	D	61,032	5,000

Siskiyou	Yes	W	92,532	0
Solano	Yes	A	182,000	—
Sonoma	Yes	D	232,080	(4,000)
Stanislaus	Yes	W	129,713	(90,000)
Sutter	Yes	I	60,532	—
Tehama	Yes	D	101,637	0
Trinity	Yes	I	42,500	—
Tulare	Yes	A	96,359	(29,000)
Tuolumne	Yes	D	50,067	(7,467)
Ventura	Yes	A	186,938	(64,635)
Yolo	Yes	D	116,284	(190,210)
Yuba	No	I	90,568	0

Sources: Department of Health Services, California Association of County Supervisors, Assembly Committee on Environmental Safety and Toxics Materials.

a. Key for plan status: A = approved by DHS; D = disapproved by DHS; W = withdrawn by county; I = incomplete or late submission.

b. Figures in parentheses are county funding totals (deficits), while figures not in parentheses are state funds the county did not spend.

plans to the state, and all have approved their own hazardous waste management plans.

The issue of siting such facilities is one of the most perplexing public policy challenges facing the state of California. If the state does not set into motion a credible system for hazardous waste reduction and management soon, not only will public health be threatened and federal clean-up monies be put at risk, but the state's economy may become crippled by yet another form of public policy gridlock.

Developing Approved Plans

The arduous tasks of producing hazardous waste inventories and developing county siting plans are only two of several major factors contributing to the lengthy delays in implementing the Tanner process. A two-year stand-off between the Department of Health Services and local governments over the meaning of the term "fair share" is now the focus of public policy debates.

David Morell, senior staff representative from DHS to the initial Hazardous Waste Management Council and manager of the Southern California Hazardous Waste Management Project, argues that the notion of fair share "was the core of the Tanner process. In order to gain any political support for treatment facilities, they had to be needed and used locally." According to Morell, author of several books on hazardous waste, the blame for the lack of progress on siting facilities lies with state officials. The Department of Health Services, claims Morell, "didn't want any size restrictions of treatment facilities. They want those decisions to be left up to the private sector, to allow them to build where they wanted to build."

Since economies of scale typically make it impractical for each county to build treatment facilities for waste generated within their borders, interjurisdictional agreements would allow groups of counties to decide among themselves how to handle particular waste streams and size these facilities to match regional needs. "These interjurisdictional agreements made these larger facilities equitable in a broader public policy context," Morell points out.

DHS has a different point of view. DHS spokesman Bob Borzelleri says that counties are going "180 degrees against the intent" of the Tanner legislation: "The intent of the legislation was to set up a reasonable, equitable hazardous waste management plan—for counties, for regions, and ultimately the state—that took into consideration that, in some counties, waste handling capabilities are limited. We need to recognize that we are not talking about industries that produce waste. We are talking about industries that produce byproducts called waste. What they mainly produce is beneficial goods and services."

Borzelleri summarizes the state's perspective by noting that since these beneficial goods and services are shared "up and down the state," the responsibility for dealing with the not-so-beneficial hazardous waste products should also be shared throughout the state.

Some environmentalists also have concerns about the Tanner process, but for other reasons. "The legislature is playing a cynical game by foisting off the responsibility of hazardous waste management to local governments," asserts Michael Picker, with the Sacramento-based National Toxics Campaign. Most counties still have "no money and precious little ability" to develop the kinds of source reduction plans needed to meet the toxics challenge, he claims.

David Willis, DHS Deputy Director of Toxic Substances Control, thinks local governments should view preemption in a more positive light: "The state can act like a heat shield for local governments, by transferring the responsibility for siting from counties to the state in order to get things done." From this viewpoint, local officials are spared the political consequences of making unpopular siting decisions, while the more impersonal and insulated state bureaucracy becomes the necessary bad guy. One individual working with local governments came close to endorsing this view, noting that, once local siting restrictions were in place, even some county officials might prefer that the state appeals board locate a controversial facility.

A Tanner Timeline

The evolution of the fair share debate and other siting issues relating to the Tanner process are outlined in the accompanying timeline. This timeline, and the following analysis, demonstrates how implementation of even carefully crafted legislation can be influenced by governments with different agendas and the peculiar politics of NIMBY. It shows how the Tanner process, in spite of the goodwill of stakeholders, became embroiled over basic issues of land use authority. Ambiguity in the legislation allowed both the state and the county to formulate policy positions at odds with each other's interpretation of "fair share."

The state, from its perspective, was addressing the threat of NIMBY by highlighting an interpretation that sets up institutional incentives to site facilities—the original goal of the Tanner process— and by continually amending its interpretation of the regulations to give local governments more of a voice.

Rural counties are particularly worried about becoming "dumping grounds" for the rest of the state. However, DHS offered assistance to counties in protecting against such an outcome by including guidelines that specify how treatment facilities could be rejected by the county because of inconsistencies with county hazardous waste management plans. These criteria include proof that the county already has sufficient treatment capacity for a particular waste stream or that agreements with generators or other counties to treat and manage waste streams can meet treatment needs.

Table 8-2 illustrates current on-site treatment capacity for counties, along with waste export and import figures. These numbers highlight the extent to which counties rely on other entities to handle hazardous waste.

Counties continue to complain that the shifting stance of DHS has made compliance with state mandates on Tanner extremely difficult.

A Tanner Timeline

September 30, 1986
Governor Deukmejian signs AB 2948 into law.

June 30, 1987
DHS issues guidelines for the preparation of hazardous waste plans, which prohibit counties from limiting the size or type of facilities that can be sited within a county. Counties are concerned that they may be forced to accept the siting of facilities the size of which will not be determined by local needs or multi-county agreements. State also releases grant funding to counties to develop county hazardous waste management plans.

April 13, 1988
DHS issues clarification of its Tanner guidelines, reaffirming its prerequisite demands for no county restrictions on facility size or type.

December 7, 1988
DHS disapproves Kern County's plan on the basis that the county, among other things, did not indicate that interjurisdictional agreements are either currently operative or enforceable. These agreements are a critical building block of the county fair share strategy, since they would allow counties to negotiate the siting of facilities for handling regional waste streams. This was the first county plan submitted and was viewed as a test of how the state would respond to county interpretations of the law.

December 27, 1988
DHS attempts to further clarify its April 13 clarification of county plan approval parameters. DHS asserts that a waste facility can be limited in capacity to meet the county's treatment needs if it: (1) meets all capacity needs of a particular waste stream; (2) is economically feasible for the proposed technology and private operator; (3) meets current and future needs identified in the county plan.

October 6, 1989
DHS issues yet another clarification of "fair share" in light of continued misunderstanding over the April and December 1988 communications. The statement reads that the state would "likely" accept fair share limitations in some instances. Effective inter-county/regional agreements may be used to meet the county's fair share obligation.

November 30, 1989
Only two counties—Los Angeles and Tulare—have their plans approved. The vast majority of county plans submitted are rejected on this date because of fair share issues, restrictions on where sites can be placed. Another issue raised by DHS: the use of the state appeals board.

January 19, 1990
DHS and county representatives hold a meeting to discuss compromise fair share language to break the political gridlock on the issue. According to one individual in attendance, DHS' Dr. Ken Kizer moved the state's position on fair share even closer to the county position. DHS also states that the focus of DHS review is no longer specific fair share language, but rather the link between the fair share concept and interjurisdictional agreements.

February 28, 1990
The state approves eleven more county plans, but does not give clear direction as to why certain plans were approved and others were not. Thirty-one county plans have been rejected over the course of the last two years.

Table 8-2. Hazardous Waste Exported and Imported for Disposal and On-Site Capacity for Hazardous Waste Management, by County, 1986

County	Exported (tons)	Imported (tons)	On-site Capacity (tons/year)
Alameda	58959	6217	0
Alpine	17	0	0
Amador	45	0	27
Butte	2544	0	22350
Calaveras	51	0	0
Colusa	25	0	0
Contra Costa	109752	204410	267187
Del Norte	2	0	0
El Dorado	110	0	0
Fresno	18646	18629	68
Glenn	61	0	0
Humboldt	223	0	600
Imperial	2351	50575	0
Inyo	11	0	134
Kern	9996	147281	0
Kings	1530	313038	0
Lake	33489	182	0
Lassen	87	0	80
Los Angeles	450571	126391	8793730
Madera	609	0	118
Marin	2508	16	0
Mariposa	1303	0	0
Mendocino	1093	0	7650
Merced	2197	0	0
Modoc	0	0	0
Mono	0.63	0	0
Monterey	12556	47	9829
Napa	1151	363	0
Nevada	129	0	0
Orange	67489	724	23988
Placer	3027	16	0
Plumas	98	0	0
Riverside	12487	71	2527
Sacramento	40483	7258	897000
San Benito	499	0	0
San Bernardino	35930	3147	0
San Diego	78101	14331	0
San Francisco	25460	354	0
San Joaquin	7954	1	55
San Luis Obispo	4078	83	0
San Mateo	32678	28629	125138
Santa Barbara	23542	131442	812
Santa Clara	76880	5352	2425529
Santa Cruz	5340	0	0
Shasta	258	558	0

Sierra	0	0	0
Siskiyou	173	0	0
Solano	129905	76998	251
Sonoma	7484	63	0
Stanislaus	14311	5234	0
Sutter	54	0	0
Tehama	98	0	0
Trinity	26	0	0
Tulare	3848	49	840
Tuolumne	77	0	113
Ventura	53020	17	107908
Yolo	4374	81	0
Yuba	840	0	62050

While counties have received encouragement and assurances from regional DHS staff about their plans, these promises of compliance with state mandates often have been contradicted by DHS headquarters in Sacramento.

A good example of how counties came to distrust DHS is the rejection of Kern County's hazardous waste management plan, the first plan submitted to DHS. Among the more disturbing positions of DHS from the counties' point of view was that a ban on deep injection wells—a form of treatment for hazardous waste—authorized by a local initiative was considered undue interference in statewide hazardous waste management planning.

In a December 21, 1988, letter to DHS, Kern County's legal counsel reveals that an applicant seeking a permit for this technology received DHS' rejection criteria before the county did. "It is incomprehensible to us that this applicant would receive preferential treatment by being provided with this document [the rejection] prior to the county," the letter reads. "This episode leads us to have serious concerns over the objectivity the department has exercised in reviewing the county hazardous waste management plan."[7]

It is interesting to track how DHS has slowly moved closer to the county view on Tanner. Yet the state repeatedly has created confusion by not being cognizant of the burdens its directives place on local governments. While its October 6, 1989, statements were designed to give guidance and assurances to local governments about how a county could reject projects that exceed fair share if

7. December 21, 1988, letter from Stephen D. Schuett of Kern County Counsel to Dr. Kenneth Kizer of the Department of Health Services, pp. 2-3.

interjurisdictional agreements are effective for transfer of the waste to other counties, this information was conveyed just twenty-four days before a DHS deadline for county plans. Though counties welcomed any additional direction they could get from DHS, many viewed this late notice as further evidence that the state did not understand how local governments work. Any major change in a county hazardous waste management plan has to be approved by a majority of cities having a majority of the county's population, a process that could take months.

Beyond fair share, the other major stumbling block in implementing the Tanner process is the use of the state appeals board. Many of the rejection notices issued by DHS on February 28, 1990, asserted that they may "jeopardize the project proponent's or interested parties' ability to appeal a local land use decision affecting the siting of a proposed facility." As originally conceived, the state appeals board was to be viewed as a last resort. DHS apparently viewed it as the likely forum for siting decisions, once again placing a greater emphasis on state preemption of local land use decisions. Given the history of siting in California and throughout the nation, this emphasis may not be completely unwarranted. Nevertheless, the original concept of the Tanner statute was to encourage local siting of facilities, not state preemption of local decision making.

While DHS gave specific reasons for the rejection of plans in 1989, many counties claim they have no adequate way of amending plans in the hope of future approval because DHS has given little guidance for required changes in rejections issued in 1990.

Meanwhile, Assemblymember Tanner introduced 1990 legislation (AB 2595) that would enable counties to revise and resubmit disapproved plans. The bill also provides for counties that have not yet submitted plans to do so. DHS has sent notices to counties that deadlines for their plans are extended to January 1, 1991. A handful of counties have responded to the DHS offer.

These extensions, say optimists, will likely result in the ultimate approval of several more county plans, providing the necessary momentum to facilitate intercounty agreements for treating hazardous waste. Pessimists, including the County Supervisors Association of California, note that communications among the various parties in June 1990 seemed to indicate that few additional county plans would be accepted in the future.

The Mechanics of Siting

While New Jersey has nine years of experience with its siting process, California has not even set into place the county plans that form the policy portion of the Tanner process. Though a siting process and associated procedures outlined by the Tanner legislation has been in effect for several years, not one facility has completed the siting process. (It is interesting to note that no facilities have completed the siting process in New Jersey either).

The Tanner legislation sets up a series of procedures for generating public input into siting decisions. They center around Local Assessment Committees. These committees, composed of at least seven people representing different interests in local communities considering the siting of a project, will be created for each project proposed throughout the state. Their function is to bring the proponent, local government, environmentalists, and citizens to the table to negotiate the terms and conditions of the proposed facility. Figure 8-2 outlines the design of the siting and local land use process. Critical issues include facility size and mitigation measures for any perceived public health impacts, such as toxic air emissions.

The Tanner legislation also expanded the responsibilities of the Office of Permit Assistance, a part of the Governor's Office of Planning and Research, which assists local agencies in implementing the procedures required to permit a treatment facility.

According to the Office of Permit Assistance, approximately fifty projects have filed required notices of intent for projects. Many of these have since been abandoned. Legislation was passed in 1989 (SB 1201) to address the open-ended nature of the notice process and other bureaucratic reforms. The bill places a one-year time limit on notice-of-intent proposals, which now also require the proponent to specify a proposed site. Some LACs have received technical assistance grants from the project applicant to assist them in evaluating the project, a policy development that underscores the private-public cooperation fostered by the process.

Case Studies

The following case studies illustrate how the permitting process works.

Figure 8-2. Hazardous Waste Facility Siting and Local Land Use Policy

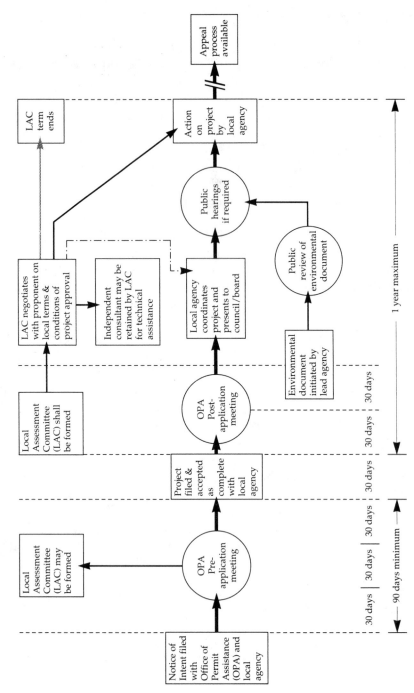

Falcon Energy Associates/San Joaquin County. Falcon Energy Associates produces fuel pellets from agricultural waste for biomass power plants throughout the Central Valley. A project proposed by Falcon for San Joaquin County would serve as a motor oil recycling station. The county desperately needs such a facility, and the oil serves as an additive required for the pellet making process.

This oil recycling station represents only 1 percent of the project's sixty-acre site, but because waste oil is considered hazardous under California's regulations, the Tanner process was triggered.

The county claimed the proposed facility is in an area zoned for agricultural use. The proponent argued that the zoning has changed since the project was first proposed. San Joaquin County has been feuding with the state over the adequacy of its hazardous waste management plan and has refused to amend it in order to meet DHS directives.

Meanwhile, well over 500,000 tons of industrial and automotive oils are generated annually in California, 7,000 tons in San Joaquin County alone. At present, DHS claims that only a fraction of the state total is sent to recyclers. According to DHS estimates, California's oil recycling capacity is three times the amount processed in 1987.

Falcon Energy Associates successfully petitioned the governor for state review of its project and was granted the first state appeal under the Tanner process. The appeals board consists of four local government officials, including one from the county where the project is proposed, and three state officials, including the head of DHS. In January 1990 the appeals board voted four to three that sufficient evidence existed to warrant further investigation of the merits of the case.

After several delays the county and proponent settled their differences outside the appeals process—yet another indication of the value of the Tanner legislation as a vehicle for problem solving. The project will be constructed, but county officials will help secure a different site.

U.S. Environmental Management Technologies/Sacramento County. U.S. Environmental Management Technologies is proposing to install a soil recycling bioremediation facility at the Sacramento County landfill. The project would treat large volumes of soil contaminated by leaking gasoline and diesel fuel storage tanks, Sacramento's largest waste stream, by the use of naturally occurring bacteria that feed on the waste. No toxic air emissions would result, as only carbon dioxide and water are generated by the process. The clean, recycled soil would then be used as fill dirt at underground tank remediation sites or as soil cover at the county landfill. The firm will lease the site from the county. This lease agreement will not be approved by the Sacramento County Board of Supervisors until an environmental impact report, currently underway, is completed.

The proposed facility will treat contaminated soil not only from Sacramento County, but from eight contiguous counties, and eventually from throughout the state. What makes this case study noteworthy is that it represents an aggressive effort on the part of Sacramento County to site a facility that would be designed to treat much more than its "fair share" of this particular waste stream. The county is supportive of this effort because the project is comparatively non-controversial and located at an existing facility.

More important, Sacramento County is strategically trying to fulfill its statewide fair share responsibilities by securing a project that has attracted little opposition. Such use of interjurisdictional arrangements demonstrates how Tanner is supposed to work and that counties actually have incentives to quickly site facilities that handle the least objectionable waste streams through relatively benign processes that do not rely on controversial treatments such as incineration.

Chemical Waste Management Inc./Kings County. Kettleman Hills has become a symbol of the state's traditional hazardous waste management practices, having allegedly contaminated local groundwater supplies. Chemical Waste Management, operator of the landfill, has filed a notice of intent to construct a new incinerator at the landfill and treatment site.

According to county studies, the public health risks of such an expanded treatment facility are minimal because local wind patterns blow incinerator air emissions away from human populations. County studies show that within a ten-mile radius of the facility, chances of residents getting cancer are approximately one in a million, a figure that is considered acceptable.

This project, nevertheless, has been attacked by Greenpeace and others on the grounds of "environmental racism." They point out that 90 percent of those living in Kettleman City, which lies approximately three miles from the proposed incineration site, are Hispanic. It is estimated that 50 percent do not speak English.

Critics, which include California Rural Legal Assistance, claim that public notices for LAC hearings on the project have been printed in English and that only one member of the seven-person Local Assessment Committee is Hispanic. In addition, CWM has ignored the LAC's recommendations for mitigating problems and plans to proceed with the project regardless of community opposition.

This project, if it goes forward, illustrates how emerging social issues such as environmental racism can impact the development of an effective hazardous waste management policy. It also questions the effectiveness of LACs when they do not have binding authority to stop or alter a project.

The issue of environmental racism is not limited to rural communities. It has been raised in San Francisco, where the county plan dictates that proposed facilities be located in areas zoned for industrial activities. Environmentalists agree that this is good public policy, but note that the plan does not provide for buffer zones between these facilities and residential neighborhoods. Communities such as Hunters Point, a predominantly African-American low-income neighborhood, may be subject to public health risks because they are located immediately adjacent to areas earmarked for future treatment facilities.

Government officials claim that the issue of environmental racism is no more than another NIMBY response to hazardous waste management. The issue highlights, nevertheless, how the issue of hazardous waste management can become linked to emotional social and political issues.

All three of these case studies address facilities that apparently will go forward. None of them has yet completed the process, however. Waste handlers such as Waste Management, Inc., parent company of Chemical Waste Management, are still worried that, despite the efforts of the state and counties to compromise over "fair share," the Tanner process may prove that "this cure for NIMBY is worse than the disease," according to Kent Stoddard, Waste Management's governmental affairs director. Buying into the concept of fair share, warns Stoddard, may make siting so uneconomic that even if the ongoing dispute between counties and the state is resolved, facilities still will not be sited. "The Tanner process," he suggests, "may ultimately provide roadblocks to siting that previously did not exist." While the process may appear to work in the abstract, Stoddard worries that the process may "institutionalize" NIMBY.

Others disagree. Tony Eulo of the Local Government Commission, an organization that has worked closely with local governments in implementing the Tanner process, observes: "The Tanner process has given local governments an incentive to initiate waste reduction programs, negotiate interjurisdictional agreements, and site needed treatment facilities. Before Tanner, local governments had absolutely no incentive to voluntarily site facilities."

Policy Choices

While the Tanner process has not yet succeeded in California, the framework it establishes is unlikely to be totally abandoned. The policy choices confronted in hazardous waste management involve improving the Tanner process, as illustrated in three areas:

Linking California's hazardous waste management policies (including Tanner) to emerging national policy. NIMBY is not confined to California's borders. The state-local disputes over siting facilities that have been occurring within California also have been occurring between states and regulators in Washington, D.C.

The national government's method of ensuring that states take care of their fair share of hazardous wastes is a carrot-and-stick approach. In order to receive funds for cleaning up sites deemed severe enough to be included on the national Superfund registry, states are required to provide the national government with biennial updates on their ability to treat and manage hazardous waste over a twenty-year planning horizon. One of the common ways states meet mandates of the Environmental Protection Agency (EPA) is through interstate or regional agreements.

California submitted its most recent plan in November 1989, emphasizing waste reduction as the primary means of meeting its Capacity Assurance Plan (CAP). The Tanner process is described in the context of how California is addressing the need to meet near-term capacity shortfalls for various waste streams. The description of California's approach to hazardous waste management highlights the value of the state appeals process and its potential role in providing for the override of local land use decisions, since such decisions may not provide sufficient treatment capacity for projected wastes.

Legislation also carried by Tanner (AB 650, Chapter 1502, section 25135.9 California Health and Safety Code) and signed into law in 1986 requires development of a state plan to assist regions in preparing their county plans and interjurisdictional agreements. Because most county plans are not yet approved, the state plan will not be completed until the next CAP submittal to the EPA. In September 1989 DHS released the data portion of what will become the state plan.

At present California is a major exporter of wastes to other states, sending 13 percent of its wastes — 219,785 tons — across state borders in 1988. Destinations in 1988 included: New Jersey (51,855 tons); Utah (48,254 tons); Idaho (39,504 tons); Texas (18,180 tons); Kansas (15,756 tons); and Arizona (13,198 tons), according to DHS records. These numbers increased dramatically throughout the latter 1980s (see Figure 8-3) and are indicative of how increased fees for treatment within the state (see Figure 8-4) provide incentives for generators of hazardous waste in California to send wastes to states that rank among the most lenient in terms of environmental standards. At present, the difference between in-state and out-of-state disposal fees is about $83 per ton.

This export practice could end soon. States such as Alabama have now banned the importing of wastes from any state or U.S. possession that has not demonstrated that it has the capacity to treat or dispose of waste generated within its borders. This law recently passed constitutional muster.[8] As of January 1990 the following states or U.S. possessions will no longer be able to ship wastes to Alabama: Alaska, Arizona, Delaware, District of Columbia, Florida, Hawaii, Kansas, Maine, Mississippi, Missouri, Montana, New Hampshire, New Mexico, Oregon, Puerto Rico, South Dakota, U.S. Virgin Islands, Vermont, Virginia, Washington, West Virginia, and Wyoming. California is among a list of thirteen additional states that may be impacted by the ban in the near future.

This same issue is being addressed at the international level. At U.S. congressional hearings on the topic held in 1988, the EPA

8. *National Solid Waste Management Association v Alabama Department of Environmental Management*, U.S. District Court for the Northern District of Alabama, No. 89-G-1722-W, January 12, 1990.

Figure 8-3. Total Exports of Hazardous Waste, 1982-88

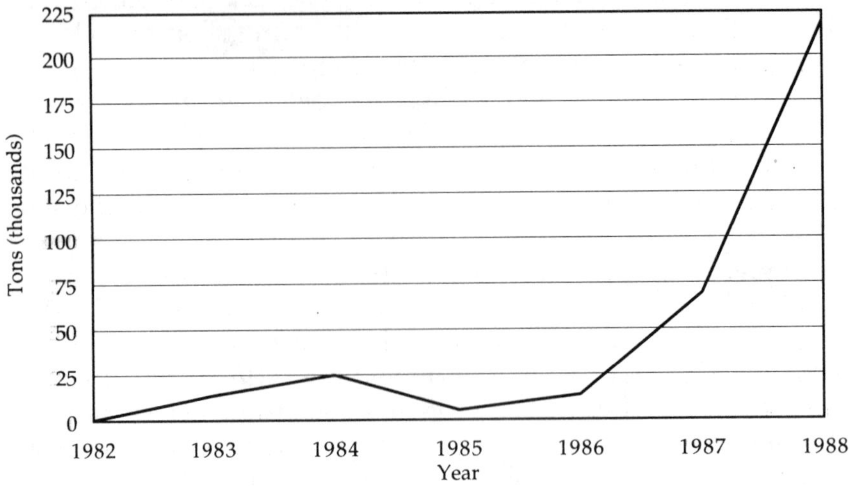

Source: California Department of Health Services

admitted that hundreds of tons of hazardous wastes have been exported without proper notification. EPA monitoring, reported EPA Inspector General John Martin, "is a program in shambles."

In a twist of fate, new health standards in Mexico are raising fears in San Diego County about the importation of wastes into California for treatment. Shipments of waste into California and Arizona from Mexico have recently jumped. By the year 2000 counties such as San Diego will fall far short of their ability to treat wastes generated within their own borders; the importation of Mexican wastes from the so-called *maquiladoras*, industrial plants that straddle the 2,000-mile border between the U.S. and Mexico, will add to the projected waste disposal problem.

Stimulating the waste reduction effort required to meet state and national goals. The best thing about NIMBY and the Tanner process is that they have focused local government attention on waste reduction, the waste management option of first choice.

For example, Santa Clara County sends over 100,000 tons of toxic waste offsite for treatment annually, according to the *San Jose Mercury News*. If Santa Clara County were responsible for its "fair share"

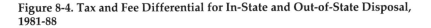

Figure 8-4. Tax and Fee Differential for In-State and Out-of-State Disposal, 1981-88

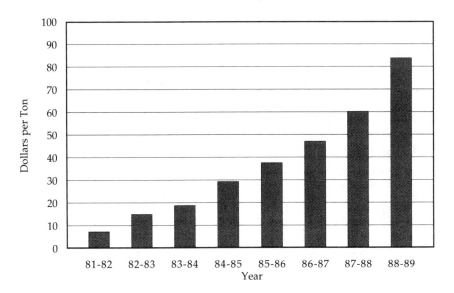

of hazardous waste, it would have to treat five times its current waste volume. The county, nevertheless, supports the concept of fair share and is gearing up to meet this challenge through waste reduction. Some of the region's largest industrial generators of hazardous waste claim certain waste streams such as solvents can be reduced by as much as 70 to 90 percent within a three-year period.

The county received a $175,000 grant from the Santa Clara Water District and began its waste reduction program in June 1989. Santa Clara is one of few counties that have developed methods to finance waste reduction through fees and incentives. The county is now trying to implement a funding formula to provide three years' financing for a county-wide waste reduction program. Half of the funds would come from cities and the county and the other half from industry by means of a $3-per-ton fee on wastes shipped off site. Although this approach has widespread support from the local industrial sector, it has encountered institutional obstacles because of restrictions on the taxing authority of counties for programs other than penalties, enforcement programs, or state mandates. All cities but one have agreed to the concept of the funding, and it appears that the tax issue has been resolved by making the program voluntary, an option negotiated with local industries.

Another way that the county is promoting waste reduction is through the South Bay Discharges Project. New EPA and regional water quality control board regulations would require costly upgrades for water pollution control facilities, which are owned by local governments and special districts. The county is therefore promoting waste minimization as an alternative, asking those who produce the waste to reduce the amounts of toxics in effluents so that the burden of compliance does not fall solely on wastewater treatment plants.

The staff is also investigating the packaging and accessibility of a direct loan program offered through the State Office of Small Business to finance waste minimization equipment. To date, few firms in California have utilized this program. The county is initiating a study to discover why the program is not being used and to identify better ways of publicizing its value.

Contra Costa County plans to require new businesses entering the county to include a waste minimization plan as an element of environmental impact reports. This, and other educational and technical assistance efforts, will require $100,000 in county funds just to set such a program in place.

Contra Costa County industries, such as The Dow Chemical Company of Pittsburg, have been supportive of the county's emphasis on waste reduction as the first step in reducing fair share waste management burdens. According to Dow's Western Division staff environmental consultant Bryant Fischback, Dow Chemical's Pittsburg plant has cut hazardous wastes from 73,000 tons in 1984 to just 3,600 tons in 1989, a reduction of over 95 percent. The facility has set a goal of reducing its air emissions by another 90 percent over the next five years. Fischback states that much of the impetus for these waste management reforms came from policies instituted by Dow's top management that are being implemented in plants at the Pittsburg site. He also praised the environmental community for its persistence in publicly promoting source reduction as the method of choice in managing wastes.

Fischback commends the Tanner process for its reliance on public input and emphasis on local control. In the past, he notes, communities such as Pittsburg existed for industry, and the local community paid much less attention to the quality-of-life issues that now dominate public policy agendas. With the large influx of residents to the area who have white-collar jobs in the Bay Area, industry has had to redefine its relationship to the community and, through processes such as Tanner, to restore public confidence in its handling of hazardous wastes. "Why should a county get dumped on?" asks Fischback, reflecting a major attitude change for industry.

There are other waste reduction success stories throughout California. Ventura County, for instance, reduced its volume of waste going to landfills by 70 percent in a two-year period with a voluntary waste reduction and on-site treatment program originally financed by state ($100,000) and county ($50,000) funds. Local industries, it is estimated, have saved $2 million annually since the program was initiated. It is now funded by fees imposed on waste generators and is not expected to make major reductions because the easy reforms have already been accomplished. The remaining work may require state technical assistance.

The development of an effective waste reduction effort for all counties is going to require state help. SB 14, by Senator David Roberti, was signed into law in 1989 and is a step in the right direction. The bill is a product of extensive negotiations between waste generators and environmentalists. It requires generators of hazardous waste of 12,000 kilograms or more per year to prepare two planning documents that describe current waste reduction procedures and future strategies and to pay user fees to the state based on hazardous waste generated. The database created by the legislation will help DHS assist firms in their waste reduction efforts.

The author of the bill summarized its importance:

This measure provides business with an option to reduce costs in disposing of hazardous waste and avoid the high costs of liability. It creates a program that includes a strong voluntary effort by business and a light administrative burden for DHS. The net effect is a positive result on the environment. In short, this legislation represents the best of government blended with the best of private interests.

Despite this start, the state, and perhaps the national government, will have to play a much larger technical assistance and information sharing role in the future.

Interjurisdictional agreements: a key to effective waste management reforms. In order for counties to retain authority over siting treatment facilities, they need to be able to prove that they have waste management capacity or have established interjurisdictional agreements to treat wastes that cannot be economically reduced through waste minimization initiatives. Local governments are scrambling to identify options for wastes generated within the county that cannot be treated with existing or proposed treatment facilities.

Since the vast majority of counties do not have approved county plans, and not one facility has yet completed the Tanner siting process, the focus of providing for a county's waste management capacity will be interjurisdictional agreements. In some cases, it may be in the county's interest to eliminate certain waste streams altogether, since state law requires treatment capacity of any waste that reaches an annual ten-pound threshold.

Due to increasing urban land costs and organized citizen opposition to treatment facilities in most cities, these agreements are particularly important for rural counties, which are especially susceptible to having facilities sited within their borders. After all, it is not uncommon for urban wastes to be managed hundreds of miles from the point of generation, typically in locations such as Kettleman City, one of the last two hazardous waste landfills in operation in California.

The primary danger for a county in not aggressively negotiating interjurisdictional treatment capacity is that the state appeals board may view inaction as a sign that the county is planning on siting its own facility to manage waste. The threat of a state appeals board override of local land use decisions provides motivation for the county to move beyond NIMBY and cooperate with other local governments.

Interjurisdictional agreements are complex and time-consuming, however. A joint powers agreement developed by the Southern California Association of Governments took several years to finalize. The Association of Bay Area Governments is now also facilitating similar agreements. Noticeably absent from programs in this area are rural counties, though some—such as Tulare, Kings, and Kern— are also initiating talks.

Interjurisdictional agreements involve tradeoffs, which may be monetary, a bartering for different types of treatment facility, or other land use exchanges. To speed up this process counties need state technical assistance in establishing equivalencies between types of waste treatment in different facilities, in analyzing what types of waste can be treated by existing facilities, and in obtaining information on health risks and cost effectiveness of the best treatment technologies now in use and those nearing commercial application.

Today, even if there is the political will for counties to share facilities, transportation routes, or geographical features, cooperative efforts often are stalled by uncertainties regarding toxicity levels. Generating a certain volume of waste oil, for instance, is not the same as generating an equivalent amount of PCBs.

Inevitably, interjurisdictional agreements will be needed both to allocate capacities of existing treatment facilities and to site new facilities. It is at this point, after all of the cost-effective waste reduction techniques have been pursued, that the integrity of the Tanner process ultimately will be tested.

The myriad complex issues that surround interjurisdictional negotiations have prompted some to propose amendments to the Tanner process to provide explicit incentives for counties to move quickly. One amendment, presented in a University of California, Davis, law journal,[9] would provide counties with a two-year time limit to identify regional facility sites. If counties do not meet the deadline, the responsibility for siting facilities will transfer to the state DHS.

Other options include new legislation clearly spelling out and codifying a fair share formula that takes into account the concerns of local governments. Such legislation could also provide for a better database management system that would feature specified systems for counties to evaluate existing treatment capacity and interjurisdictional agreements. A matrix of waste reduction and treatment options for different regions of the state could be formulated, allowing the state to play the role of technical advisor, with counties given deadlines for meeting capacity needs or risk the loss of this state technical assistance.

Conclusion

The evolution of the Tanner process displays the best and worst aspects of democratic government. The process used to formulate it—face-to-face consensus decision making among impacted inter-

---

9. Cathy L. Crothers, "Tanner Hazardous Waste Streams—Controversy over 'Fair Share' Responsibility," *University of California, Davis, Law Review*, 3(4): Summer 1990.

est groups—is now being employed in other policy areas dominated by knotty political issues. Nevertheless, the process of implementing Tanner displays how the checks and balances of American democracy can stagnate even the most promising reforms.

While the overall assessment of the Tanner process in moving California beyond NIMBY is hardly a ringing endorsement of the law, there are many useful lessons still being learned from the ongoing debate surrounding its implementation. Along with the negatives attached to delays, Tanner has also produced models of entrepreneurial public policy making at the local level.

"Democracy is not fast," observes Sunne McPeak, Contra Costa County supervisor and one of the key local government leaders credited with changing the focus of the Tanner bill from simply siting waste facilities to creation of a process for local governments to buy into alternatives such as waste reduction. "We decided we would advocate at the local level for things not explicitly stated in the legislation. We would do waste reduction even if that was not the state mandate," says McPeak.

Public-private partnerships show promise in developing funding for needed programs in times of fiscal stress. Such partnerships are "a total shift in mentality about how we solve tough policy issues," continues McPeak. "Instead of keeping the liability of proposed solutions solely in the hands of government officials, all those participating share in the responsibility of resolution." The partners become "jointly responsible for an outcome, and then contractually agree to carry out provisions of that outcome. The key is moving from an attitude that folks at the table are advisors to government, to stakeholders in implementing a plan."

The true test of whether the Tanner process works is yet to come. The delays may have shattered the trust that is required to create good systems to balance current economic needs with public health. Financial incentives embodied in the Tanner legislation in the form of a 10 percent take of gross receipts of off-site treatment facilities, may appeal to those counties seeking new funding sources. A note of optimism resides in the prospect of a more environmentally attuned and proactive governor.

No matter what new administration takes over in January 1991, however, the focal point of progress is the ability of all stakeholders to move beyond the distractions of issues such as state versus local authority and NIMBY, and use the tools of the Tanner process to achieve both waste reduction goals and the siting of safe treatment facilities.

ELECTRICITY REGULATION REFORM

Tim Duane

9

State-level electricity regulation in California currently is the jurisdiction of both the California Public Utilities Commission and the California Energy Commission. This regulatory structure has been effective in preventing the development of unneeded power plants, which until the 1980s were dominated by large, centralized, utility-owned generating sources. The industry structure has increasingly shifted to smaller, decentralized, non-utility owned generation sources since passage of the national Public Utility Regulatory Policies Act in 1978. The result is a regulatory system that is ill-suited to the policy challenges facing the state in the 1990s. This chapter calls for consolidation of the electricity regulatory functions of the two agencies to improve state energy policy.

Electricity regulation is in a state of transition in California, and wholesale restructuring of the present regulatory system may be required. The electricity industry has changed dramatically since establishment of the present system, causing serious strains for the regulatory environment. These strains led the legislature more than a decade ago to create a Joint Committee on Energy Policy and Implementation to reconsider the structure of electricity regulation. That committee issued a study in March 1979, calling for separation of the "line" and "adjudicatory" functions of the California Energy Commission (CEC) into a department of energy and a regulatory commission.[1] The legislature did not adopt these recommendations. The Little Hoover Commission (Commission on California State Government Organization and Economy) then released a study in February 1984, calling for better coordination between the CEC and the California Public Utilities Commission (CPUC).[2] Despite good

---

1. *Energy Administration and Regulation in California: an Analysis,* Staff Report to the Joint Committee on Energy Policy and Implementation, by Bob Foster, Project Director, March 1979.
2. Commission on California State Government Organization and Economy, *A Study of the Organization and Coordination of Electric Energy Planning and Electric Utility Regulation in California,* February 1984.

intentions, however, conflicts between the two agencies' jurisdictions and mandates have been compounded since then.

In adopting Senate Concurrent Resolution No. 7 (SCR 7) in 1988, the state legislature observed that the current regulatory system "has resulted in significant fragmentation, duplication, overlap, and confusion in the formulation and execution of state energy related functions."[3] To address potential conflicts between the CEC and the CPUC, and to consider alternate organizational structures for electricity regulation in the state, SCR 7 established the Joint Committee on Energy Regulation and the Environment. The joint committee is also addressing potential conflicts between California's energy and environmental regulatory agencies and policies.[4]

Before these energy-environmental linkages can be addressed, however, the legislature must resolve the jurisdictional conflict that exists between the CEC and the CPUC. "I am concerned," stated Joint Committee Chairman Senator Herschel Rosenthal (D-Los Angeles) at a recent workshop, "that linking air quality issues and planning to our existing uncoordinated energy structure may exacerbate our environmental problems rather than help to resolve them."[5] Dr. Patricia Nemeth, deputy planning director for the South Coast Air Quality Management District (SCAQMD) agreed: "From an air district vantage point," she observed, "our job is undoubtedly more difficult because there are two energy agencies in this state that have overlapping and sometimes conflicting functions."

Meeting the state's ambitious air quality goals while continuing to provide reliable, cost-effective electricity to California ratepayers clearly will require more than improved coordination between the regulatory agencies. Even with sincere efforts by both regulatory commissions, new circumstances facing the industry raise fundamental questions about continuing under the present regime. The following conditions are significantly different from those under which the present regulatory structure was established.

---

3. Senate Concurrent Resolution No. 7 (Rosenthal), Resolution Chapter 20 of 1989.
4. Craig R. Roach, Edward P. Kahn, and David L. Modisette, *Electric Resources and Environmental Impacts, Phase I: Defining the Issues and Problems*, Joint Committee on Energy Regulation and the Environment, Sacramento, CA, April 13, 1990.
5. Joint Committee on Energy Regulation and the Environment, *Workshop on Electric Resources and Environmental Impacts, Phase I: Defining the Issues and Problems*, Palo Alto, CA, April 27, 1990.

Utilities no longer own most generation resources proposed for development. The present regulatory system was structured when all new electric generation resources were owned and operated by utilities, which were under direct rate regulation by the CPUC. The federal Public Utility Regulatory Policies Act (PURPA) of 1978 has since resulted in most new generation resources being proposed by unregulated developers.

The CEC no longer has siting authority over all new thermal power plants. When the CEC was created, it was given siting authority for all new electric generation resources over 50 megawatts (MW) in size. The typical utility-built plant at that time was 500 to 1,000 MW; small independent generation projects were essentially non-existent.[6] Most new thermal power plants today are smaller than 50 MW, exempting them from CEC regulation.

Utilities now have an interest in lower demand forecasts to limit competition. The present regulatory system was established when utilities were forecasting significant growth in demand, which would make construction of new utility resources necessary. Because utilities are no longer the primary providers of new resources, they now have an interest in lower demand forecasts—-which would tend to limit competitors' market opportunities.

A non-utility constituency now exists for high demand forecasts and high rates. The present regulatory system was established when only the utilities had an interest in high demand forecasts and high rates; today this result would primarily benefit a non-utility constituency of independent power producers.

Selection of new generation resources will be based upon bidding-oriented systems. The present regulatory system was established when utilities determined new resource additions through centralized planning and site selection, offering more direct regulatory oversight by both the CPUC and the CEC. The emergence of a semi-competitive market for providing new electric generation resources has led to bidding-oriented selection systems.

Environmental policy concerns are not captured by bidding systems based only on direct financial costs. The current regulatory system was established when centralized regulatory oversight offered opportunities

---

6. Decentralized generation prevailed in the earliest days of the U.S. electric utility industry, but economies of scale and technological developments led to domination by large, centralized utility plants by the 1960s.

for incorporation of environmental concerns into the resource selection process. Bidding systems based only on direct financial costs do not incorporate environmental concerns.

Historical Context

Created by the Warren-Alquist Act of 1974, the California Energy Resources Conservation and Development Commission (commonly called the California Energy Commission, or CEC) was born at a time when the state's electric utilities were forecasting rapid growth in demand and a need to build large new power plants up and down the California coast. Faced with serious environmental and rate impacts from such construction, the legislature established the CEC to develop a four-pronged strategy for reducing the need for and alleviating the impacts of new facilities. While Governor Ronald Reagan vetoed legislation establishing the CEC in 1973, he signed similar legislation after the Arab oil embargo in 1974.[7]

The CEC was established essentially to prevent the development of unneeded power plants, but it was not given direct authority over utility resource planning. Instead, it had an independent demand forecasting capability, with authority to adopt an official state forecast of electricity demand; centralized siting authority for all thermal power plants over 50 MW, whereby projects could be approved only if they met established need; authority to establish conservation standards and incentives to obviate future need; and a technology development function to promote conservation and renewable energy. These four functions were translated into action by the four main divisions of the CEC: Assessments, Siting and Environmental, Conservation, and Development.[8]

Electric utilities have been regulated as "natural monopolies" in the United States by state public utilities commissions for over half a century. The CPUC determines retail rates for the investor-owned utilities in the state,[9] dominated by Pacific Gas and Electric (PG&E),

7. See *supra* note 1 for a thorough discussion of the legislative origins of the CEC. Statutes are in Warren-Alquist State Energy Resources Conservation and Development Act, Public Resources Code Section 25000 *et seq.*, updated in P160-89-001, California Energy Commission, January 1989.
8. The CEC's historic organizational structure is summarized in Suzanne Reed, *California Energy: Policy Development and Administration*, Touche Ross & Co., January 6, 1984.
9. Municipal and publicly owned utilities are exempt from CPUC oversight, held accountable to voters via local governing bodies.

Southern California Edison (SCE), and San Diego Gas and Electric (SDG&E).[10] Municipal utilities set their own retail rates.

Environmental regulation has traditionally been separate from public utility regulation. Utilities do need advance CPUC approval through a Certificate of Public Convenience and Necessity before beginning construction of a new project, but the regulators rarely challenged utility proposals before the mid-1970s. Demand was growing steadily at 7 percent per year until the oil embargo, while costs were generally declining until the late 1960s. New facilities met a growing need while also lowering prices. Resource planning decisions were deferred to utility planners, who then had to ensure project compliance under all environmental laws. The California Environmental Quality Act of 1970 required an environmental impact report to be completed for all new power plants, but no special state-level environmental permits needed to be obtained by power plant developers before 1975.

Despite significant rate increases required to pay for more expensive oil, utilities expected continuing demand growth when the oil embargo shocked California consumers. Environmentalists and some state legislators challenged this assumption, and they questioned the need for dozens of large new power plants proposed for construction. The CPUC staff, however, had little expertise in environmental regulation, and it already had a heavy load of rate-setting regulatory responsibilities: electricity, natural gas, water, telecommunications, and transportation (trucking and buses). The legislature therefore created a new energy policy agency, with independent demand forecasting capabilities and siting authority.

Unlike the CPUC, the new agency focused only on energy issues. While the CPUC mandate was primarily one of protecting ratepayers and shareholders through the establishment of "fair and equitable rates," the CEC was required to examine more than just the direct ratepayer economics of energy project development. The CEC's resource planning process focused on determining the "need" for new resources, "which, in the judgement of the commission, will reasonably balance the requirements of state and service area growth and development, the protection of the public health and

---

10. Southern California Edison and San Diego Gas & Electric have agreed to merge but are still awaiting regulatory approval. The CPUC is expected to issue a decision on the merger in late 1990.

safety, the preservation of environmental quality, the maintenance of a sound economy, and the conservation of resources."[11]

The CEC has not been explicitly directed how to balance these sometimes competing considerations, but it has been given an explicit mandate to consider environmental issues. If the CEC's "integrated needs assessment"—which includes consideration of these various mandated criteria—does not find that a proposed facility is needed, it cannot be built.

This centralized siting authority does not necessarily translate into an ability to define specific utility resource plans, except through the negative act of rejecting a siting application. The CEC is explicitly forbidden to compel any utility to adopt any specific resource plan, making demand forecasting and the issue of need the primary focus of the commission's regulatory processes. For this reason, the earliest debates focused on demand forecasting methodologies and determination of overall need.

Forecasting Demand

Because the CEC-adopted demand forecast determines the official need for new power plants, the demand forecasting exercise is a critical part of the Electricity Report planning process.[12] The large investor-owned utilities have traditionally relied on econometric demand forecasting techniques, which forecast future electricity demand based upon historically established relationships between energy use and economic activity. The CEC staff offered an alternative approach, which examined the potential for affecting demand in specific energy end uses through price changes and regulatory policies. New state appliance efficiency standards, for example, could reduce the electricity demand associated with the typical new refrigerator, which could translate into a significant reduction in overall demand. This end-use approach was data-intensive, but captured the impact of new regulatory policies. Such a policy intervention would not be captured by the historical econometric relationships, which relied upon broader economic indicators.

The utilities therefore tended to forecast higher growth rates than did CEC staff. Electricity demand was essentially treated by the

---

11. Public Resources Code 25309(b).
12. Professor Lyna L. Wiggins of MIT offered valuable insights about this critical early modeling debate.

utilities as given, beyond the control of either the utility or the regulators. This approach focused on the historical obligation of the utility to meet all demands for its services, which led to an emphasis on development of new supplies. Utilities argued that failing to anticipate future needs could leave the utility system vulnerable to shortages. Moreover, new utility investments had historically served as the foundation of utility company growth and increased profits.

CEC staff preferred to highlight opportunities to dampen load growth. Demand-side management—through standards, price incentives, and direct utility investments to improve the efficiency of customers' end-use equipment—could be treated as a source of new supply to meet the growing economy's electricity needs. Although not widely anticipated at the time, structural changes in the economy from basic manufacturing to service industries would also diminish energy needs per unit of economic output. The CEC believed these options were considerably more cost-effective than building new power plants. They also offered environmental benefits, conserved resources, and reduced dependence on highly vulnerable, imported fossil fuels. CEC staff forecasts therefore emphasized conservation-oriented policies in their integrated needs assessment.

The early utility and CEC staff forecasts differed widely for long-term electricity demand. Comparing their results was difficult, moreover, since they used different forecasting techniques. A common forecasting methodology was therefore sought, and much of the earliest debate focused on technical modeling issues.

Subsequent biennial forecasting proceedings led to a convergence between the two forecasts: CEC staff forecasts generally got higher, while utility forecasts got lower. The optimistically low CEC staff forecasts were pushed higher by the failure to achieve complete saturation of end uses with more efficient technology, which reflected the importance of many subtle factors in determining customer equipment investments. The lowered utility forecasts reflected the relative success of demand-side management programs, price-induced conservation, and a slower state and national economy.

The end-use versus econometric modeling debate was put to rest in 1988, when PG&E submitted an end-use model as the basis for its demand forecast and a common forecasting methodology was finally in place. Actual demand growth has proved to be significantly lower than the utility model's forecasts, and efficiency programs have played an important role in controlling demand growth. Other regulatory factors may have also been at work, however, which made a lower demand forecast advantageous to PG&E. In particular, low demand forecasts limit competition. This is in sharp contrast with the past, when utilities had incentives to offer higher demand forecasts, thereby justifying construction of new utility facilities.

Even with this new incentive for low demand forecasts by utilities, the increased importance of energy efficiency as a strategy for meeting both energy and environmental policy goals must still be recognized.[13] Unlike the conditions that existed in 1974, these strategies now have widespread acceptance by both utilities and regulators. Because there is such widespread support, consistency between broad CEC "need" policy and CPUC funding of utility-sponsored efficiency programs is critical. Utilities and others recently went through an exhaustive collaborative process to define new energy efficiency targets, leading to a near-doubling of utility expenditures over the next three years.[14] Some environmentalists argue that even more demand-side gains can be made. Unless state energy policy and funding decisions are consistent, however, even the gains expected under the collaborative process may not materialize.

Emergence of Independent Power Producers

The most significant change in the regulatory environment has been the passage in 1978 of the federal Public Utility Regulatory Policies Act (PURPA), which established the foundations for independent, non-utility-owned generation. While it did not have a significant effect until the early 1980s, PURPA has proved to be the most far-reaching structural change in the electric utility industry in half a century. Its impacts on the structure of the electric utility industry have exacerbated the CEC-CPUC conflict. As it is the dominant paradigm for new resource development today, understanding the

13. Dian M. Greunich, Arthur Rosenfeld, and David L. Modisette, *Energy Efficiency as a Coordinated Energy and Environmental Strategy*, Joint Committee on Energy Regulation and the Environment, Sacramento, CA, April 6, 1990.
14. See *An Energy Efficient Blueprint for California, Report of the Statewide Collaborative Process*, by Barakkat and Chamberlin, Oakland, CA, February 1990. Utilities filed funding applications with the CPUC in March 1990.

history of its implementation in California is critical to facing the policy challenges of the 1990s.

Originally intended to promote the development of renewable energy and cogeneration technologies, PURPA has proved to be an important force for broader deregulation of the electric utility industry. The Federal Energy Regulatory Commission (FERC), which regulates all wholesale power transactions and hydroelectric project licensing, adopted regulations in February 1980 that allowed state regulatory commissions to implement PURPA. California regulators at the CPUC chose to pursue implementation aggressively. The CEC had authority only over demand forecasting and new facility siting, while the CPUC had broader jurisdiction over public utility regulation, including implementation of PURPA's important reforms. As utilities stopped building major new power projects (they were struggling against high inflation, cost overruns, and other financial constraints) the balance of regulatory power for electricity policy shifted from the CEC to the CPUC.

Section 210 of PURPA requires utilities to purchase the power output of Qualifying Facilities (QFs), which are exempt from regulation as public utilities, at the utility's "avoided cost"—defined as what it would have cost the utility to produce the power in the absence of the QF purchase. A QF must be a renewable energy technology (e.g., wind, solar, geothermal, hydroelectric) that is less than 80 MW in size or a cogeneration project that meets minimum standards for efficient production of both electricity and thermal energy (e.g., steam or hot water).

By producing both thermal energy and electricity, cogenerators are more efficient than independent production of the two forms of energy by industrial processes and utilities. Renewable energy advocates argued that utilities were failing to invest in cogeneration and promising new technologies in the 1970s due to a conflict of interest. PURPA was intended to create a utility-independent market for investments in those technologies by allowing investors to avoid direct regulation. It also limited utility ownership of any individual QF to 50 percent.

Initial investment in renewable-based electric generation technologies was small under PURPA. Federal and state tax credits made highly leveraged investments financially attractive to many investors, but uncertainty about future purchase rates made power revenues risky. Utilities paid QFs based upon a simple calculation of avoided fuel costs, which fluctuated with both fuel price variations and changes in the resource mix. Negotiation of sales contracts with utilities was also time-consuming and sometimes difficult. Utilities fought PURPA in the courts, and they were generally not enthusiastic about supporting potential competitors who were not subject to direct CPUC oversight. Prospective QFs complained about utility foot-dragging and obstacles to development, such as high charges for back-up power. The CPUC encouraged more receptive utility behavior through rate-of-return penalties totaling millions of dollars in utility rate cases, and California utilities began to promote QF development in the mid-1980s.

The CPUC ordered the utilities to develop "standard offers" to prospective QFs, which would simplify negotiations and minimize transactions costs. Three basic standard offers were developed, including one for small QFs under 100 kilowatts. The other two standard offers differed in terms of whether or not the QF could supply "firm capacity." Demonstrating the ability to provide such reliable capacity increased utility payments, since the utility then avoided the need to build new capacity. These contracts were made available at a time when California utilities faced a critical need for new capacity. Completion of several large, utility-owned investments had been delayed, and system reserve margins were dangerously low during periods of peak demand.

The standard offer contracts primarily addressed the important problem of transactions costs. Many of the most promising renewable technologies were highly capital-intensive, but had minimal operating costs once constructed (e.g., wind, solar, geothermal, and hydroelectric). Even with a standard offer, the variable price of future energy payments made it difficult for these projects to obtain low-cost financing. Investors demanded higher returns to compensate for the increased revenue risk. This contrasted sharply with utility investments, on which utility shareholders were authorized to earn a preset rate of return regardless of changes over time in the value of a plant's energy. QF representatives therefore sought CPUC approval of a "fixed price" contract.

PG&E had negotiated similar contracts with some wind-power developers, who received a fixed-price payment for their energy based upon average anticipated avoided costs. These payments were expected to cost ratepayers no more than long-term payments under the short-run avoided costs rate, but they were front-loaded to allow capital-intensive wind projects to meet their debt service obligations. Other QFs wanted similar arrangements, since avoided costs were then expected to escalate rapidly along with the oil price increases that were widely forecast. Ratepayers would remain "indifferent."

The CPUC began to investigate development of such contracts in April 1982, but their complexity and disagreements had prevented resolution of the issue a full year later. There were critical short-term needs for power, expectations of continuing cost escalation, continued delays in completion of key utility plants, and, in anticipation of the forthcoming fixed-price contract, a virtual stall in QF development under the existing standard offers. The CPUC ordered its staff, the utilities, and QF representatives to negotiate an "interim standard offer four" (ISO4) that could be in place while the CPUC conducted hearings. After five weeks of negotiations, they reached a compromise. The innovative ISO4 was approved by the CPUC in September 1983, to be available for one to two years.[15]

The new ISO4 contract offered fixed-price payments for up to ten years of a thirty-year contract, while cogenerators (whose fuel costs could vary over time) had special options that fixed the non-fuel component of the payment calculation. Both firm and "as-available" capacity payments were offered, but the implicit forecast of avoided costs assumed continuing escalation of fuel costs. Ratepayers would bear the burden of forecasting errors, which could be either high or low. In return they would receive QF power at fixed prices for up to ten years. After that, the ISO4 called for payments at prevailing short-run avoided cost rates. The contract did not include provisions for revising the terms, however, if conditions changed dramatically during the period of its availability. This proved to be a fatal flaw in design of the otherwise attractive interim measure.

While the QF industry was initially cautious about ISO4, the response was overwhelming in 1984 and 1985. Even as fossil-fuel prices started to collapse on world markets, prices stayed fixed under the ISO4 contracts. Even after thousands of megawatts of prospective QF projects had signed up to supply power to the

---

15. See various decisions in CPUC Application (A)82-04-044, *et al.*, also known as the OIR-2 proceeding.

utilities, the reduced value of further additions was not reflected in new ISO4 prices. And even when large utility-owned facilities were finally completed and operational, the reduced value of capacity and energy purchases did not change ISO4. Fearing such sweet terms would not be available for long, prospective QFs generated a veritable "gold rush" to sign contracts. They had few obligations under the contracts, so speculative paper projects also signed up. Utilities sought CPUC help, and the CPUC suspended the availability of ISO4 on April 17, 1985. Major utility facilities came on-line shortly thereafter, yet hundreds of QF projects already had ISO4 contracts. Suddenly California was awash in new electric supply opportunities—and a potential excess of commitments. It also had a healthy QF industry—which was now competing with the utilities to supply the state's future needs for electric power.

Excess Generating Capacity

The collapse in world oil prices, the unexpected level of contract commitments under ISO4, and the completion of large, centralized, utility-owned power plants (e.g., the Diablo Canyon and San Onofre nuclear plants and the Helms Pumped-Storage Hydro plant) led to a reversal of the utility position on independent power between 1983 and 1985. Whereas the utilities had encouraged their development (with prodding by the CPUC) when the system faced shortages, the independent power producers were blamed for an electricity supply glut once the utility additions were on-line. Moreover, the QFs under ISO4 were relatively expensive: oil prices had dropped, yet the fixed-price contracts were built on an assumption that they would increase. Finally, the new utility resources had high fixed costs and low operating costs. Their short-run marginal costs were therefore considerably less than the ISO4 QF purchases, yet the utilities could curtail QF output only under limited conditions under PURPA. The utilities wanted some way out of the contracts, since they were no longer needed in the short term.

Utilities feared that the result of further QF development under ISO4 would be significant rate increases, driving industrial customers to bypass the utility system by installing self-generation or cogeneration systems. This might necessitate further rate increases as fixed costs were allocated to fewer and fewer sales, which could negatively affect all other utility ratepayers and utility profits.

The CPUC and CEC were also concerned about the rate implications of this "excess capacity." CEC forecasts showed no demonstrable need for the power, since the new utility resources and excess out-of-state capacity could easily meet the state's demand. Furthermore, many of the QF projects were smaller than 50 MW in size—making them exempt from the CEC-regulated siting permit process.[16]

These "non-jurisdictional" projects therefore were not regulated in the same way as larger projects, even if they executed their ISO4 contracts with the utilities at the same time and for the same terms. The cumulative impacts of the smaller projects were potentially greater than the larger projects, both economically (the CPUC concern) and environmentally (the focus of CEC regulation). It seemed as if everyone involved in the regulatory process except the QF industry itself wanted to limit further QF development under ISO4. The legislature responded by passing SB 1970 in 1986, calling for joint CEC/CPUC hearings on the "excess capacity." Testimony was filed in the summer and fall of 1987 for joint action by the two commissions.

Positions in the proceeding were fairly predictable. The utilities blamed the QFs for the unanticipated glut, highlighting the "overpayments" being made under ISO4. The QF industry responded with an analysis demonstrating that the excess capacity was only temporary, noting that QFs had filled a valuable role during the recent period of narrow reserve margins. They demonstrated that even the ISO4 contracts were less expensive than the new utility-built additions, which were considerably over budget. While ratepayers were "overpaying" under the fixed-price contracts relative to short-run avoided costs, they might still be benefiting relative to utility construction. The utilities countered that the marginal operating costs of the new utility-owned resources were low.

The real problem was neither new utility-built projects nor the ISO4 contracts: it was a failure by the regulators to link availability and price terms of the ISO4 to need. This failure materialized largely because of the overlapping and sometimes conflicting jurisdictional responsibilities of the CEC and CPUC. The CEC had responsibility for determining need, but no authority to implement QF develop-

---

16. The QF industry informally estimated the cost of going through the CEC siting certification process at around $1 million and an extra year of delay, so many cogeneration projects were sized at 49.9 MW.

ment policy through the establishment of contract terms. The CPUC had responsibility for promoting QFs through those contracts, but no responsibility for matching the resulting supply and CEC-determined need.

The QF industry could easily pass the blame to the utilities and the regulators. They were independent, unregulated businesses—with no legal obligation to meet retail customer demands or to ensure low, stable retail rates. The experience demonstrated the importance of linking supply opportunities with responsibilities, as the historical "regulatory compact" once did with the regulated utilities. Who would exercise that responsibility in a deregulated market for electric generation? Given the industry-wide deregulation discussions of the 1980s, it was an appropriate question. The FERC continues to explore deregulation proposals today.[17]

The final report on the joint CEC/CPUC hearings was submitted to the legislature in April 1988.[18] The commissions advocated a "tough but fair policy of contract administration" for limiting the number of ISO4 projects that would eventually go forward, with a focus on achieving ratepayer benefits before approving contract changes. In particular, they recommended that the requirement that QFs be on-line within five years of the date of contract execution be rigorously enforced "because of the planning certainty this gives the utility and the planning discipline it imposes on QFs." Special exceptions were made for "force majeure" events (e.g., a CEC license condition that the project's on-line date be extended beyond the five-year deadline) and where "it would benefit ratepayers to defer the on-line date of a project." Following a proposal by this author, PG&E had advocated paid deferrals and negotiated contract buy-outs to discourage development under the ISO4 contract. The joint report gave reluctant approval of such efforts, but no enthusiastic support. It did not want to endorse paying QFs not to produce power, even if ratepayers might benefit.

---

17. Paul L. Joskow and Richard Schmalensee discuss alternative deregulation scenarios in *Markets for Power: an Analysis of Electrical Utility Deregulation*, Cambridge, MA, MIT Press, 1983. For a more recent analysis see U.S. Congress, Office of Technology Assessment, *Electric Power Wheeling and Dealing: Technological Considerations for Increasing Competition*, OTA-E-409, Washington, D.C., May 1989.
18. California Energy Commission and California Public Utilities Commission, *Report to the Legislature on Joint CEC/CPUC Hearings on Excess Electrical Generating Capacity (SB 1970)*, P150-87-002, 1988.

The commissions also recommended that they continue efforts to achieve an integrated Electricity Report and standard offer update process and that a broadly based blue-ribbon committee be appointed to evaluate California's energy regulatory institutions and procedures and to make recommendations for enhancing coordination, consistency, and efficiency.

Despite efforts to improve coordination, however, the regulatory structure remains unwieldy. The current system for acquiring new generation resources is sequential. The CEC determines need and identifies a "base case" resource plan through its biennial Electricity Report process. The CPUC then determines whether to offer long-run standard offer contracts to QFs through the Biennial Resource Plan Update proceeding. In this proceeding utilities submit resource plans to the CPUC, and the commission determines if there is an Identified Deferrable Resource (IDR) that QF purchases could potentially "avoid." If there is an IDR, prospective suppliers are asked to submit bids to win the right to a contract.

In theory, this should prevent excess capacity from being acquired; in practice, it has created a forum-shoppers' paradise for encouraging conflicting electricity policies. "As presently constituted," CEC Chairman Chuck Imbrecht notes, "it takes as much as four years to reach a decision...and this is only the start of the actual permit application process. Moreover, due to a lack of coordination between the state's lead agencies, a reasonably high likelihood exists that one or the other agency will not actually approve the project permit because of inconsistent assumptions...used in the process of determining appropriateness."[19] The result is a leadership vacuum in state electricity policy—and potential conflicts with important environmental policies.

Energy and the Environment

Environmental issues resurfaced in the public consciousness in the late 1980s, and they are now becoming a driving consideration for energy regulators and utility planners. Whereas the primary energy policy concerns of the 1970s were associated with ensuring reliable supply, environmental issues—especially air quality—will dominate energy policy in the 1990s. That new focus follows the remark-

19. *Supra* note 5.

able emergence of a viable non-utility generation industry in the 1980s, along with the completion of major utility-owned generating plants. It is doubtful that the present energy regulatory system is equipped to handle these new environmental policy challenges.

The CEC recognized the failure of the current regulatory system in a recent report to the legislature addressing the importance of "non-price" factors in energy policy:

> While the Commission still has the authority to perform integrated energy planning, it must rely on the CPUC to produce the right kind and quantity of resource additions secured through bidding in investor-owned utility service areas. It is essential that the value of nonprice factors be included in planning decisions which set the level of conservation, achieve a diverse fuel mix, address environmental problems, and ensure adequate electricity supplies to sustain the state's economy. It is equally important that the same factors be included when candidate resource additions are valued. Otherwise, the planning process of the CEC and the implementation process at the CPUC will result in wasteful duplication of effort, inconsistency in results, and unjustified delay in securing needed energy resources. The respective roles of the CEC and the CPUC must be better delineated if the state hopes to have an energy planning and acquisition process which respects the value of nonprice factors, and is capable of implementing an overall energy strategy.[20]

The CEC also highlighted its diminished authority over power plant siting in Electricity Report Seven (ER-7), adopted in June 1989: slightly more than one-half of total proposed capacity additions were for projects less than 50 MW, outside CEC control. Because there are a large number of small projects, 90 percent of the nearly 1,700 identified projects would not come before the commission for siting approval.[21]

Unlike the conditions existing when the CEC was established by the legislature in 1974, the integrated needs assessment is no longer conducted for most power plants proposed for development in California (nor is it conducted for out-of-state plants). This requires the CEC to exercise indirect control by adopting "base case" resource plans for individual utilities—and then hoping that the CPUC will abide by them. The CPUC has agreed only to give the CEC recommendations "great weight" in its process of determining whether to require the utilities to offer a long-run QF contract.

Under the currently adopted framework, QF bids are offered as a percentage of the fixed costs of the IDR; energy payments will then

20. California Energy Commission, *Report to the Legislature in Response to Assembly Concurrent Resolution 160 (Resolution Chapter 147, September 15, 1988)*, Sacramento, CA, April 11, 1990.
21. *Ibid.*

be made according to the IDR's variable costs. This eliminates the risk to ratepayers of "overpayments" associated with overestimating future avoided costs, but they must now bear the risk of "underpaying" otherwise cost-effective QFs. Capital-intensive generation technologies are at a distinct disadvantage, so the bidding system is unlikely to yield a diversified mix of winning bidders. The winners are likely to be dominated by gas-fired cogenerators and gas-fired combined-cycle plants. This exposes ratepayers to increased reliance on natural gas, which already accounts for over one-third of electric generation in California. Moreover, even projects that are not fueled by gas will be paid according to variations in natural gas prices. Based upon the Draft Electricity Report 90,[22] over 90 percent of all three investor-owned utilities' production costs will be tied to natural gas prices by the year 2002.[23] This could expose ratepayers to even more significant price risk than oil did in the 1970s.[24]

Hence the CEC's concern about the present regulatory system and the CPUC's adopted bidding system for acquiring new generation resources. None of the non-price factors in the CEC mandate will necessarily be captured by bidding. The CEC has therefore supported utility proposals for CPUC consideration of a "multi-attribute bidding system," which would assign explicit values to non-price factors as bid selection criteria. The CPUC staff has been considering special "adders" to capture these values.[25] In the past neither the CEC nor the CPUC has explicitly assigned values to the reduction of residual emissions or control costs.

The CEC is examining air quality impacts in the Electricity Report 90 proceeding. Focusing on air emissions in the South Coast Air Quality Management District (SCAQMD) region, the commission is considering assigning values to residual emissions released by power plants. Analytic approaches to valuing these emissions reductions have focused on the marginal cost of meeting existing

---

22. Released in April 1990. The final ER90 will be adopted in October 1990.
23. Karen K. Edson, Peter Kyle, and Kevin Woodruff, "Rebuttal Testimony of the Geothermal Resources Association Regarding Fuel Diversity Policy and Demand Conformance Issues in ER 90," July 13, 1990.
24. The CPUC issued an order on June 8, 1990, to reconsider the adopted bidding system in I.89-07-004. Hearings will be held in October 1990 and a final commission decision is expected by the end of the year.
25. The CPUC held workshops on incorporation of non-price factors into the bidding system on November 2, 1988, March 6, 1990, and May 8, 1990. Hearings will be held on this in October 1990 in I.89-07-004.

standards.[26] The utilities have generally objected to assigning any value to residual emissions, claiming that existing environmental regulations already capture the value of emissions controls to society. The CEC is likely to assign some small value, however, and it plans to extend the analysis to other regions in future electricity report proceedings.[27]

Coordinating CEC and CPUC treatment of these environmental values is another matter altogether. The CEC could approve a project for its environmental benefits, for example, yet the CPUC may not approve the necessary contract for utility purchase of its power output. Alternatively, natural gas-fired non-jurisdictional QFs may win a bidding competition at the CPUC—yet the CEC may want to discourage natural gas dependence. Integration of environmental and other non-price factors is therefore a critical issue. It holds the potential for serious conflicts between CEC and CPUC energy policy in the state.

Differences between the agencies may also be more fundamental. The definition of need differs between the two, since they were established with different mandates. The CPUC has a long history as a rate-making agency, entrusted to protect ratepayers against excessive rates for the provision of essential public utilities. The CEC, on the other hand, has a short history built on promoting conservation, protecting the environment, and limiting the development of large, centralized power plants. The CPUC defines need in terms of reducing ratepayer costs; the CEC takes a broader view to include environmental values, but is also more restrictive regarding the siting of plants. It is doubtful that these two conflicting regulatory roles can yield consistent policy that will adequately address both the need for reliable supplies of energy at reasonable costs and environmental protection issues.

Future Options

The crisis in state electricity regulation has led the Joint Committee on energy Regulation and the Environment to examine various pro-

---

26. See CEC staff testimony in Docket 88-ER-8: Chris Tooker, "Valuing Emission Reductions for Electricity Report 90," Staff Issue Paper No. 3, August 8, 1989, and Robert Therkelson, "Valuing Emission Reductions for Electricity Report 90," Staff Issue Paper No. 3R, November 21, 1989.

27. The CEC is scheduled to adopt the final Electricity Report 90 in October 1990 (Docket 88-ER-9).

posals for agency reorganization.[28] Single-agency structures under consideration include consolidation of the existing CEC into an expanded CPUC, or consolidation of the CPUC's energy-related functions with the CEC into a new regulatory agency. Proposals for dual-agency structures include consolidation of the CEC's existing adjudicatory functions into the CPUC, with maintenance of the remaining CEC functions in a new Department of Energy (with a single executive director appointed by the governor). Alternatively, the CPUC's energy-related functions could be consolidated with the CEC's adjudicatory functions to form a California Energy Regulatory Commission, while the new Department of Energy would be structured as above. Advocates of the dual-agency structure argue that accountability for state energy policy will be clearer if a single appointee heads the Cal-DOE, while the CERC or CPUC would be more independent. Moreover, they note that the present line and adjudicatory roles of the CEC often conflict.[29]

Each of the proposals has merit. What is clear is that consistent state electricity regulatory policy—and related energy and environmental policy—can be achieved only if the opportunities for conflicting policy direction are minimized. A diversity of policy forums is much less valuable than a diversity of participants and policy viewpoints; in fact, a diversity of forums tends to reduce participation to only those large players (e.g., utilities) able to be at both the CEC and CPUC simultaneously. The present system fails this important test. Even if jurisdictional turf could be clearly delineated, the potential will continue for significant conflicts between CEC and CPUC policies. Fundamental restructuring is therefore necessary to ensure consistency and improved regulatory efficiency.

The call for organizational restructuring is not new. In 1984 the Little Hoover Commission observed:

Based on our study, we believe that the organization and coordination of energy planning and electric utility regulation is inadequate. In general, the activities of these two commissions are poorly coordinated. As a result, there is virtually no linkage between the development of State energy policy, as conducted by the Energy Commission, and the implementation of that policy through the PUC's rate-setting process. Additionally, there is duplication and confusion about jurisdiction

---

28. The Joint Committee was scheduled to release a discussion paper describing reorganization options in late summer or early autumn 1990. The paper was unavailable at press time.
29. See *supra* note 1 for discussion of the conflict between line and adjudicatory roles.

for some energy responsibilities…The Energy Commission and PUC unnecessarily duplicate certain activities.[30]

Despite these concerns, the commission recommended only minor changes in organizational structure, finding "no rationale which has not been previously presented that supports a realistic reorganization proposal." Instead, improved coordination between the CEC and CPUC was proposed.[31]

The failure of that effort for improved coordination suggests that reorganization is now appropriate. For purposes of consistency, a single-agency structure seems preferable. Despite some concern about distinguishing line and adjudicatory functions within an agency, most regulation in state government occurs within single agencies. If commissioner staff can be adequately differentiated from advocacy staff (e.g., the Division of Ratepayer Advocates is separate from commissioner advisors at the CPUC), both functions should be able to operate within a single organization. Establishment of equitable and comprehensive procedures for public participation will also ensure that commissioners are not unduly biased in favor of staff positions. Development of an adequate record—as now occurs under the CPUC's quasi-judicial hearings process—is essential.

The origins and corporate cultures of the CPUC and CEC suggest that concerns about energy-environment policy linkages would best be addressed within a planning-oriented agency like the CEC. In particular, the balancing of critical environmental considerations is unlikely to be adequately considered in a pricing-oriented agency like the CPUC. CPUC attention is also often riveted on telecommunications and other non-energy policy issues, including trucking, busing, and water utility regulation. This suggests that the CPUC's energy regulatory and policy functions (for both electricity and natural gas) should be removed for consolidation with the CEC. The new agency would be in a position to address overall state energy policy, including the fuel substitution impacts of alternative policies. This is likely to become increasingly critical as a strategy for achieving environmental policy goals. The SCAQMP proposals for electrification, for example, could improve air quality within the Los Angeles basin, decrease fossil fuel demand for the state, and

---

30. *Supra* note 2.
31. *Ibid.*

increase both emissions and the need for new generating facilities outside the SCAQMD air basin.[32] Inter-fuel substitution issues cut across all energy sources.

Such a consolidation should be a merger, however, not an acquisition: the CEC should not swallow up the CPUC staff. Instead, the new energy regulatory agency should combine the best of both agencies' corporate cultures. The reorganization should not abandon important strengths of the existing CPUC system, such as its quasi-judicial evidentiary process. At the same time, however, the CEC process allows for policy direction from commissioners. A reasonable balance must be struck that meets both the need for due process and the need to establish leadership on state energy policy.[33]

It is unclear whether this proposed consolidation of the CEC and CPUC energy policy and regulatory functions will have much political support. It is nevertheless the necessary medicine for improving state energy and environmental policy. Effective regulatory policy cannot be implemented if success requires support from a competing regulatory agency. Consolidating the two agencies would improve policy consistency and reliability, reducing a manageable source of uncertainty in resource planning. Continuing the present system could cost California ratepayers, the environment, and the economy billions of dollars and irreparable harm through either unnecessary generation investments or future shortages.

---

32. *Supra* note 19, and South Coast Air Quality Management District and Southern California Association of Governments, *South Coast Air Basin Final Air Quality Management Plan*, March 1989.

33. The Little Hoover Commission also expressed concern about the CPUC's constitutional mandate to regulate investor-owned utilities, which would need to be addressed in any consolidation legislation.

REPRESENTATIVE GOVERNMENT AND THE INITIATIVE PROCESS

Eugene C. Lee

10

In response to the dominance of state political life by a single monopoly—the Southern Pacific Railroad—Californians in 1911 voted into the state constitution the right of the people by petition to place a statute or constitutional amendment directly on the ballot. The threat to representative government at that time was real, and the response—the ballot initiative—was a reasonable one.

In 1990 representative government again is threatened, this time by the initiative process itself. Instead of serving as a safety valve, the initiative has become an uncontrolled political force of its own. It has produced occasional benefits, but at extraordinary cost. This chapter examines the fundamental weaknesses of the initiative process and suggests ways of overhauling the system to deal with them.

In the 1980s a political revolution took place in California—the frequent substitution of plebiscitary democracy for representative government. More people voted directly on more issues than anywhere else in the world. The largest number of state ballot propositions originated with the California legislature, in submitting constitutional amendments and bond issues to the voters. But many of the measures in the 1980s were the result of the initiative, that institution of "direct democracy" that has so dramatically altered the California political landscape. The trend is continuing into the 1990s as the governor, the legislature, and the courts find their agendas and calendars increasingly involved with ballot measures and captured by forces over which they have little control.

The initiative represents the right of the people by petition to put a statute or constitutional amendment directly on the ballot.[1] This is a right that Californians voted into their constitution in 1911, as part of a larger effort to wrest control of the political and economic institu-

---

1. Petitions must be signed by registered voters equal in number to 5 percent in the case of a statute and 8 percent in the case of a constitutional amendment of the votes cast for governor in the most recent gubernatorial election. To qualify for the ballot in 1990, 372,178 and 595,485 valid signatures, respectively, were required.

tions of the state from the domination of the Southern Pacific Railroad. The move was led by a faction of the Republican Party, the Progressives, a group of professionals and businessmen who conceived of the initiative as an instrument to neutralize the power of special interests, to provide a vehicle for civic education on major policy issues, to create pressure on legislators and governors to act on specific measures, and, when they failed to act, to bypass these representative institutions altogether.[2]

In twenty-two other states, sixteen west of the Mississippi River, citizens are similarly empowered. All but one of these states, as in California, also employ the referendum, through which citizens may petition to refer legislative action to the voters at the polls.[3]

Most of these states permit both constitutional and statutory initiatives. In California in recent years, the ratio of statutory to constitutional measures reaching the ballot has been about two to one, a possible reflection of the higher signature threshold for constitutional amendments.[4] California is one of only five states that do not allow legislative amendment or repeal of statutory initiatives. This has led to the creation of a quasi-constitutional body of law, subject to change only by a vote of the people unless the measure itself authorizes legislative action.

Uses of the Initiative

Writing in 1939, Key and Crouch observed:

...the groups using the initiative have not differed from the organizations lobbying before the legislature. They range all the way from blocs advocating legislation with obviously selfish motives to groups promoting measures which are the product of sincere and relatively well-thought-out schemes for the general welfare.[5]

The subsequent record has been essentially the same. In the last twenty years, for example, voters have confronted such diverse

2. Eugene C. Lee, "California," in David Butler and Austin Ranney (eds.), *Referendums: a Comparative Study of Practice and Theory,* American Enterprise Institute, 1978, pp. 88-9.
3. For discussion of the initiative process in the United States see: Thomas E. Cronin, *Direct Democracy: the Politics of Initiative, Referendum, and Recall,* Cambridge, MA, Harvard University Press, 1989; and David B. Magleby, *Direct Legislation: Voting on Ballot Propositions in the United States,* Baltimore, The Johns Hopkins University Press, 1984.
4. This record contrasts sharply with the period from 1912 through 1978, in which over 60 percent of the initiatives on the ballot were constitutional measures.
5. V.O. Key, Jr., and Winston W. Crouch, *The Initiative and Referendum in California,* Berkeley, University of California Press, 1938, p. 487.

issues as a lottery, property taxes, marijuana cultivation, public salaries, AIDS, legislative districting, rent control, campaign contributions, and criminal justice. Volunteer grassroots organizations, single-interest economic groups, political parties and elected officials, farmers, organized labor, environmentalists, doctors and lawyers — all have been a part of the contemporary initiative scene.[6]

The frequency with which such groups have employed the initiative has varied over the decades. Although widely used in the first half of the century, the initiative was little employed in California in the 1950s and 1960s. But between 1970 and 1990, as indicated in Table 10-1, over 400 ballot measures were proposed, 60 percent of all petitions taken out in the nearly eighty-year history of the initiative, including over 40 percent of all initiatives ever adopted. In 1988 alone a record-breaking eighteen initiatives qualified for the ballot, and this was repeated in 1990. In sharp contrast to the record of earlier years, only one-sixth of all circulated measures qualified for the ballot in the 1970-89 period. But nearly half of those that did qualify were approved by the voters, a marked increase over the record of previous decades. The initiative revolution was in full swing.

Why the Increase?

The reasons for the upsurge are varied, complex, and overlapping. Perhaps the most obvious reason is the role of state government itself. More than forty years ago, Carey McWilliams wrote: "Interests, not people, are represented in Sacramento...the market place of California where grape growers and sardine fishermen, morticians and osteopaths bid for allotments of state power."[7]

Many of the interest groups have changed, but the overall trend has been an increasing intrusiveness of state government into societal and economic affairs. This is not peculiar to California, of course, but the existence of the initiative has provided a powerful incentive for a wide variety of groups to become involved directly in McWilliams' "market place."

---

6. In his study of private-sector political involvement Thomas concludes that, of the fifty initiatives in the 1976-88 period, corporate interests were the primary backers of nine, the primary opponents of sixteen, and nonactive in twenty-five cases. Tom E. Thomas, "Corporate Political Strategy in the California Initiative Process," unpublished doctoral dissertation, Graduate School of Business, University of California, Berkeley, 1989, p. 52.

7. Carey McWilliams, *California: the Great Exception,* New York, Current Books, 1949, p. 213.

Table 10-1. California Initiatives Titled, on Ballot, and Adopted, 1912 through 1989 (according to year of election)

Decade Submitted	No. Titled[a]	Titled Initiatives Qualified for Ballot		Qualified Initiatives Adopted	
		No.[b]	%	No.	%
1912-19	44	30	67	8	27
1920-29	53	35	68	10	29
1930-39	67	37	55	10	27
1940-49	42	20	48	6	30
1950-59	17	12	71	2	17
1960-69	38	9	24	3	33
1970-79	139	22	16	7	32
1980-89	263	44[c]	17	22	50
Total	663	209	32	68	33

Notes

a. Titled initiatives include all proposals officially submitted to the attorney general prior to circulation of petition, whether or not the proposal subsequently qualified for the ballot.
b. Includes four "indirect" initiatives submitted to the legislature, one each in 1936 and 1942 and two in 1952. Only the 1936 measure was approved by the legislature.
c. Excludes two measures removed from the ballot by the California Supreme Court.

The state can also create new opportunities for private gain, an attractive inducement to use the initiative. In 1984 Scientific Games, Inc., the nation's largest manufacturer of lottery tickets, provided $2.2 million of the $2.6 million spent by Californians for Better Education to qualify and promote a lottery initiative. The proposition "...contained certain provisions that virtually guaranteed that the firm would be awarded the lucrative contract to supply the state's lottery tickets."[8]

The increasing use of the initiative process involves far more than the role of state government in societal and economic affairs. For many observers, much of the explanation rests in the unresponsiveness of the legislative and executive branches of state government. According to Republican Assemblyman Ross Johnson, "We've seen increased partisanship and bitterness in the Legislature, which has led to deadlock and frustration with the process."[9] Martin Smith noted in the *Sacramento Bee* that "elected lawmakers are cautious, even paralyzed in dealing with major controversial matters. State

8. *Supra* note 6, pp. 299-300.
9. Charles Bell and Charles Price, "Are Ballot Measures the Magic Ride to Success?" *California Journal*, September 1988, p. 382.

legislators are ideologically polarized, in part because they've gerry-
mandered themselves into overall safe electoral districts, [where
they do not have to compromise to gain reelection]."[10]

California's requirement of a two-thirds vote of each house to pass
all appropriation measures, a rule shared with only two small states,
has further weakened the ability of the majority party to develop its
own programs, as has the fact of divided party control of the legislative and executive branches.[11] The lack of strong programmatic
leadership by governors of either party for the past quarter-century
further defines the context in which "direct democracy" has flour-
ished. Political columnist Dan Walters concludes: "Virtually every
major issue presented to the voters via initiative in the last decade
has been before the Legislature without being resolved, or sometimes even addressed."[12]

In such a context of fragmented political power, the initiative has
been increasingly used, not just by groups to offset the failures of the
legislature and the governor—the original intent of the Progressives—but by governors unable to get their way with the legislature,
by members of the minority party in the legislature unable to pass
their bills, and by individual legislators of both parties unable to
overcome the opposition of powerful lobby groups.[13] In 1988 Bell
and Price estimated that, beginning in 1970, approximately 15 percent of all proposed initiatives had been filed by state office
holders.[14] And in 1990 candidates for governor sponsored ballot
measures, attempting to tie their fortunes to the popularity of initiatives with expected broad public appeal—environmental protection, ethics in government, and criminal justice. It was also a

---

10. *Sacramento Bee*, September 6, 1989.
11. Thomas adds that in a context of fiscal limits the budget allocation process is a zero-sum
game. Funding a new program may require a cut in an existing one, placing state agencies and
programs in direct competition and increasing the intensity of political conflict within the
legislature. He suggests that "affected agencies and their client groups should be increasingly
likely to bypass the legislative agenda by taking their appeals directly to the voter." *Supra* note
6, pp. 351-2.
12. *Tribune*, February 8, 1989.
13. Thomas notes that "sponsors thus tend to turn to the initiative only after their favored
legislation has been killed previously in committee, defeated on the floor of the assembly or
senate, or vetoed by the governor. The initiative agenda therefore tends to depend upon the
relative distribution of power within the state legislature." *Supra* note 6, pp. 55-6.
14. *Supra* note 9, p. 380.

strategy that escaped restrictions on campaign finance that affect candidates but not initiatives.[15]

Lobbyists were also spending an increasing portion of their time on initiatives, meeting with clients and political leaders to shape the language and strategy of ballot measures or to head off the threat of one—time formerly spent in seeking legislative support for or against specific bills. In 1990 Dan Walters reported another strategy—the counter-initiative or preemptive strike: "Increasingly, those who find their interests adversely affected by ballot measures are not content merely to campaign for their defeat. Rather they are devising alternative proposals that would either supersede the undesirable measures or hopelessly confuse the issue so voters would reject all measures."[16]

The Initiative Industry

Elected officials and lobbyists have not been acting on their own. Rick Kushman of the *Sacramento Bee* notes that "California's initiative process, which has exploded in recent years, has spawned a cottage industry of signature gatherers, initiative writers, lawyers who specialize in challenging or protecting initiatives and, of course, political consultants—all lured by the promise of expensive campaigns that absolutely dwarf what is spent on mere candidates."[17] Thomas adds: "Though these professionals may not actually create political issues, they seem to have made it more likely that disgruntled groups will seriously consider using the process, and have certainly improved the likelihood of success, if they do."[18]

The initiative industry is in an enviable position. It profits regardless of the success or failure of the ballot measure. Nearly $130

15. The strategy was not without controversy. Following the June 1990 primary, Jerry Roberts reported that there had been strong disagreement within the Van de Kamp campaign over its emphasis on the November initiatives; some saw this as a drain on money, time, and energy as the candidate was "forced, in effect, to run four separate campaigns." *San Francisco Chronicle,* June 8, 1990.
16. *Sacramento Bee,* February 20, 1990. For example, in the 1988 insurance war, insurance industry officials "qualified Prop. 106 in part to siphon off money from the CTLA's pro-100 campaign, and to sow dissension in the ranks of the trial lawyers." *Supra* note 6, pp. 355-6. In 1990 competing initiatives dealt with the regulation of logging, one sponsored by an environmental coalition called Forests Forever, the other a counter-initiative sponsored by the timber industry.
17. Rick Kushman, *Sacramento Bee,* February 12, 1990.
18. *Supra* note 6, p. 69.

million was spent on the twenty-nine ballot measures in 1988. As reported in the *San Francisco Examiner*, the insurance industry's five-way initiative war cost $70 million; Proposition 104, the no-fault measure, alone cost over $55 million, of which the chief consultant made over $6 million; petition firms grossed nearly $2 million; and two law firms billed over $600,000.[19] "That kind of money makes people sit up and take notice," observes Kushman. He quotes David Townsend, a Sacramento consultant who has handled a number of major initiatives: "If you're in it as a hobby, you do presidential campaigns, because you usually run those at a loss. If you are in it as a business, you do initiatives."[20]

It is a business that, according to John Balzar of the *Los Angeles Times*, is creating a "gold rush of campaign consultants...a west-ward-ho migration of professional campaign talent without precedent ...for the money and thrills, California's biannual orgy of ballot initiatives is tops in the consulting world, both for the homestaters and the newcomers. Here is a chance to get rich and do battle over driving issues of the day—insurance, political reform, transportation—all without the distraction of a candidate."[21]

The initiative process also involves logrolling (variously described as auctioning, trading, coalition-building, or populist pork barreling) typical of the legislative process. For example, in 1988 and 1990 sponsors of increased tobacco and alcohol taxes and bond issues for parks and rail transit wrote their proposals with an eye on campaign contributions and political support from those who would directly benefit from the distribution of the proceeds.

The Initiative Process

Designing, qualifying, campaigning for, and implementing an initiative is a complex, multi-step process. While the political context of the 1990s is not the same, the formal steps are those established in 1911.

The Petition

Although many initiatives have originated in the legislature, any citizen seeking to amend the state constitution or to add a new

19. *San Francisco Examiner*, February 19, 1989.
20. *Supra* note 17.
21. *Los Angeles Times*, June 12, 1989.

statute to California law can start the initiative process. Most serious sponsors seek the assistance of experienced attorneys and other experts in drafting their measures, and a few law firms specialize in this activity. While citizens may obtain assistance in drafting from the state's legislative counsel, few make use of this service.

Regardless of source, a draft of the proposed measure must be submitted to the attorney general, accompanied by a payment of $200. That office prepares an official title and 100-word summary of the proposed measure, including, where relevant, a fiscal analysis of the estimated impact of the measure upon state and local government revenues and costs. All of this information must appear on each petition to be circulated to the voters.[22] When this official summary is complete, the signature race commences. Sponsors have 150 days to seek and file the necessary petitions.

Qualification for the Ballot

At the heart of the initiative industry is the paid petition-gatherer, an essential part of a process that requires the signatures of a half-million to a million voters:

'Hey, this is a good one. Stop political corruption. Sign right here.' Dan Jansen, 28, is going to repeat this 1,000 times in the next ten hours as he stands in front of a Santa Rosa supermarket behind two ironing boards and eight clipboards...Jansen is one of a few people with the almost robotic persistence to make a good living circulating initiative petitions. Ten hours a day, six days a week, he gathers signatures that he sells for an average of 40 cents apiece...Jansen brings in 300 to 400 signatures a day, clearing about $600 a week. 'The average person burns out after about a week and a half,' Jansen says.[23]

Although observers have identified some thirty-five firms in the business of gathering signatures, successful petitions are generally the work of two California firms—Kimball Petition Management, Inc., and American Petition Consultants, headed by Mike Arno. Of the twelve initiatives on the November 1988 ballot, nine were qualified by one or the other of the two firms. Although differing in the character of their clients—Kimball's more liberal than Arno's—their methods are virtually identical.

---

22. Titling can be controversial. In 1980, for example, then Attorney General George Deukmejian initially put the title Rent Control on an initiative that, if passed, would have repealed all existing rent control laws. The title eventually was changed under pressure from tenant groups. *Supra* note 6, pp. 286-7.
23. *California*, February 1990, p. 13.

Both firms put thousands of paid petition circulators into the field and organize the signature-collection effort; assist volunteer groups in organizing petition campaigns (typically while the paid drive is proceeding); process signatures to assure their validity, using elaborate computerized listings of registered voters; and work with political consultants and organizations using direct mail to obtain signatures (and campaign contributions that are often used to pay petition gatherers). Specialists in the laws and regulations that govern the content and timing of initiative petitions, both firms virtually guarantee qualification of the initiative. And both are politically and financially successful.

The paid signature gatherers are independent contractors, who move from campaign to campaign—and from firm to firm— depending on timing and who is paying the most per signature. As the petition season heats up, they may bid up the price for their services. And if there are competing initiatives—as for example in the "insurance war" of 1988—petition firms may increase the price per signature and attempt to lure the opposition's forces into their own camp.[24]

Thomas reports that in the 1980s nearly all initiatives not sponsored by business qualified with the help of some sort of organizational backing, such as consumer advocacy or environmental groups.[25] However, with few exceptions in recent years, petition gathering involving only unpaid volunteers has not proved successful; the volume of signatures required is simply too large. While volunteer efforts may be politically effective in creating an atmosphere of grassroots involvement, they are generally not cost-effective. Organizing a volunteer effort can be expensive, with the employment of trained supervisors and the inevitable processing costs. And in the end, "mercenaries" frequently must be employed to complete the job of signature gathering in the limited time available, leading on occasion to territorial squabbles with the remaining volunteers.

One alternative remains—direct mail, aimed at both gathering signatures and soliciting campaign contributions. However, while

---

24. For a discussion of the desirability of regulating petition gathering and enhancing the role of unpaid volunteers, see Daniel Hays Lowenstein and Robert M. Stern, "The First Amendment and Paid Initiative Petition Circulators: a Dissenting View and a Proposal," *Hastings Constitutional Law Quarterly*, Fall 1989, pp. 175-224.
25. *Supra* note 6, p. 72.

such an approach is often beneficial in developing lists of supporters who contribute to the campaign, it is not always an economical way of obtaining signatures. "Unless it can be done for less than $1 per name," says one consultant, "it is not competitive with paid petition gatherers."

Regardless of the approach—volunteer, paid petition gatherer, or direct mail—the petition campaign has become increasingly costly, sometimes involving more than a million dollars, although Thomas reports that non-corporate access to the initiative agenda "does not seem to have become overly constrained."[26] Whatever the case, Berg and Holman conclude that "initiative efforts today, even at the qualification stage, resemble candidate campaigns."[27]

The Campaign and the Voter

The comparison could be reversed. Candidate campaigns have adopted political tools, most particularly radio and television commercials and direct mail, already exploited with respect to ballot measures. Candidate or initiative, the target is the voter. However, David Magleby notes: "Voting on ballot propositions places voters in a distinctive decision making role...[requiring] more information and involvement than does voter decision-making in a candidate contest...candidate appeal is irrelevant, partisanship is less important, and public opinion on current public-policy issues assumes greater significance."[28]

However, voter awareness of most ballot measures is often lacking. On the eve of the June 1990 primary election, 40 to 50 percent of registered voters polled had not heard of several of the key ballot propositions.[29] A survey of pre-election *California Polls* from 1978 to 1986 indicated that some three months before the election an average of 64 percent of the registered voters polled had neither seen nor heard about the proposition in question. A few days before the election, the average was 30 percent, but on some propositions voter ignorance of the measure was still more than half. Education best

26. *Ibid*, p. 73.
27. Larry L. Berg and C.B. Holman, "Losing the Initiative: the Impact of Rising Costs on the Initiative Process," *Western City*, June 1987, p. 30.
28. David B. Magleby, "Opinion Formation and Opinion Change in Ballot Proposition Campaigns," in Michael Margolis and Gary Mauser (eds.), *Manipulating Public Opinion*, Pacific Grove, CA, Brooks-Cole, 1989, p. 98.
29. Field Institute, *The California Poll*, June 4, 1990.

explained awareness of the propositions, leading Magleby to conclude that "direct legislation is a political process best understood
and used by those voters who are better educated or better off
financially."[30]

Absent candidate and party cues, proposition voters generally
decide much later. For most ballot measures, according to Magleby,
the pattern is one of growing voter indecision as the campaign
proceeds: "What typically seems to happen is that as the campaign
starts up and media coverage begins, information for and (especially) against the measure surfaces, and voters become uncertain or
undecided in their opinions...However, in the final pre-election polls
and in the actual voting the proportion of undecided drops as the
election forces a decision."[31]

There are exceptions. On issues such as the death penalty, opinions change little during the campaign. But most propositions face a
shifting electorate, which moves most often from a "yes" to a "no"
vote.

Successful or not, initiative campaigns increasingly involve television commercials. Thirty-second television spots are typically the
product, with the emphasis on a quick emotional or symbolic message for or against the measure in question. The timing of commercials is critical. Based on their knowledge of audience characteristics,
political consultants attempt to marry their message to potentially
receptive viewers.[32]

While television commercials are aimed at a more general audience, direct mail attempts to target those voters most likely to be
sympathetic to the particular cause. As suggested above, direct mail
is used not only to mobilize support but to raise funds. Political
consultant David Townsend described his system: "I have the entire
state, every voter, on computer...I know their party, sex, age,
whether they own their home or rent, what elections they vote in,
whether they vote absentee. I can send mail to a specific group, say
18-to 49-year-old Democratic women who rent, with a very specific

30. *Supra* note 28, p. 103.
31. *Ibid*, pp. 105, 107.
32. Not all television commercials are paid for. Many stations have accepted an obligation to
provide fair coverage, even when a campaign is unable to match its opponent with paid
commercials. On October 2, 1988, the *San Jose Mercury News* reported that backers of both
Propositions 99 and 103 were able to secure "tens of thousands of dollars worth of advertising
from more than half of California's thirty-five television stations."

message. If you have to pull back and make your message so general it doesn't offend anybody, it also doesn't say anything."[33]

Paid political advertising is not unique to initiatives. The ballot pamphlet is. Sent to every registered voter about three weeks in advance of the election, the pamphlet includes the complete wording of each measure (whether originating in the legislature or by initiative petition), a summary prepared by the attorney general, an analysis prepared by the legislative analyst, and arguments submitted by proponents and opponents of the measure. The end result for the November 1988 election was a 159-page publication, considerably larger than a weekly news magazine, costing several million dollars to publish and mail and requiring several hours to read.

Detailed procedures governing both the substance and the timing of the ballot pamphlet are prescribed in the elections code, leaving little discretion to the secretary of state, the officer responsible for production of the pamphlet. The final pre-publication step allows a brief period for public review of the pamphlet and, upon complaint, for court deletion or amendment of language that it finds false or misleading. The secretary of state's office reports a recent increase in the number of challenges and court-ordered changes, not only to arguments but to titles, analyses, and the attorney general's summary. In March 1990, for example, opponents of Proposition 115—a sweeping revision of criminal law—petitioned the court to require the legislative analyst's summary to include a statement that the initiative would cost taxpayers $500 million a year. The judge rejected the request, but did substitute his own language.[34]

The basis for this increased interest in the ballot pamphlet does not rest solely on its importance to voters. Indeed, "the available survey evidence indicates that most voters do not read the handbook or use it as a source of information for decisions on propositions."[35] The reason is clear. Citizens require a reading level of a third-year college

---

33. Rick Kushman, *Sacramento Bee*, February 18, 1990.
34. The legislative analyst's summary had concluded that "the net fiscal effect of this measure is unknown...and impossible to quantify." In contrast, the judge's language stated that "there may be only a minor fiscal impact on state and local governments, or there may be a major fiscal impact." In commenting from the bench, the judge said: "The tenor of the legislative analyst's fiscal impact statement to voters is not to worry...[However,] costs could be enormous and I don't think the voters are keen on thrusting their hands deeper into their pockets." Quoted in *The Los Angeles Times Daily Journal*, March 21, 1990.
35. *Supra* note 3, p. 136.

student to understand the pamphlet; more than two-thirds of those who receive the document cannot read it.[36]

But judges can and do. Despite evidence to the contrary, the state supreme court has held that the ballot pamphlet "is an important aid in determining the intent of the voters in adopting a constitutional amendment or a statute"[37] and that it "represents, in essence, the only 'legislative history' of the constitutional amendment available to us."[38] Attorneys who represent initiative sponsors say they are increasingly being asked to review arguments in advance in anticipation of legal challenges, with respect to both court review of the ballot pamphlet and, as discussed below, post-election litigation involving successful initiatives.

Television, direct mail, ballot pamphlet—all are aimed at encouraging the citizen to vote. But as Mervin Field observes, voter turnout has been steadily declining. Furthermore: "Taxpaying voters represent a declining proportion of all taxpayers and are, increasingly, a different breed of people. They are older, much more white than the rest of the population, they earn more, they have accumulated more wealth, and have different needs than the large majority of taxpayers who happen not to vote."[39]

The record noted by Field relates to turnout generally, affecting the vote for both candidates and ballot measures. However, Magleby concludes that there is an additional bias with respect to those who go to the polls but fail to vote on ballot measures: "In the absence of party cues or economizing devices, poorer and less educated voters confronted by most statewide propositions are less likely to participate and do not have their preferences recorded. For these citizens, at least, voting on propositions does not lead to a more accurate representation of the popular will than the traditional candidate election."[40]

Low voter participation is also the result of changes in the law permitting initiatives to appear on the June primary ballot. This practice, which started in 1970, was initiated without serious discussion of the implications of the much lower primary turnout, less than

36. *Ibid.*, p. 138.
37. *Lungren v Deukmejian*, 45 C.3d 729 (1988).
38. *White v Davis*, 13 C.3d 775 (1975).
39. "Falling Turnout—a Nonvoting Majority," *Public Affairs Report*, University of California Institute of Governmental Studies, March 1990, p. 9.
40. Magleby, *supra* note 3, p. 121.

one-third of eligible voters in 1990. Reduced participation compared to the November election is not the only issue. Depending on the presence or absence of contests, the primary election turnout may also be skewed heavily in the direction of Democrats or Republicans and will almost certainly involve a greatly reduced share of independent voters, who are ineligible to participate in partisan primary races. This uneven turnout can affect the results of a closely contested initiative, again casting doubt on the representativeness of the outcome.

Absentee Voting

Until the mid-1980s virtually all attention and publicity concerning initiatives was devoted to securing the preferred vote on election day. As suggested above, two-thirds and more of the citizenry are not familiar with most ballot measures until a few days before the election, necessitating a heavy emphasis on last-minute inducements to support or oppose an initiative. Increasingly, however, voters are being encouraged to cast mailed ballots from their homes, well in advance of election day. The paradox of seeking the vote of the "pre-informed" citizen is only now being recognized. The implications for the initiative process are profound.

Campaign Finance

Even though election turnouts are low, they still involve millions of citizens, each of whom must be persuaded to go to the polls (or mail in a ballot), to proceed far enough down the ballot to vote on the initiatives that follow the candidate races and legislative measures, and to vote the way the initiative sponsor or opponent wants. In a world of information overload, this is a large order, and millions of dollars are required to fill it.[41]

---

41. Daniel Lowenstein criticized decisions of the U.S. Supreme Court that overturned limitations on initiative campaign spending. After reviewing twenty-five California ballot propositions in which significant one-sided spending occurred between 1968 and 1980, he concluded that "the power of some groups to raise enormous sums of money to oppose ballot propositions, without regard to any breadth or depth of popular feeling, seriously interferes with the ability of other groups to use the institutions of direct democracy for their intended purpose. Remedial measures are available. Legislatures should adopt them and courts should uphold them." Daniel H. Lowenstein, "Campaign Spending and Ballot Propositions: Recent Experience, Public Choice Theory and the First Amendment," *UCLA Law Review,* 29 (February 1982), p. 608.

Thomas reports that during the 1976-86 period initiative proponents spent (in 1986 dollars) an average of $2.5 million, while oppo-
nents' expenditures averaged $3 million. Less than one-fifth of the
thirty-two initiative campaigns during this period were characterized by roughly equal spending, while the rest were divided
evenly between one-sided negative and one-sided positive spending. Of the thirteen campaigns with one-sided negative spending,
only one passed, while of the six campaigns characterized by rough
parity in spending, the pass-fail ratio was an even fifty-fifty. Nine of
the thirteen one-sided positive spending campaigns were successful. Thomas concludes that the role of money must be qualified by
the type of campaign. Where corporations are not heavily involved,
"campaign spending ratios tend to reflect public sentiments rather
than guide them." High-levels of spending on both sides in campaigns involving rivalry within the business sector tend to neutralize each other, while "no amount of campaign spending by business
interests seems to be able to win a majority of voters in [business-
backed] 'pro-active' campaigns." Where non-business groups seek
to impose new regulations or costs on the business community, one-
sided negative spending by corporate interests seems to turn public
opinion against the propositions. However, excessive spending can
backfire by focusing media attention on the corporate opposition
itself, as evidenced by industry failure to defeat the "toxics" initiative
in 1986 and the tobacco tax initiative in 1988.[42]

Implementation

The initiative process does not end on election day. Ballot measures
frequently require statutory implementation. This can be both complex and controversial as, for example, in the case of Proposition 99,
the tobacco tax initiative overwhelmingly supported by the voters in
1988. Funds from the new tax were to be used to supplement but not
to replace existing levels of service. However, faced with a perceived
funding crisis, the result of another initiative — Proposition 98 dealing with school funding, the governor proposed to use these tobacco
tax receipts to support existing state programs for the medically
indigent. A storm of protest emerged, with charges of sleight-of-
hand budgeting. The governor was forced to shift course.

---

42. *Supra* note 6, pp. 94-104, 369.

The battle was not over. As reported by Greg Lucas in the *San Francisco Chronicle*, the joint legislative committee seeking a compromise was "finding its job difficult because dozens of health and environmental groups are seeking shares of the tax money...'In a deal of this size,' one legislative staff member said, 'no one is going to get exactly what they want.'"[43]

Increased Judicial Review

The product of direct democracy, presumably the most "popular" of political institutions, frequently requires interpretation by the courts, the least "popular." The end of the line for initiatives is frequently not the election, nor legislative implementation, but the supreme court of California. In recent years many successful initiatives have been challenged in court. The judicial outcome has often been quite different from voter expectations. The result has been, in the words of former justice Joseph Grodin: "...to expose courts to the winds of politics more than they ought to be exposed. Initiatives, because of the unilateral nature of the drafting process and the zeal of the drafters, are much more likely to produce questions of constitutional dimension than legislatively adopted statutes. In addition, the constitutional questions are much more likely to be political hot potatoes for the judicial branch."[44]

Court challenges occur both before and after the election. Grodin suggests that for both political and judicial reasons, the court has developed a rough but useful distinction: "A court will not intervene before an election to decide a constitutional challenge to the *substance* of an initiative measure...A court will, however, intervene before an election to consider *procedural* objections to a measure...[and] will intervene to consider an objection that the *subject matter* of the measure, without regard to its merits, is not appropriate to the initiative process."[45]

Under this rule of thumb, the court has, in recent years, removed from the ballot a proposed redistricting of the legislature and Congress on the grounds that the state constitution permits only one redistricting per decade; ruled inappropriate a proposed measure

---

43. *San Francisco Chronicle*, August 1, 1989.
44. Joseph R. Grodin, *In Pursuit of Justice: Reflections of a State Supreme Court Justice*, Berkeley, University of California Press, 1989, p. 105.
45. *Ibid.*, p. 107.

ordering the legislature to petition Congress for a balanced budget; and removed a proposed insurance initiative because it contained two subjects. In general, however, the court has allowed measures to go on the ballot before entertaining challenges as to their constitutionality.[46]

Post-election challenges are quite another matter. In recent years many initiatives have either been totally invalidated by the court or invalidated in part or so narrowly construed as to defeat at least part of what the proponents intended. In other cases, the court has had to interpret ambiguous or inconsistent language. Measures passed by the voters in 1988 threw the issue of court involvement into high profile. In upholding the constitutionality of Proposition 103, the auto insurance measure, the state supreme court ruled that its most drastic provision, an automatic 20 percent rollback on insurance rates, could not be imposed if the insurance companies were prevented from earning a "fair and reasonable" return. In 1990 litigation continued, involving multiple lawsuits.

The court faced an equally complex problem in meshing two initiatives dealing with campaign finance, propositions 68 and 73, both of which passed in the June 1988 election. The California constitution requires that if provisions of two or more measures approved at the same election conflict, those of the measure receiving the highest affirmative vote shall prevail. The passage of two initiatives on the same subject, drafted by different parties with entirely different motives, has led, in the words of Mark Barabak of the *San Francisco Chronicle*, "to little evidence of reform...but plenty of work for lawyers and accountants."[47] In a world of competing counter-initiatives, this may well be a portent of things to come.

The court has been put in a difficult position: "It is one thing for a court to tell a legislature that a statute it has adopted is unconstitu-

---

46. Gordon and Magleby find that in a number of states initiatives increasingly are being challenged in court prior to the election. They conclude that courts generally should not conduct pre-election reviews of a measure's substantive validity, except when "the election causes a present, significant irreparable injury to a fundamental public interest," although "challenges alleging failure to comply with procedural requirements or subject matter limitations should be reviewable before the election." James D. Gordon III and David B. Magleby, "Pre-election Judicial Review of Initiatives and Referendums," *Notre Dame Law Review,* 64(3):1989, p. 320.
47. *San Francisco Chronicle,* January 29, 1990.

tional; to tell that to the people of a state who have indicated their
direct support for the measure through the ballot is another."[48]

Grodin suggests that justices are well aware of the potential
impact of an unpopular decision on a forthcoming confirmation
election.[49] Stephen Barnett comments: "The fears sketched by
Grodin, excessive though they seem, help to explain why the court
goes to such lengths to sustain initiative measures...post-1986
trauma may explain the court's 1989 decision rewriting Proposition
103, the initiative regulating the insurance industry, in order to
uphold it."[50]

Writing with a particular concern for minority rights and the
responsibility of federal courts, Eule summarizes the dilemma facing the state judiciary. Where the "filtering system" of the legislative
and executive branches of state government has been removed, he
observes, courts must play a larger role, "not because direct democracy is unconstitutional, nor because it frequently produces legislation that we may find substantively displeasing or short-sighted, but
because the judiciary stands *alone* in guarding against the evils
incident to transient, impassioned majorities that the Constitution
seeks to dissipate." However, the electoral accountability of judges
discourages them from playing a filtering role with respect to ballot
initiatives:

> In no area would judges seem more at risk than when they overturn plebiscites
> ...Judicial review is most essential in the presence of unfiltered majoritarianism. Yet
> it is precisely the examination of voter action that puts elected judges at greatest
> risk...In spite of the obstacles to empirical validation, it hardly seems far-fetched
> that the most principled of jurists will hesitate—consciously or unconsciously—to
> void an electoral mandate in the face of a pending election...Direct democracy thus
> poses a peculiar threat to state judicial independence.[51]

A politicized judiciary, or at least the public's perception of such, is
one possible outcome of the court's involvement. Another outcome is
equally troubling:

> Democratic politics ideally revolves around the compromises needed to secure
> widespread consent for government actions. Representative government...leaves
> the loser in a political contest with part of what they asked for or at least a feeling that

---

48. *Supra* note 44, p. 105.
49. *Ibid*. California appellate justices are appointed by the governor subject to voter approval at
the next general election. Renewal for a twelve-year term is also subject to voter confirmation.
50. Stephen R. Barnett, "California Justice," *California Law Review*, 78 (January 1990), p. 213.
51. Julian N. Eule, "Judicial Review of Direct Democracy," *The Yale Law Journal*, 99 (May 1990),
pp. 1525, 1580-4.

their interests were considered. A judicialized politics, in contrast, bypasses public consent...[It] alienates voters by placing public policy in the private hands of lawyers and litigants...it polarizes by producing winner-take-all outcomes, in which the losers are likely to feel embittered.[52]

In part, the court has brought this on itself. The California constitution provides that "an initiative measure embracing more than one subject may not be submitted to the electors or have any effect." But the court has interpreted this single-subject rule so broadly as to seriously weaken its usefulness. As described by Justice Stanley Mosk in dissenting from the court's approval of the Victim's Bill of Rights in 1982:

> [The single-subject provision of the constitution] is now virtually a dead letter. If an initiative that adds seven separate subdivisions to the Constitution, repeals one section of the Constitution, adds five new sections to the Penal Code and three more sections to the Welfare and Institutions Code can be held to contain 'one subject,' then any rubric of 'general welfare' or 'pursuit of happiness' can be deemed one subject...Orwellian logic has become the current mode of constitutional interpretation.[53]

Grodin explains that the court majority has consistently interpreted the single-subject rule as requiring only that the provisions of a measure be "reasonably germane" to one another. However, he notes, Justice Wiley Manuel believed that:

> ...in the initiative process a more stringent application was appropriate to protect voters against undue complexity and against a distortion of the popular will through political logrolling in which a majority of votes is garnered by offering something for everyone. Justice Manuel proposed, and a minority of other justices accepted, a requirement that in order to pass the single-subject test, the various provisions of an initiative be not merely 'reasonably germane' to one another but also 'functionally related' to one another.[54]

Writing in 1983, Lowenstein disagreed, arguing that the "reasonably germane" test had served the court well. He suggested, however, that in order to give greater coherence to the single-subject rule, the court should regard provisions of a measure as acceptable if:

> ...in the public understanding, they bear some relationship to each other. Reaching a decision would not be an exercise in logic, but would be based on a reading of the public mind...[based on evidence] such as articles, books, television and radio programs, and the legislative or political programs of various groups...The question would be whether, discussion of the initiative itself aside, public discussion suggests that the matters dealt with are regarded as related to one another...The

---

52. Fred Siegel, "Nothing in Moderation," *The Atlantic Monthly,* May 1990, p. 108.
53. *Brosnahan v Brown*, 32 Cal. 2d 298 (1982).
54. *Supra* note 44, p. 108.

'popular understanding' variation of the 'reasonably germane' test is recommended as the most coherent interpretation of the single-subject rule consistent with the rule's language, history, and purpose, and with the court's precedents.[55]

Without amplification, it is difficult to test the practicality of Lowenstein's proposal, attractive as it may sound. His UCLA colleague Julian Eule asks, "how can a court accurately gauge what the voters knew? Although I am prepared to testify as to the enormous voter confusion—including my own—regarding the four insurance reform initiatives [in 1988], do we really think the courts can monitor confusion on a systematic basis?"[56]

Whatever the case, and despite Justice Mosk's "dead letter" prediction, the single-subject rule has recently been resurrected. While noting that no court had ever undertaken such prior review, an appeals court stopped the petition process in 1988 for a no-fault insurance initiative sponsored by the insurance industry. The court held that a clause in the 120-page measure excluding insurers from most campaign contribution limits was "a paradigm of the potential deceptive combination of unrelated provisions at which the constitutional limitations on the scope of initiatives is aimed." Not only voters but those who signed petitions to qualify the ballot measure were deemed likely to be confused: "We believe it is extremely unlikely that the average voter or signer of a sponsoring petition, or even one more conscientious and sophisticated, would take the time to study the initiative in such detail as to discover this obscure campaign funding provision."[57]

In its opinion the court cited both the "reasonably germane" and "functionally related" tests. That the Manuel rule may be reconsidered is suggested by the supreme court's refusal to review the appellate court's decision. And in line with Lowenstein's proposal, it is noteworthy that the court recognized the reality of voter confusion and deception and the issue of voter understanding.

---

55. Daniel H. Lowenstein, "California Initiative and the Single-Subject Rule," *UCLA Law Review*, 30 (June 1983), pp. 970-5.
56. *Supra* note 51, p. 1571.
57. *California Trial Lawyer Association v Eu*, 200 Cal. App. 3d 351 (1988). In 1990 both the tobacco tax (Proposition 99) and "consumers' right to know" initiative (Proposition 105) were under legal challenge as violating the single-subject rule. Proposition 115, the criminal law measure passed by voters in June 1990, was immediately challenged in court as violating both the single-subject rule and the constitutional bar against use of the initiative to revise, as opposed to amend, the state constitution.

The single-subject rule is related to another legalistic but highly significant term, the "severability clause." Found in many initiatives, the clause provides that if any portion of a measure is found unconstitutional, it may be "severed" to permit the rest of the initiative to take effect. In their attack against Proposition 103 before the supreme court, insurance industry advocates focused their arguments on this issue. If the rate rollback were to be struck down, they argued in their brief, the whole measure should be invalidated: "Proponents should not succeed with their attempt to use unconstitutional provisions in a 'bait and switch' to obtain approval and effective enactment of the balance of their initiative."[58]

However, in putting limits on the rollback, the court held that the clause in question could be severed from the rest of the rate-setting provisions and that the remainder of the initiative, after deleting the insolvency standard, would likely have been adopted by the people. Not all agreed:

The trouble is, the measure approved by the court is not the measure passed by the voters. And there's good reason to doubt that they would have passed this one...The court did not consider the likely impact on voters of *what came with* its invalidation of the insolvency standard—the undoing of the rollback and freeze. If the voters had known that insurers could choose to cut *no* rates immediately, and might never have to cut any, Proposition 103 surely would have lost some support.[59]

Eule adds: "It is not immediately evident what warrants judicial deference to electoral policy judgments that the electorate never actually made...To suggest that the voters approved, let alone understood, the many facets of Proposition 103 is pure mythology."[60]

Preble Stolz concludes: "The Supreme Court can decide only about 140 cases a year, and the justices would be less than human if they did not focus the bulk of their attention on the big cases. A challenge to a successful initiative, especially after a hotly contested election, is almost by definition a big case...The judicial preoccupation with ballot measures seems certain to continue."[61]

One wonders whether the ballot pamphlet, that little-read document, will continue to be used by the court as the basis for determin-

---

58. As reported by Philip Hagar, *Los Angeles Times*, February 1, 1990.
59. Stephen R. Barnett, "Is This the Will of the People?" *Los Angeles Times*, May 16, 1989.
60. *Supra* note 51, pp. 1570-1.
61. Preble Stolz, "Say Goodbye to Hiram Johnson's Ghost," *California Lawyer*, January 1990, p. 44.

ing the intent of the voters with respect to initiatives brought before it.

The Initiative in the Twenty-First Century

In 1911 the initiative was a practical institutional response to the dominance of California political life by a single monopoly—the Southern Pacific Railroad. The threat to representative government was real; the public's reaction was rational.

In 1990 representative government is again threatened, not by a private monopoly, but by the initiative process itself. In a paradoxical turn of events, the initiative, instead of serving as a safety valve, has become an uncontrolled political force of its own. It is a force that has produced occasional benefits but at an extraordinary cost—an erosion of responsibility in the executive and legislative branches of state government, a simultaneous overload in the judiciary, and an excessively amended state constitution alongside a body of inflexible quasi-constitutional statutory law. At a time when the ultimate in statecraft is required to achieve even a minimum of coordinated public policies, the initiative offers the politics of simplification.

To be critical of the initiative is not to ignore the fact that the threat of its use has led to legislative compromises, that it "may be useful as a mediating tool between competing economic interests,...even when it is not actually used."[62] Nor is it to excuse the failings of the legislature, the weaknesses of the executive branch, or the excesses of the electoral process: negative campaigning, incumbent-dominated safe districts, and the problems surrounding campaign finance and honoraria, to name the most prominent contemporary criticisms. It is to suggest, rather, that instead of being a positive response to these shortcomings, the initiative itself contributes to them. Elimination or reform of the initiative would not, of course, eliminate these weaknesses. But it is no longer realistic to accept the initiative as necessary to offset them. The initiative is part of the problem. Turned on its head, "direct democracy" is no longer democratic.

Important aspects of the state's political agenda are being set, not by its elected leaders, but by unaccountable single-interest groups operating in a fragmented, uncoordinated, and frequently contra-

62. *Supra* note 6, p. 328.

dictory manner. Proposition 13 and Proposition 4 (the Gann appropriations limit) are classic examples. Each conceivably reasonable by itself, they have in combination radically altered the relative roles of state and local government to an extent not anticipated by their authors or by the voters who approved them. The recent tobacco tax, education, lottery, and wildlife bond initiatives are further illustrations of "ballot-box budgeting," which complicates any attempt to rationalize the $55 billion-plus state budget.

It is not just successful initiatives that preoccupy the elected branches of state government. It is the impact of all those that appear on the ballot, forcing attention, time, and energy onto those few measures that have attracted signatures and providing an excuse for legislators and governors to abdicate their leadership roles in deference to a spurious "voice of the people." In reality that voice reflects a special interest that often develops its proposal in private and, without meaningful publicizing of its financial backing, seeks qualification of its measure.

It is also a "voice of the people" to which the courts have paid homage, without evaluating its authenticity. The court stresses its "solemn duty jealously to guard the sovereign people's initiative power...one of the most precious rights of our democratic process."[63] But this "precious right" has become obscured in a world of million-dollar campaigns and thirty-second television spots and a declining electorate unrepresentative of the adult citizenry. The initiative process adds special gravity to Mervin Field's concern that "the more that non-voters become different than voters in color, in class, in attitudes toward life, we create and build threatening pressures which could easily explode and alter for the worse the future course of our precious democracy."[64]

Despite the enormity of the impact of the initiative process on California's political life, it is doubtful that the resulting product has been worth the candle. Only about half of the successful initiatives in the last decade have made a significant difference in the life of the average citizen, not always for the better. In part, this is because the courts have ruled unconstitutional or narrowly interpreted important provisions of many measures—the insolvency standard of Proposition 103, provisions of Proposition 8 relating to criminal

63. *Supra* note 53.
64. As quoted in *The New York Times*, June 12, 1990.

evidence, or Proposition 24 concerning rules of the legislature. Other measures—the inheritance tax, income tax indexing, a resolution on nuclear weapons, English language requirements—have had limited application or would have been adopted anyway. To be sure, the state's tax system has been fundamentally altered through the initiative process, and stricter controls on toxic substances have been introduced. But at what cost to representative government?

Alan Rosenthal of Rutgers University's Eagleton Institute of Politics, a long-time observer of the state legislative scene, provides one answer: "...the initiative serves the interest of a growing number of political actors: those impatient with the pace of the legislative process and the means by which it is necessary to build consensus, those who see no reason for compromise, those who want to use initiative campaigns to advance their own careers, those who want to avoid responsibility by passing the buck to the voters, those in the minority legislative party who are frustrated by their status, and those who do not get all they want from the legislative game and run to the nearest petition."[65]

Eule characterizes the likely result of bypassing representative institutions:

Considered judgments, sensitive to the interests of all, require time, debate, deliberation, information, and shared power. Substitutive plebiscites [i.e., initiatives] shortchange the decision-maker on all these accounts...Public debate is infrequent. Exposure to minority perspectives occurs accidentally if at all. Voters may be confused and overwhelmed by the issues placed before them. Any efforts at self-education are thwarted by manipulative campaigns designed to oversimplify the issues and appeal to the electorate's worst instincts. Most important, voters register their decisions in the privacy of the voting booth. They are unaccountable to others for their preferences and their biases. Their individual commitment to a consistent and fair course of conduct can be neither measured nor questioned.[66]

If the initiative is to play a constructive role in California in the twenty-first century, several changes—at a minimum—must be considered. Precedents exist in one or more states for most; some have

---

65. "An Outsider's View of the California Initiative," in *Summary Proceedings of a Conference on the California Initiative Process: Current Controversies and Prescriptions*, Davis, University of California, University Extension, March 23, 1990, p. 24.
66. *Supra* note 51, pp. 1555-6.

been introduced in previous sessions of the California legislature. Together they might salvage a badly flawed institution.[67]

- Initiative proposals should be improved technically. Pre-petition review by some qualified agency should be mandatory.
- The sponsorship of initiatives should be made clear on the petition itself, with a listing of any organization providing more than a specified amount, say $25,000, to pay for signature gathering.
- Public hearings, required under existing law with respect to any initiative that qualifies for the ballot, should be reorganized, providing a meaningful opportunity for press and media coverage and analysis of both the substance and sponsorship of each measure.
- The ballot pamphlet should identify the major financial supporters of the initiative campaign, pro and con, and the amounts of their contributions. To the extent possible, it should be required that campaign contributions be made prior to publication of the pamphlet.[68]
- The initiative should be restricted to the November ballot, as was the case until 1970, thus ensuring a more representative vote. In June 1990, for every two citizens voting, five did not; measures passed by a vote of only 20 percent of registered voters, less than 15 percent of eligibles.
- Consideration should be given to requiring a minimum threshold in turnout (e.g., 50 percent of registered voters) as a condition of passage, to ensure that the "people's voice" is more than marginal.
- Most importantly, as is true in most initiative states, the legislature and governor should be empowered to amend and repeal statutory initiatives after a specified period.

---

67. Proposition 137, on the November 1990 ballot, requires voter approval of any statute regulating procedures or requirements for statewide or local initiatives or referendums. Described as the Right to Vote Initiative, the petition was sponsored by the Howard Jarvis Taxpayers Association, an organization that derives much of its support from the funding of initiative campaigns. The petition was attached in the mail to another petition, which also qualified, increasing voting requirements for state and local taxes.

68. SB 1495, passed in 1990, required identification in the ballot pamphlet of any campaign contribution or expenditure of $10,000 or more. The governor vetoed the bill, apparently because of disagreement over the wording of a second provision requiring disclosure in the pamphlet of written evidence of any agreement to include provisions in the initiative in exchange for a campaign contribution or a pledge to collect a specified number of signatures.

- Simultaneously, the requirements for initiatives involving constitutional amendments should be made more stringent,
  enhancing the importance of that document and reducing the
  temptation to utilize it for matters better left to statutory form.
  (Eleven of the seventeen constitutional initiative states require a
  petition of 10 percent or more, in contrast to California's 8
  percent.)

All of the above and more would be aided if the legislature were
required to consider measures prior to their placement on the ballot.
Failing that, the signature requirement for an indirect initiative could
be made sufficiently attractive (2 to 3 percent) that sponsors would
choose this route if it were made an alternative to the direct
initiative.

The state supreme court must play a greater part in preserving the
integrity of the initiative process. Both voters and petition signers
must be protected from the confusion, ambiguity, and misrepresen-
tation that characterizes many ballot proposals. Tests governing
both the single-subject and severability rules must be redesigned
and reapplied. The democratic process will be best protected if the
court applies a higher standard of construction to initiatives than to
measures that have been subject to legislative and executive
scrutiny.

Finally, as suggested by Daniel Lowenstein, the realities of voter
understanding and intent must be addressed if the principles of the
state constitution are to be validly applied. Political scientists may
have something to contribute to constitutional law and practice.

The people of California face one of the most dramatic and challenging political futures in world history—a state in which no racial
or ethnic group constitutes a majority, an economy of staggering
complexity but enormous potential, an environment of unparalleled
beauty under siege from the pressures of unprecedented growth, a
society of rich cultural differences trying to forge a common destiny.
Citizens look to our representative political institutions to address
these challenges, to our political leaders to try to develop consensus
out of diversity.

But can these challenges be successfully addressed in the face of
an initiative process designed to freeze into the constitution or law
some special program or benefit without regard for its impact on the

larger society? Not without a radical overhaul. As in 1911, it is time for Californians to act to salvage their representative government.

The author is grateful to the many practitioners and observers of the initiative process who read and commented on earlier drafts of this chapter. Special acknowledgment is extended to four seniors at the University of California, Berkeley, who contributed to the research: Amy Albright (signature gathering); Krista Atteberry (implementation of Proposition 99); Kenneth Button (ballot pamphlet); and Jennifer Steen (absentee voting).

REDISTRICTING: PUBLIC POLICY OR JUST POLITICS?

Bruce E. Cain

The current procedure for redrawing political boundaries—which relies on legislators to define the districts from which they will be elected—is unpopular with many Californians, but no alternative proposal has been able to garner sufficient support to replace it. Uneven rates of population growth and changes in the racial and ethnic composition of the population continue to make redistricting necessary, yet disagreements over how to adjust to such demographic changes have repeatedly resulted or threatened to result in reapportionment deadlock.

This paper examines the nature and effects on electoral outcomes of various districting arrangements and the characteristics of several recent proposals for altering redistricting procedures. Options for California in designing a broadly acceptable redistricting policy are outlined.

It is now so commonplace to say that redistricting is inevitably political that the expression has lost any well defined meaning. Redistricting is certainly political in the sense that Californians have legitimate disagreements about who should be represented in what proportions, and therefore about how districts should be drawn. However, redistricting is not political in the sense that it affects only the interests of politicians, or that it must always be contentious and bitter. Californians can try to forge a more sensible reapportionment public policy.

In fact, redistricting is implicitly at least as much about public policy as it is explicitly about political power. The decennial census and the supreme court's doctrine of "one man/one vote" force California to have a procedure for drawing district boundaries. Redistricting methods and criteria influence the types of districts drawn and the kinds of representatives who are elected to the legislature. Thus, the first-order effect of drawing new political boundaries is its direct relation to political representation, i.e. to the composition of districts and the representatives who are elected to office from them. At the same time, since these factors affect legislation, the second-order redistricting effect is its indirect impact upon policy issues such as spending priorities, environmental protection, education, and abortion rights.

There is a tendency in the debate over redistricting either to overlook these public policy linkages or to exaggerate their importance. Redistricting can change a state's public policy by altering the legislature's composition, potentially causing a reversal in political control. On the other hand, only a fraction of the total number of districts are really vulnerable to transformation by redrawing boundaries because so many areas in California are socioeconomically and racially homogeneous. Redistricting, for instance, cannot create Republican seats in south-central Los Angeles or Democratic seats in southern Orange County.

The greatest impact of changing district boundaries is usually felt in the most politically marginal and competitive areas. Since this median voter effect induces representatives to converge towards the middle of the ideological spectrum, a change caused by redistricting in a marginal area often means trading a moderate from one party for a moderate in another—a difference that may matter even if it does not shift the ideological spectrum of the legislature dramatically.

Although it is rarely if ever stated this way, the critical redistricting reform question is whether it is possible or desirable to resolve procedural redistricting questions (i.e. how to decide how to draw district lines) without reference to or concern for the first- and second-order effects various procedural reforms would produce. A number of those who have supported redistricting reform over the last decade believe that first- and second-order issues should not be considered, and that procedural fairness pure and simple (often based on a legal model) is the desired policy goal. Those who have opposed these reforms either have doubted the premise that redistricting procedures can be intrinsically fair, or have objected to the probable first- and second-order effects that these procedures would induce (e.g. the effect on minority communities, coastal protection, the relative balance between the parties).

In the end, there is no public policy about redistricting in California. The status quo prevails, not because it is popular, but because all departures from it are opposed by some majority of political interests.

This chapter explores the various problems that people have with the current method of drawing California district boundaries and the numerous reforms that have been proposed to deal with them. Although few will admit it, interest group expectations about representation have moved progressively in recent years towards roughly proportional representation. Many racial, ethnic, and political group leaders increasingly think that a fair outcome is one that gives them a share of seats roughly equivalent to their share of votes. It is my belief that no reform will be accepted unless, in one way or another, it deals directly with "fair outcome" expectations.

The Problem of Redistricting

Political actors have always known that process and outcome are intimately linked in redistricting. Prior to the California Supreme Court's rulings in *Baker v Carr*[1] and *Reynolds v Sims*,[2] population malapportionment served to delay and moderate the policy consequences of sectional and demographic change in California. From 1850 to 1880 the balance of the state's population favored the north, but by 1879 regional dominance had become a constitutional issue. As California's population shifted from north to south (16.6 percent in 1890 to 50 percent in 1930) and from rural to urban areas (7.4 percent in 1850 to 61.8 percent in 1910), the debate over whether, and to what degree, district lines should reflect population changes became more salient. The legislature was able to forge a compromise in 1911, but was unable to do so in 1921, 1923, and 1925.

The resulting malapportionment had adverse policy consequences for the newly populated areas. The northern and rural-dominated legislature rejected a water project favored by the south and restricted southern county access to state highway funds.[3] The implementation by initiative of the so-called federal plan (apportioning the lower house by population and the upper house by county) constitutionally locked in a compromise between geographic and population-based representation that lasted until the one-man/one-vote decisions of the 1960s.

---

1. 369 U.S. 186 (1962).
2. 377 U.S. 533 (1964).
3. A thorough description of California redistricting is found in David L. Wilkening, "Political History of California State Legislative Reapportionment," unpublished masters' thesis, California State University, Sacramento, 1977.

Despite significant changes in legal doctrine, political climate, and technology since the late nineteenth century, certain features of California redistricting have remained remarkably constant. Just as in the earlier period, uneven rates of population growth during the last two decades have altered the fragile balance of electoral power across the state. Since 1970 California's population has grown fastest in suburban and rural areas, and more slowly in older urban areas such as San Francisco, Los Angeles, and Oakland. In 1980, for instance, Riverside, San Bernardino, Orange, and San Diego counties gained while other counties, such as San Francisco, lost representation. One constant in California's reapportionment history is that losing representation is always painful and difficult to accept. Just as in 1911, 1921, 1923, and 1925, the inability to agree over how to adjust to demographic shifts caused redistricting deadlocks in 1971 and 1973, and would have done so again in 1981 except that outgoing Democratic Governor Jerry Brown signed the Democratic-controlled legislature's second set of redistricting bills just before leaving office.

The reapportionment stalemate of the 1920s eventually was broken by an initiative introducing the federal plan to California, but this is where the historical parallels end. Although a number of redistricting reform initiatives were placed on the ballot during the 1980s—the Sebastiani initiative, Propositions 39, 118, and 119—none was ultimately successful.

While the identities of the interests affected by redistricting have changed from sectional and geographic to partisan and racial over the course of the last hundred years, the basic principles of redistricting have remained the same. First, one cannot properly identify a gerrymander without referring to electoral outcomes.[4] A redistricting plan with ugly shapes yielding proportionate shares to competing parties might not be called an unfair gerrymander, and for the same reason a plan with compact shapes producing grossly disproportionate outcomes might be called unfair and even declared unconstitutional under the Voting Rights Act if the affected community is black or Latino. A good example of the latter is the 1981 Los Angeles County Board of Supervisors redistricting, which the federal district court declared was in violation of the Voting Rights Act in

---

4. See, for instance, Bruce E. Cain, *The Reapportionment Puzzle*, chapter 3, Berkeley, University of California Press, 1984.

May 1990, even though the districts were compact and in conformity with the one-man/one-vote doctrine.

Second, it is important to realize that the term gerrymander can refer to either bias or unresponsiveness in the relationship between seats and votes.[5] Critics of the current system often fail to distinguish between the two, causing considerable confusion. Bias refers to how equally the electoral system treats various groups and parties. Outcomes may be disproportionate but the system unbiased if each party/group could hypothetically receive approximately the same share of seats for a given share of the votes. Needless to say, since this proposition rests on a conjectural assumption (i.e. what would have happened to seat shares if vote shares had been different), it is hard to measure bias with any statistical certainty. The concept, however, is at least clear in theory. Responsiveness refers to the degree to which a change in vote shares results in a change in seat shares. A highly responsive system is one in which small changes in the statewide vote lead to large changes in the distribution of seats, and a highly insulated system is one in which large vote swings are needed to produce moderate or even small changes in seat shares.

When people complain about partisan gerrymandering in California, they implicitly mean that one party is favored by the system over another. They are likely to base this inference on the degree of disproportionality between seat and vote shares. This can be misleading since electoral systems such as that used in California (i.e. single-member, simple plurality) have the properties of not yielding proportional outcomes and tend to exaggerate the majority party's seat share. The most efficient partisan gerrymander would create as many winnable seats as possible for a given party without wasting votes. It would be biased and highly responsive at the same time — in essence, sinning in one dimension but excelling in another.

Consider Figure 11-1, in which Party A controls three seats by a 13-12 margin and Party B controls one seat by a 25-0 margin. Party A has gotten a great deal of bang for its electoral buck, winning 75 percent of the seats with only 39 percent of the vote. Party B has 61 percent of the vote but only 25 percent of the seats. Clearly, this districting arrangement treats the parties unequally, and in this

---

5. This distinction is best discussed in Gary King, "Representation Through Legislative Redistricting: a Stochastic Model," *American Journal of Political Science*, 33(1989): 787-824.

Figure 11-1. Types of Districting: Efficient Partisan Gerrymander (biased, responsive)

Party A (13) Party B (12)	Party A (13) Party B (12)
Party A (13) Party B (12)	Party A (0) Party B (25)

Party A: 3 seats with 39% of vote
Party B: 1 seat with 61% of vote
Total voters: 100

Figure 11-2. Types of Districting: Bipartisan Gerrymander (unbiased, unresponsive)

Party A (25) Party B (0)	Party A (0) Party B (25)
Party A (25) Party B (0)	Party A (0) Party B (25)

Party A: 2 seats with 50% of vote
Party B: 2 seats with 50% of vote
Total voters: 100

sense is biased. A compensating virtue is that it leaves the majority vulnerable to electoral disaster if circumstances change the voting balance of the efficiently drawn seats, a consequence of high responsiveness.

The so-called incumbent's gerrymander is at the exact opposite of the spectrum: in its pure form it is simultaneously unbiased and unresponsive. Parties are treated equally in the translation of votes to seats, and there is little or no seat change in response to shifts in vote shares. Figure 11-2 demonstrates a hypothetical example of such a case: both parties are inefficiently grouped at 25-0, and only the most drastic partisan transformation can alter the outcome. Either party could do better by a more efficient arrangement of the voters, but the incumbents who represent these districts can do no better:

Figure 11-3. Types of Districting: Reformer's Ideal (unbiased, responsive)

Party A (13) Party B (12)	Party A (12) Party B (13)
Party A (13) Party B (12)	Party A (12) Party B (13)

Party A: 2 seats with 50% of vote
Party B: 2 seats with 50% of vote
Total voters: 100

wide partisan margins ensure their reelection in November. The trade-off between the advantages of a partisan and bipartisan gerrymander demonstrates that individual candidate and party incentives are not always identical. The political party will tend to prefer the favorable partisan gerrymander, whereas individual incumbents will tend to prefer the bipartisan gerrymander.

The reformer's ideal would be a system in which there is little or no bias and relatively high responsiveness. Both parties would be treated equally, but both would also be highly vulnerable to small perturbations in the vote. This can be seen in Figure 11-3. Here each party controls two seats 13-12, and the balance can be swung by small changes in the vote. A curious feature of this example is that the outcome can become quite disproportionate if the vote swings uniformly in all districts just one point in the direction of one party. A party could end up with 46 percent of the vote and no seats under this arrangement. Thus, the reformer's ideal may be fair in the technical sense that any seats-votes discrepancy produced is even-handed in its distortion, but, quite obviously, it is not fair in the sense of yielding seat shares in proportion to vote shares.

The final possibility is a biased, unresponsive system, or what we might term an inefficient partisan gerrymander. As illustrated in Figure 11-4, Party A controls three seats by comfortable margins, but by so doing, passes up on the chance to control the fourth seat. This most closely characterizes what partisan gerrymanders tend to look

Figure 11-4. Types of Districting: Inefficient Partisan Gerrymander (biased, unresponsive)

Party A (18)	Party A (18)
Party B (7)	Party B (7)
Party A (18)	Party A (0)
Party B (7)	Party B (25)

Party A: 3 seats with 54% of vote
Party B: 1 seat with 46% of vote
Total voters: 100

like in the real world.[6] They are never as efficiently partisan as they might be due to a number of factors such as the aversion to risk and idiosyncratic preferences of incumbents, the homogeneous concentrations of like-minded voters in California, and adherence to constitutional and other criteria.

Even if one accepts that bias and responsiveness are the problems that need to be fixed (ignoring the proportional representation critique for the moment), it is important to see that a solution for one does not guarantee a solution for the other. For instance, Proposition 118, which, though defeated, made its way onto the primary 1990 ballot, and the so-called Ross Johnson initiative, which did not, both proposed that the redistricting vote be changed from simple majority to a two-thirds vote of the legislature. Critics pointed out that while a two-thirds vote addressed the problem of bias by giving the minority party a veto over plans it opposes, it would most likely lead to an incumbent/bipartisan gerrymander, or in our earlier terminology, an unbiased/unresponsive system.

Proposition 119, the so-called Huening initiative, tried to address both problems. It required a supermajority vote from a redistricting commission composed of five Democrats, five Republicans, and two independents, and it also stipulated that as many competitive districts be drawn as possible, which in theory might lead to an unbiased, responsive system. Unfortunately, it proposed a definition of

6. Bruce E. Cain, "Assessing the Partisan Effects of Redistricting," *American Political Science Review,* 79(1985): 320-33.

"competitive" that was severely flawed, equating districts that were plus or minus two registration points of the statewide registration spread with competitive seats. Not only did people question whether this would result in truly competitive seats under the current 49 percent Democrat and 39 percent Republican state split, but it was never explained how this definition would hold up if the state became overwhelmingly partisan in one direction or the other. More fundamentally, it is difficult to come up with a simple but accurate definition of a competitive seat, especially in a state as complex and variable as California. Registration figures rarely tell the whole story.

The disposition of the decline-to-state voters, the presence or absence of a well known incumbent, the racial, ethnic, and ideological composition of the electorate, and the quality of the candidates all critically figure in electoral outcomes. In San Diego a pro-choice Democrat won a 1989 state senate seat in a district with less than 50 percent Democratic registration, while a moderate black Democratic challenger lost a 1986 assembly election for a seat with greater than 60 percent Democratic registration. The most accurate definition of a competitive seat would have to be flexible and conditional. Yet such flexibility would make it harder to objectively implement "competitive" criteria than a simple, inflexible rule.

None of the redistricting reforms proposed to date has dared to recommend roughly proportional representation for political parties, or even for racial and ethnic minorities. While there is no constitutional right to proportional representation, as the supreme court has reiterated on a number of occasions, it is not unconstitutional to seek proportional partisan fairness (e.g. *Gaffney v Cummings*, 1973),[7] or to use redistricting for affirmative action goals (e.g. *United Jewish Organizations v Carey*, 1977).[8] In theory, then, one of the criteria mandated by reform could be rough proportional fairness for major parties and for minority groups protected under the Voting Rights Act. In other words, such reforms would view fairness in a sense other than an unbiased, responsive system. Even though the identification of electoral equity with proportional representation increasingly underlies the rhetoric of contemporary interest group politics, I strongly doubt whether a majority of California voters

7. 412 U.S. 735 (1973).
8. 97 U.S. 996 (1977).

would support an explicit proportional-fairness redistricting requirement at this moment in time.

But even if public attitudes were to change, there would still be formidable difficulties inherent in trying to achieve fairer outcomes under the current electoral system. Single-member district systems are ill suited to the task of producing proportional results. Rather, optimally located political interests are favored and highly dispersed groups are severely punished by these rules. Women, for instance, cannot "control" geographically based political districts because their population is too interspersed with men. The other extreme, over-concentration, is also politically damaging, although not to the same degree. Areas that are densely packed with supporters of one party are "inefficient" in the sense described earlier. They will at least elect a representative of their own, but their geographic inefficiency will prevent them from maximizing their total representation.

Using redistricting to compensate for dispersion or concentration is always cumbersome and sometimes not effective. It is particularly difficult if there are criteria such as compactness or respect for city and county boundaries that must also be observed. In the end, a single-member district system will be "fairer" to some groups than to others, no matter what affirmative actions are contemplated, and especially "fairer" to the majority and to geographically oriented interest groups. To some degree, people still think of their political identity in geographic terms: northern versus southern Californians over water issues, coastal versus inland interests on oil drilling, rural versus urban interests on prison location. But to an increasing degree, Californians also think of themselves in terms that are non-geographic (e.g. as women) or semi-geographic (e.g. as Latinos). Semi-geographic interests can sometimes be assisted by "friendly" redistrictings, but non-geographic interests are out of luck. As a second-best strategy, non-geographic interests focus on making sure that their incumbent allies in the legislature are well taken care of in redistricting. Thus, women's groups look with interest on the fate of female incumbents, and planned parenthood groups lobby on behalf of those who have supported their causes over the years. But, apart from this indirect interest in redistricting, non-geographic groups cannot look to the redesign of district boundaries as a means of enhancing their political power, and in this sense California's voting system is necessarily arbitrary.

Table 11-1. Features of Selected Redistricting Proposals

Features	Alternatives			
	Status Quo	Prop 118	Prop 119	Cumulative/ Limited Vote
Equal population requirement	court guidelines	< 1% deviation	< 1% deviation	court guidelines
Minority rights	federal standards	federal standards	federal standards	more proportional results
Competitiveness	none	none	within 2 points of state registration	none
Compactness	none	population based	population based	none
City/county splits	advisory	numerical limits	numerical limits	none
Redistricting agent	legislature	legislature	commission	legislature or commission
Decision rule	majority	2/3	7/12	—

Procedural Approaches to Fairness

Dissatisfaction with California redistricting has led to a number of reform proposals, several of which are summarized in Table 11-1. Most reforms proposed have been procedural in orientation, aspiring to make redistricting better by making the process fairer. There are several variations of this approach. The first is to use a random method for drawing district lines. The best example of this in recent years is the Stanaland proposal, which dictated that redistricting should start in a corner of the state and proceed laterally across the top picking up census tracts until a district reaches its ideal population. The next district would then start at the adjacent census tract and continue in the same fashion. Because the process would be automated and arbitrary, it would guarantee that district lines would not be intentionally manipulated for partisan, racial, or other purposes. It does not guarantee, however, that the outcome would be "fair" in any of the senses discussed so far.

Proceeding in this automated, random fashion might by chance lead to an unbiased, responsive, or proportional system, but it might not. In addition, it would probably be necessary to deviate frequently from the strict application of this procedure in order to avoid carving up inner-city black and Latino seats and thereby violating section 2 of the Voting Rights Act, or in order to minimize unpopular city and county splits. What seems like a straightforward, simple procedure would likely be difficult, if not impossible, to implement in its purest form, and at some point exceptions might become more numerous than the rule.

Another approach to making the process fair is to strive for neutrality. The most common example of this is the nonpartisan commission proposal. What is wrong with legislative redistricting, some suggest, is that incumbents have a conflict of interest when they design the districts that they run in, and thus a fair line-drawing process is one controlled by disinterested individuals, not by incumbents. Neutral commission proposals have surfaced several times in the last decade, including a 1982 initiative to set up an independent reapportionment commission, a 1984 scheme backed by Governor Deukmejian to establish a reapportionment panel of three retired appellate judges, and the 1990 Huening plan, which amalgamated the two by proposing an independent commission appointed by a panel of three retired appellate judges from a list of names put forward by nonpartisan groups.

Objections to this kind of approach fall into two categories. First, the fairness issue discussed earlier in the context of randomized redistricting applies equally to neutral procedures. A disinterested process, like a random procedure, does not guarantee an unbiased, responsive, or proportional set of district lines. At best, it eliminates potential motives for creating unfair district lines. An independent or neutral commission presumably would make more of an effort to be fair-minded.

But a second objection to the neutral commission proposal challenges the fair motive assumption as well. Some, especially those closely connected to politics, are skeptical of the assertion that commissions can be truly neutral. Removing incumbents from the line-drawing process addresses one potential conflict of interest, but not all the other ones commissioners might have. All Californians are potentially affected by the first- and second-order effects of redistricting, sometimes as tangibly as are incumbents. Moreover, it would be extremely difficult to insulate commissioners from outside influence. What would prevent a party or group from later rewarding commissioners who defend their interests during a redistricting, or from signaling their preferences in the press and through informal channels? The Huening plan attempted to make it illegal for commissioners to communicate with outside groups about the workings of their commission, but it is unlikely that this would have successfully insulated them from outside influence.

The problem of achieving true neutrality is further complicated by the reformer's dilemma over the level of knowledge needed by commissioners. In an effort to get commissioners with pure motives, it is sometimes proposed that they be totally apolitical, or that they be given no political information such as party registration figures or previous voting results to work with. On the other hand, one can never be sure that commissioners are really ignorant, or even that the process would work better if they were. At best, an ignorant commission would be like a random procedure; at worst, it might be easily manipulated by staff or outside groups into adopting "unfair" lines.

Neutral commission proposals have not fared well in initiative campaigns. By clever advertising, opponents have been able to sow doubt in the minds of the public about the accountability, representativeness, neutrality, or competence of each proposed redistricting commission or panel, especially those that would use judges. The charge that judges serving on a redistricting panel would consciously or unconsciously favor the party that appointed them to the bench has seemed plausible to many voters. A traditional Madisonian premise underlying American politics is that people are not angels, and therefore political institutions should be designed to withstand both the good and the bad of human nature. A political process that depends on individuals of high moral character goes against the ingrained skepticism of American political philosophy. The language of lobbying and campaign finance reform refers to both corruption and the appearance of corruption as important targets of state regulatory action. Similarly, the appearance of institutional naivete can be as damaging to public confidence as the existence of naive institutions. Whether or not neutral commissions are politically naive, they have certainly appeared so to many Californians.

Commissions, however, do not have to be neutral. A third procedural approach would be an explicitly political panel composed of non-legislative party members or elected officials and representatives of major racial and ethnic groups in the state. The purpose of this body would be to fashion a politically stable solution through compromise and negotiation. This alternative might be more acceptable to those who object to the conflict of interest incumbents may have when they draw district lines. If the panel is sufficiently representative of the diverse interests in the state, and if the commission's product is the result of bargaining and compromise, the process will be consensual. That is to say, there is no guarantee that the explicitly political commission's plan would satisfy objective measures of fairness such as bias, proportionality, and responsiveness, but at least it would have some reasonably broad base of support.

The critical issues in designing a political commission are who should be included on such a panel and by what rule they should make collective decisions. The safest compositional principle would be proportional representation for the major groups and parties in the state based on census numbers, but there would have to be minimum size requirements, and these would no doubt be controversial. An even trickier problem is the commission's decision rule. As mentioned earlier, supermajority rules have the advantage of leading to unbiased results and the disadvantage of leading to deadlock. Consider the experiences of 1971 and 1973 when the governor's office and the legislature were in different hands. Reagan vetoed the legislature's bills, ultimately forcing the court to appoint a special master to draw district lines. Something similar may happen in 1991 if the Republicans retain the governor's office. I have argued for some time that some mechanism is necessary to force consensus if a supermajority rule is used—for instance, imposing a court-drawn plan until the legislature comes to some agreement or, more radically, not allowing elected members of the commission, if there are any, to run for reelection until they complete their redistricting duties.

Redistricting Criteria

A second approach to redistricting reform has been the construction of so-called "good government" criteria. These are standards that prescribe what boundary lines should look like, how they should relate to city and county borders, the size of allowable population deviations, and the like. They do not usually directly address the issue of fairness in any of the three senses previously defined; they do not mandate proportional representation or require that district lines conform to formulae measuring minimum bias or maximum responsiveness. Rather, the idea is that these formal standards encumber any attempts to draw lines unfairly while at the same time promoting so-called good government values. This can be called the "handcuffs" approach to redistricting reform.

The implicit assumption of the handcuffs approach is that the greater the degree of freedom a linedrawer has, the higher the degree of potential abuse. For instance, if new district lines did not have to be drawn every ten years after a census, then, as was the case in some state legislatures prior to *Baker v Carr* and *Reynold v Sims*, it would be possible to dilute the votes of some individuals by allowing high variations in district populations. If malapportionment were permitted, a group could find all of its voters concentrated in large districts and those of other groups efficiently spread out over much smaller districts, producing an arrangement with high bias and low responsiveness. Requiring one man/one vote deprives the would-be gerrymanderer of a technique that might lead to unfairness, but it also eliminates the possibility of malapportionment for some good purpose, such as preserving a rural voice in the legislature of a rapidly urbanizing state. The doctrine of one man/one vote has in fact been applied in an increasingly strict and absolute manner by the courts. In the 1981 redistricting the conventional wisdom was that congressional district population deviations had to be plus or minus 1 percent of an ideal population to pass the court's scrutiny, but that state legislative districts could vary by 10 percent since they, unlike Congress, were not governed by Article I, section 2 of the U.S. constitution. Whereas one can point to instances, such as *Brown v Thomson*[9] in which states were given a great deal of population leeway in the 1980s (in that case, up to 23 percent), the decision in *Karcher v Daggett*[10] will give linedrawers pause before they deviate very far from exact population equality. In that case the court struck down a congressional plan with less than 1 percent population deviations in favor of an alternative with even smaller deviations

---

9. 462 U.S. 835 (1983).
10. 462 U.S. 725 (1983).

because it could find no good reasons for the larger deviations and suspected that the plan was politically biased.

To its credit, the handcuffs approach to redistricting reform has certain advantages. Measuring outcomes (especially hypothetical ones such as are needed for bias and responsiveness measures) is difficult and potentially contentious, whereas measuring whether redistricting plans conform to these formal criteria is relatively simple. Moreover, the concepts of equal population, compactness, and preserving city integrity are easier for many people to grasp than outcome standards such as bias, responsiveness, and proportionality.

On the other hand, the handcuffs approach also has a number of disadvantages. To begin with, the correlation between formal criteria and outcome fairness is at best random. No one argues that a plan with compact, contiguous, equally populated districts that respects city and county boundaries will necessarily yield fair outcomes. Rather, the argument is that a plan that maximizes these criteria has less freedom to create intentionally unfair lines. Although it might lead to undesirable results, it would do so randomly and unintentionally.

In fact, some critics doubt whether it even does this. They contend that certain criteria — e.g., compactness — can have predictable short-run partisan and racial effects, and thus that preferences for them are based on strategic calculations of political advantage rather than on notions of good government. For this reason Democrats and minority groups, for instance, opposed the peculiar compactness measures proposed by Propositions 118 and 119. Of the numerous possible compactness definitions one might choose from, most are based on area or perimeter calculations. The ones proposed in Propositions 118 and 119 were population-based (i.e. they prescribed that the ratio of population inside a district to the population inside a polygon drawn outside a district could not be less than 60 percent in any instance or less than 75 percent on average). Critics pointed out that a population-based measure necessitates more compact shapes in areas of high and uniform population density than in areas of lower and less uniform population density.[11] Since Democrats and

---

11. A complete survey of compactness measures in general and of the ones in Propositions 118 and 119 can be found in Wendy Tam, "Preventing Gerrymandering: the Flynn and Huening Initiatives," unpublished honors' thesis, University of California, Berkeley, 1990.

non-white minorities in California tend to reside in the more densely populated inner-city areas, they opposed this measure based on its potentially adverse political consequences for them.

A second disadvantage of the handcuffs approach is that one has to be able to specify when it is permissible to make exceptions to the simple application of the criteria. Formal criteria often conflict with one another. Equal population sometimes requires that a city or county be split. Preserving the integrity of racial and ethnic neighborhoods may occasionally mean drawing jagged lines that violate the norm of compactness. Proposition 119 recognized this possibility, and stipulated that some criteria take priority over others. This, however, assumes that there is a consensus in support of such an ordering, which is probably not true in a complex state such as California.

Finally, while handcuffing the line-drawer with formal criteria constrains intentional manipulation for partisan, incumbent, or other advantages, it does not eliminate gerrymandering. The Burton plan, regarded by many as one of the most partisan plans in the state's history, had the lowest population deviations of all the plans submitted by the legislature and was quite good by historical standards in minimizing the number of split counties and cities (although some of these splits were quite imaginative). If redistricting priorities are not explicitly enumerated, it is possible to be strategic about which handcuffs one chooses to accept. A plan maximizing compactness and the number of whole cities within districts might be more favorable to one party than a plan emphasizing minority representation and respecting communities of interest. At best, a well intentioned handcuffs approach only indirectly and accidentally leads to fair outcomes; at worst, formal criteria can be used to justify political manipulation for purportedly good government reasons.

A separate justification for formal criteria and redistricting fairness is that these criteria are in themselves good for representation. Equal population, the supreme court has reasoned, gives individuals equal voices in elections, lending legitimacy to public decisions. Compactness, it is said, places adjacent areas and neighborhoods in the same district and thereby fosters a sense of political community. A similar argument can be made for respecting the borders of coastal, desert, and mountainous regions. A number of criteria allegedly simplify lines of representation, such as the so-called "nesting" of assembly and senate seats or the requirement that cities and counties be kept wholly within a single district.

There is some merit to almost all of these arguments, although one might question whether the criteria are as closely matched to their representational goals as it is claimed. For instance, reasonable people might disagree over whether a city is better off wholly contained in one district or divided among several. Some maintain that larger district components have a greater voice than smaller ones, and others suggest that it is better to have several representatives, each with a share of a city or county, than to have only one. There are so many variables in this area that I doubt that one side or the other is right. The correct answer is that it depends. It is probably a good thing to try to include some of these considerations in any plan. If there is a question as to whether a community would be better off divided or united, the sensible thing to do is to ask them.

The representational value of all these criteria, except for equal representation, is secondary to the fairness issues discussed earlier. It might be nice to simplify the lines of representation or to give cities the greatest degree of political influence allowable, but these goals are distinctly secondary in importance to the perceived and actual fairness of district boundaries for significant racial, ethnic, and political groups in the state.

Racial and Ethnic Representation

The legacy of the bitter 1981 redistricting has directed much attention to partisan gerrymandering, but the more serious and potentially controversial issue is fair racial and ethnic representation. A number of the major racial and ethnic groups in this state do not believe that they are fairly represented. Latinos, for instance, will constitute about a quarter of the population in 1991, but less than 10 percent of elected members in the state legislature. The problem is even more acute at the local government level, particularly where the impact of immigration has been the greatest. Until the federal government brought suit to remedy the situation, Latinos constituted a third of Los Angeles city's population and a quarter of the county's, but only 7 percent of the elected representatives on the city council and none on the board of supervisors. By a standard that equates fairness with proportionality (as opposed to simply unbiased and responsive translation of seats to votes), this appears to be unfair.

It would be wrong to blame the underrepresentation of minority groups on redistricting and electoral arrangements alone. Latinos in California have a number of electoral disadvantages. Their population has a higher than average fraction of age-ineligible persons and non-citizens as well as generally lower aggregate levels of education and income. This depresses participation levels, causing the percentage of Latinos in the electorate to be substantially lower than their percentage in the population. In 1980 Latinos comprised 19 percent of the population and 9 percent of registered voters. Because Latinos and certain Asian groups are less concentrated geographically than blacks in California, a single-member, simple plurality electoral system will naturally be less favorable to them. Affirmative districting and electoral arrangements can only partially compensate for these natural handicaps.

Expected major increases in California's percent nonwhite population in 1990 and major revisions in the Voting Rights Act will increase the salience of racial and ethnic issues in the upcoming redistrictings at all levels. That is not to imply that race and ethnicity were insignificant in 1972 and 1982, but only that legal requirements have changed in such a way as to make it easier to prove violations now. In addition, minority group expectations about representation will be higher in 1991 than before. The Voting Rights Act was amended at its periodic seven-year renewal in 1982. Prior to this, plaintiffs had to show that a voting mechanism or districting arrangement was put in place with the intent of diluting the votes of protected minority groups. New language prohibits any procedure or rule that results in denial or abridgement of the right to vote based on a "totality of circumstances" test. In a critical case involving state legislative districts in North Carolina,[12] the supreme court upheld the amended language. Among the various elements in the totality of circumstances test, the court singled out three as being particularly relevant to proving a violation. First, does a group have a sufficiently large population in a geographically compact area to constitute a majority? Second, is the group politically cohesive? Third, is there evidence of racial polarization in voting? In other

---

12. *Thornburg v Gingles*, 478 U.S. 30 (1986).

words, do white voters tend to vote for the white candidate and minority voters for the minority candidate when given the choice?

California witnessed two kinds of these so-called section 2 cases in the 1980s. One type, exemplified by cases in Watsonville and Pomona, challenged at-large election systems.[13] Watsonville had adopted at-large elections in 1952, but had experienced a 127 percent increase in Latino population during the 1970s. Nine Latino candidates had run for the offices of city council and mayor from 1971 to 1985, but none had been elected. Plaintiffs argued that it was possible to create two districts that would be at least 75 percent Latino, and that under an at-large arrangement, racial polarization prevented Latino candidates from winning. The district court conceded that there was evidence of lack of electoral success and racial polarization, but questioned whether Latinos were a cohesive political force given socioeconomic variations within the Latino community and the large number of non-voters. This decision was reversed by the Ninth Circuit Court of Appeals in 1988, and the city was forced to adopt a district system.

The Watsonville case could prove to be a landmark because of the prevalence of at-large mechanisms in California. Many of them were adopted either to conform with the requirements of general law cities or as a part of Progressive urban reforms, but not as conscious attempts to dilute the votes of Latinos. It would have been nearly impossible to have challenged these arrangements under the pre-1982 intent standard. The 1982 amendments to the Voting Rights Act now make cities vulnerable to legal challenges if their long-established electoral practices have the consequence of diluting minority votes, whatever the intent. This may affect a number of California cities in the 1990s in two ways. First, they may have to abandon their at-large form of elections if they have large minority populations and low minority representation. Secondly, in drawing district lines they will have to pay more attention to the integrity of minority neighborhoods.

This brings us to the second type of section 2 cases, those involving redistricting challenges. The two best examples of these are the

---

13. *Gomez v City of Watsonville*, 863 F.2d 1407, 1419 (9th Cir. 1988). A good discussion of the case can be found in Barbara Phillips, "Minority Political Empowerment: the Legacy of *Gomez v City of Watsonville*," paper prepared for the Conference on Representation, Reapportionment and Minority Empowerment, Pomona College, Claremont, CA, March 29, 1990.

Los Angeles city and county cases.[14] Although the city case did not go to court, it was settled under the threat of a trial. Only one Latino had been elected to the fifteen-person council for over twenty years, even though the Latino population had grown to just under a third in that period. Faced with evidence of polarized voting in the Art Snyder recall elections and the observation that existing lines divided the Latino community into at least five significant parts, the city settled by drawing a new Latino district, eventually won by Gloria Molina. The justice department's challenge to the board of supervisors' district lines, however, did go to court, and in June 1990, the court held that the board's lines violated section 2 of the Voting Rights Act. In both cases, Latinos had little (in the city case) or no (in the county case) success in electing one of their own, and it was possible to draw at least one majority-population Latino district. Once again, the questions of Latino cohesiveness and non-voting arose, but the plaintiffs prevailed in both instances.

These cases set important precedents for redistrictings at all levels in California. It would be unwise for those who redistrict at either the state or local level to divide large, compact minority populations for any good or bad political purpose. Two controversial questions in the 1990s will be what is a sufficiently large minority population and how compact must it be? As mentioned earlier, even though the Voting Rights Act can be used to prevent vote dilution, it does not legislate a right to proportional representation or mandate strongly affirmative redistricting plans. These goals will have to be won in the rough and tumble of redistricting negotiations.

Toward a Sensible Redistricting Policy

The foundation of a sensible public policy towards redistricting rests on a clear and explicit theory of electoral fairness. Reforms that indirectly deal with electoral fairness (e.g. procedural neutrality, randomness, or handcuffing criteria) can work because a redistricting plan will inevitably be judged on its first- and second-order effects. A plan is not legitimate simply because the redistricting procedures used inhibit ill will. In politics legitimacy hinges on the outcomes of procedures as much or more as on the fairness of the process.

---

14. *U.S. et al. v City of Los Angeles*, No. CV 85-7739 JMI (C.D. Cal. 1985) and *U.S. et al. v County of Los Angeles*, No. CV 88-5435 KN (C.D. Cal. 1989).

As was stated before, there are at least two competing views of political fairness California could adopt. The first, traditionally associated with district-based plurality rules, is an unbiased, responsive system. The power of incumbency and residential patterns in the state might prevent California from ever fully realizing this ideal, but in theory districting could be explicitly oriented towards this goal. Assuming agreement could be reached on a procedure for measuring bias and responsiveness, the critical consideration would become not who draws the lines or why, but is the plan within acceptable limits of bias and responsiveness? Primary criteria such as equal population or contiguity would have to be respected, but others such as preserving city and county boundaries would come into play only if they did not throw a plan outside the acceptable fairness parameters.

Alternatively, California could adopt a proportional representation standard of fairness. This concept of fairness does not fit as easily with the kinds of electoral systems we currently employ at the state and local level in California, but districts could nonetheless be made to conform more closely to a proportional standard. Most likely, this would require relaxing certain criteria of compactness and city and county preservation in order to achieve the desired outcomes. Groups that are sufficiently large to warrant representation would also have to be determined.

If popular expectations in this country continue to evolve towards the second notion of fairness, California may be forced to change its electoral system in the future. This does not necessarily mean that California will have to adopt a European-style, party list, proportional representation system (although that might be an option), but rather that cities, counties, and the state may want to consider experimenting with some less drastic electoral innovations.

Two possibilities that deserve closer scrutiny are indexing the size of representative bodies at various levels of government in California and adopting so-called semi-proportional electoral rules. The first is really a matter of common sense. The state has grown at an annual rate of 2.5 percent in recent years, or more than twice the national average, but the size of most city councils, boards of supervisors, and the state legislature has remained the same. A simple law of political science is that larger bodies generally will be more descriptively representative than smaller ones. The least descriptively representative system is one in which one person represents many, and the most is a direct democracy in which each person is his or her own representative. It is hard for the Los Angeles Board of Supervisors to be descriptively representative when each supervisor represents 1.5 million people. Some thought should be given to providing guidelines for expanding or contracting the number of elected officials in accordance with population changes. This alone would go a long way towards relieving perceptions of unfairness among California's minority communities.

In addition, there should be some institutional experimentation with semi-proportional rules, perhaps initially at the local level to head off potential section 2 challenges. Examples of these mechanisms are limited and cumulative vote systems.[15] In a limited-vote scheme, candidates run in multi-member districts, but unlike the usual at-large format, each voter has fewer votes than offices up for election. This prevents the majority from always prevailing. The cumulative vote system is based on a similar principle: each voter can choose to place all his or her votes on one candidate, or give single votes to a number of candidates, which in effect allows a minority to express its intense preference. The effect of limited-vote systems is to give more proportional results without departing from the historical district-based tradition of Anglo-American democracies. Such systems have been used effectively elsewhere in the United States, including Illinois and Chilton County, Alabama, and may provide a more amicable solution to what will otherwise become a bitter controversy in the future.

When I wrote *The Reapportionment Puzzle*[16] nearly a decade ago, I thought that an openly political but consensual and accountable redistricting process was the best that California could hope for. That would still be an improvement over what we have today, or what has been proposed so far by Common Cause and the League of Women Voters. However, it may be that a consensus favoring proportional fairness will emerge in California as the best way to deal with diversity during the 1990s, and if so, some political experimentation may be in order.

---

15. See Edward Still, "Cumulative and Limited Voting in Alabama," paper prepared for the Conference on Representation, Reapportionment and Minority Empowerment, Pomona College, Claremont, CA, March 29, 1990.
16. *Supra* note 4.

CALIFORNIA IN WASHINGTON

Beryl A. Radin

12

Despite the sizable presence in the nation's capital of representatives of approximately eighty California public organizations, the state has not been as effective as it might be in making its case in Washington. In part this is due to the widespread perception among non-Californians that this affluent state can take care of itself, but it is also a result of the failure to communicate to the U.S. Congress a unified statewide agenda. This chapter describes the current system within which Washington-based California representatives operate, the impact of that system on California issues, and current proposals for change.

In 1972 then San Francisco Mayor Joseph Alioto commented: "No mayor can really do his job unless he spends at least one day per month in Washington."[1] For Alioto as well as other state and local chief executives around the U.S., Washington representation was an essential form of grant entrepreneurship during a period of extensive proliferation of national programs. For some states and localities, obtaining grants required a personal presence in Washington. In 1973, for example, the Office of the Governor of California had a full-time staff person in Washington who served as the eyes and ears of the chief executive. In the late 1960s Speaker of the California Assembly Jesse Unruh set up a Washington office for the California Legislature. Both the City of Los Angeles and Los Angeles County had representation in Washington in the 1970s.

Others found it was sufficient to depend on the information and influence developed by the myriad government interest groups that represented the states, cities, counties, and specialized governmental functions. The National Association of Counties, the U.S. Conference of Mayors, the National League of Cities, the National Conference of State Legislators, the National Governors' Conference (now called the National Governors' Association), the Council of

---

1. Quoted in Donald H. Haider, *When Governments Come to Washington*, The Free Press, 1974, p. 98.

State Governments, and a host of specialized organizations played important and visible roles in the development of intergovernmental policy in the U.S.

Much has changed in the field of intergovernmental relationships since the 1970s. National grant dollars are available to states, cities, counties, and special districts in greatly diminished amounts and in many fewer programmatic areas. At least some of the available dollars have been designed to maximize discretion at the state level, with minimal strings and a reduced role for national agency officials. Other dollars flow in tightly prescribed directions. But those directions are determined by Congress, not by agency officials. The Reagan as well as the current Bush administration have emphasized the devolution of authority and decision making beyond the Washington beltway.

Despite these changes in the intergovernmental landscape, Washington offices and representation for groups around the country seem to have increased. New York—California's major competitor in terms of population and public activism—has staff and offices operating in Washington that represent the governor, New York City, the New York-New Jersey Port Authority, the state assembly, the state senate, the minority in the senate, the New York City Metropolitan Transit Authority, the New York State Board of Education, and the New York City Board of Education.

But no other state matches California in the extent of representation in Washington. As Figure 12-1 indicates, California public organizations with some form of Washington representation include thirty-three cities, fourteen counties, seven state organizations (six state agencies are subsumed within the Office of the Governor), four education agencies, twenty special districts, and three umbrella agencies.

Yet, despite the sizable presence of representatives of approximately eighty California public organizations, the Golden State has not been as effective as it might be in making its case in Washington. California is 3,000 miles from Washington, D.C., but the state's political culture creates another sort of distance—a tension between the way Californians view their role in the federal system and how it is viewed by others. There are a number of unresolved issues in this area:

Figure 12-1. California Jurisdictions, Organizations, and
Agencies with Representation in Washington, D.C.

Cities	
Alhambra	Oxnard
Anaheim	Park
Bell	Pasadena
Colton	Rancho Palos Verdes
Fresno	Redondo Beach
Garden Grove	Richmond
Hayward	Riverside
Huntington Beach	San Bernardino
Inglewood	San Diego
Laguna Beach	San Francisco
Livermore	San Jose
Long Beach	San Leandro
Los Angeles	Santa Ana
Newport Beach	Santa Barbara
Norwalk	Santa Monica
Oceanside	Victorville
	West Hollywood

Counties	
Alameda County	San Mateo County
Fresno County	San Jacinto County
Los Angeles County	San Joaquin County
Orange County	Santa Clara County
Riverside County	Stanislaus County
San Bernardino County	Tulare County
San Diego County	Ventura County

State Organizations	
Office of the Governor	State Senate
including representatives from:	State Assembly
World Trade Commission	Public Employees
Department of Finance	Retirement System
Department of Energy	State Teachers
and Water Resources	Retirement System
Department of	Board of Equalization
Food and Agriculture	Franchise Tax Board
Department of	
Transportation	
Department of Health	
and Social Services	

Education Agencies

California State University system
University of California system
California Community Colleges
California State Department of Education

Special Districts

Transportation:

Bay Area Rapid Transit
Long Beach Transit
Los Angeles Transportation Commission
Los Angeles Rapid Transit District
Metropolitan Transportation Commission
Orange County Transportation Commission
San Diego Transit District

Water:

Imperial Valley Irrigation District
Napa Flood Control and Water Conservation District
Riverside County Flood Control District

Ports:

Long Beach
Oxnard
Los Angeles
San Francisco

Other:

Anaheim Public Utilities
Long Beach Department of Oil Properties
Los Angeles County Community Development
Los Angeles Department of Conservation
Northern California Power
South Orange County Drug Prevention

Umbrella Agencies:

County Supervisors of California
County Welfare Directors of California
League of California Cities

Note:

This list was developed from sources of information released between 1988 and 1990. It may not be complete or fully up to date because of multiple and informal sources of information.

- Californians in Washington have to contend with a perception that it is able to take care of its own problems. Known in Washington as the ABC (Anybody But California) syndrome, this is a problem in many different policy areas.
- It is difficult to develop a unified, aggregate California position on many issues because of the diversity and conflict within the state. Partisanship, geography, and specialized functions accentuate that diversity and conflict.

- The changes in national programs during the 1980s mean that jurisdictions no longer can depend on their individual relationships with agency officials. Agency-level discretion has been replaced by a shift to two very different actors: the U.S. Congress and the California Legislature, two entities that also are characterized by diversity and conflict.

These factors have a major impact on the way that the state can assure that its special interests are effectively articulated on a wide range of policy matters. The challenge is to reshape California's representation in Washington in order to better articulate future policy needs and choices.

Based on interviews with Washington-based representatives of California public organizations in spring 1990, this chapter examines the reasons for the increase in California representation in Washington and analyzes the ways they deal with their clients, as well as with the California congressional delegation and staff of national agencies. The chapter concludes with an examination of the impact of this system of representation on California issues and problems and current proposals for change.

Building a Washington Presence

California public organizations have been at the forefront of representation in the nation's capital for many years, and representation has increased over the past decade. This increase can be explained by shifts in national policy making and special characteristics of the Golden State.

As the availability of grants to state and local governments has decreased, agencies have less discretion in the allocation of funds. Available dollars are earmarked through program design, largely as a result of congressionally designated formulae for distribution. Devolution of authority to the states has also been a factor. As the role of Congress has increased, it has become more crucial for state and local governments to follow the national policy debate and attempt to influence congressional decision processes. As legislation wends its way through multiple committees and subcommittees, it requires constant monitoring and scrutiny. Seemingly trivial legislative provisions designed to meet a set of concerns for one jurisdiction may create a new set of problems for another.

Jurisdictions have found that congressional debate focuses increasingly on technical issues and requires those who seek to influence the process to have considerable expertise in related fields. This is required not only to assure that jurisdictions can qualify for available funds, but also to minimize negative impacts of regulatory, taxation, or other new programs—a function that Washington representatives call "damage control."

The need for specialized expertise has increased at the same time that professional associations representing state and local government have experienced steep reductions in budget and staff. One study estimated that the reduction in federal funding from 1980 to 1985 for the seven major state and local government associations ranged from almost 29 percent to 100 percent.[2] At the same time, some of them, especially local organizations, were frozen out of the policy process by the Reagan White House as budget cuts and policies tilted the intergovernmental balance away from local government to the states.

Special circumstances in California served to exacerbate the national problems. The size and diversity of the state is unparalleled within the U.S., and the fragmented and diffuse nature of authority and decision making within California made it difficult for either the state legislature or the major cities and counties to accept the national government's assumption that the governor, alone, speaks for the state.

California local governments—especially those in southern California—had learned that national policy could be used to circumvent what they believed to be anti-urban and anti-southern biases in Sacramento. When local governments recognized the implications of the pro-state focus in Washington, it became clear that they needed to find a way to assure that their interests were articulated at the national level. The California congressional delegation—the largest in the nation—provided a point of access. Not only did the delegation offer an alternative political voice, but its members were strategically placed in a number of leadership roles in both the House

---

2. Charles H. Levine and James A. Thurber, "Reagan and the Intergovernmental Lobby: Iron Triangles, Cozy Subsystems, and Political Conflict," in Allan J. Cigler and Burdett A. Loomis, (eds.), *Interest Group Politics,* Congressional Quarterly Press, 1986, p. 212. See also Ardith Maney, "What Else Happens When Governments Come to Washington: Intergovernmental Lobbying and the Dominance of Institutions," paper presented at the annual meeting of the Midwest Political Science Association, Chicago, April 5-7, 1990.

and the Senate. This resource could be tapped—but it required an investment of time and expertise beyond that afforded by flying mayors into Washington once a month. When debate is cast in technical terms, participation in the process requires both expertise and a staff investment of time to ensure that a jurisdiction's voice is effectively heard.

During the past several years a set of national policy decisions were made that provoked a reexamination of the type and extent of California representation in Washington. Several local governments—particularly Los Angeles County—were not pleased with the outcome of the 1986 Tax Reform Law. Institutions of higher education as well as the business community were dismayed by California's failure to receive funds for the Earthquake Engineering Research Center, Sematech (the semiconductor consortium), and the supercollider. Increasingly, it appeared that California was experiencing the results of the ABC syndrome. Today, at the same time that California public organizations seek to maintain their share of a shrinking national budget, they are facing new resistance in Washington.[3]

California Representation in Washington

More than eighty California public organizations are represented in Washington by a diverse array of individuals who speak for them on Capitol Hill and in the agencies. Staff range from employees of California organizations with expertise and knowledge of the client's world to lobbyists hired because of their personal influence with members of Congress and their staffs. Current forms of representation include:

One client with multiple staff members responsible to the client. The Office of the Governor has a staff of fifteen; the City of Los Angeles operates with a staff of six;[4] the University of California has a staff of five professionals.

One client with one staff member directly responsible to the client. Operating in this fashion are the representatives for the California

3. See Matt Rothman, "Who's Fighting for California?" *California Business*, 1 February 1990, p. 40.
4. Although the City of Los Angeles staff operates through a consultant contract with the Center for Municipal Development, its mode of operation is similar to that of a staff directly on the city payroll.

State University system, the League of California Cities, and the County Supervisors Association of California.

One client represented by a full-time person in a lobbying, public relations, or law firm. The representative for the California Department of Education is located within a firm but works full-time for the department.

Multiple clients represented by one person. This mode is used by a number of cities and counties who want a Washington presence but lack either the resources or the demand for a full-time lobbyist. Several lobbying firms fill this need.

Multiple clients represented by a firm or group. This is the way that law firms with public organization clients are usually organized; it allows a firm to utilize a diverse array of experts within the group for specialized projects. Several lobbying firms use this format.

As one might expect, the Washington representatives who operate within these diverse settings come from a variety of backgrounds. In some cases these people trade on their ability to gain access to various decisionmaking settings. In few instances, however, is access alone adequate; representatives also emphasize the importance of being able to make a substantive case for their clients. A few California public organizations have chosen to package their representation in multiple forms. When issues are debated in highly technical terms they may contract with a specialist in that policy area. In some cases that specialist will supplement the more general representative; in other cases the jurisdiction or organization may choose to replace the generalist with a package of specialists.

Although many contracts between clients and representatives emerge from a competitive bid process that values expertise and knowledge of the Washington policy world, connections in California are also important. Many representatives are California natives or received their education in a California institution. Still others spent a portion of their careers in the state; a few of them worked for the organization they now represent in Washington.

One aspect of the California culture that appears to have been adopted by the Washington representatives is bipartisanship or—in some cases—nonpartisanship. Thus, a firm that is headed by a strong and visible Republican may represent a city or county that has a Democratic member of Congress. This pattern is due to several factors. The requirement for nonpartisan municipal elections minimizes the tie between local politics and national politics. In addition, since the Reagan years, Washington representatives have dealt with a Republican administration and a strong Democratic delegation in Congress. In this circumstance, it would be counterproductive for them to trade on a partisan set of relationships and arguments.

In a few cases representatives have a combination of public and private clients, and several of them noted that the style and focus of representation is different for these two groups. "While both the public and private sectors are bottom-line oriented, I've been surprised how sensitive the public agency is to increased mandates without federal funding," commented one representative.

Over the years there have been some changes in the profile of California's Washington representatives. More women are now representing public agencies, and there appears to be a movement toward specialization. For example, Los Angeles County, the largest local government jurisdiction, has engaged a law firm with specialization in finance and immigration.

Relationships with Clients

Most Washington representatives have an official reporting line back to a single individual in the California organization. However, the complexities of intra- and intergovernmental structures within the state mean that relationships are often more complex than the official structure may suggest.

Many representatives try to assure that their reports and analyses are routinely sent to all interested individuals and interests within the organization they represent. The University of California Washington office, for example, reports directly to the office of the university president; however, reports to that office also are sent to contacts on each of the university campuses.

Local government representatives for both cities and counties also have to contend with a multiple cast of characters. While the contract or reporting link may be through the city manager or the chief administrative officer, most representatives know that these individuals must balance the differing perspectives of mayors, city councils, and boards of supervisors. Washington representatives try to avoid becoming involved in political machinations within the jurisdiction, and especially to avoid allowing local politics to be aired in the

Washington political arena. One of the representatives has a slogan that he proclaims regularly to his Bay Area clients: "Wash your dirty laundry in the Bay, not in the Potomac."

There are instances, however, where the Washington representative becomes embroiled in issues in which members of Congress or national agency representatives play a role. This has occurred when a member of Congress disagrees with a California jurisdiction and uses the leverage of money or policy to punish that jurisdiction. The structure of California government makes it difficult for representatives to avoid these issues entirely. Conflict between statewide agencies (especially those represented within the Office of the Governor) and local jurisdictions can take place around the design of national programs, such as those for drug prevention or for vocational education. The statewide agency wants to protect the state role, while the local entity seeks to maximize its autonomy in the allocation of funds and determination of program elements.

Most representatives assume that there will be differences among members of the California corps of representatives and proceed with an acceptance of that diversity. For example, the disagreement between the University of California and the California State University systems about authority for doctoral programs has not been surfaced in a Washington policy context. Similarly, it is assumed that northern California and southern California may have different views on some issues.[5]

To some degree, the increase in the number of Washington representatives reflects the variety of California institutions and the different approaches that they take. Although there had been a single office for the California Legislature in the past, the differences between the state assembly and senate are acknowledged in the decision to have separate Washington representation for those legislative bodies.

Sacramento Versus Washington

Those representatives who report to their clients through a legislative affairs function or office are often struck by the differences

---

5. As the list of cities and counties indicates, more southern California jurisdictions have some form of Washington representation than do those in the north. This reflects not only the population distribution within the state but the nature of the issues and diverse approaches taken by the two parts of the state in terms of intergovernmental relationships.

between the Sacramento and Washington modes of operation. These differences become obvious because it is common for jurisdictions to establish parallel reporting systems for their Washington and Sacramento representatives. According to one Bay Area representative, the differences stem to some degree from the initiative and referendum system in California because "everything is on the ballot in California." Others look to various aspects of the decision process to explain the differences. One representative commented: "People in California assume that Washington is like Sacramento. They have to learn that different advocacy techniques and methods of operation are at play. The game in Washington is one of relentless coalition building." Another noted: "Washington has a much slower process. It is a much bigger pond than Sacramento. There are so many actors and there are no real clues as to who has left 'fingerprints' in many areas."

Differences between the systems can be the basis for problems with a client. "People often do not understand the differences between the two settings," observed one representative. "In Sacramento, every bill gets a hearing. Our clients often want us to cover hearings and don't understand the difference between the two regarding the role of hearings. Staff play an important role here; the most powerful lobby in D.C. is congressional staff. We lobby staff who, in turn, lobby other staff. Sacramento staff don't have the license or numbers they have here. Remember, there are 10,000 Capitol Hill staff in Washington."

At least one representative noted that it is often difficult to get local jurisdictions to focus on national issues because they view their time and effort as a tradeoff between national and state questions. These jurisdictions are caught in a resource conflict that requires them to choose between affecting the discretion exercised at the state level and participating extensively in national policy development.

Working in Washington

Despite the diversity of their interests, California's Washington representatives seek to maximize their effectiveness in common ways. All of the representatives emphasize the importance of working in coalitions to accomplish their goals, and they accentuate their ability to deal with issues in substantive as well as political terms. Some representatives turn to other California colleagues for information and support. Others draw on the national organizations to which their clients belong as the basis for information exchange and development of strategy. Still others seek support only after they decide what substantive policy and strategy to employ.

Maintaining Networks

Despite differences in policy approaches and agendas, almost all of the Washington representatives interviewed are linked in networks that provide for the exchange of information at both state and national levels. Partisan politics sometimes intrudes and blocks these efforts. "During the past decade Republican governors have often tried to be supportive of Republicans in the White House," noted one veteran representative, "and as a result we have not been given the help we needed from the governor." But, as another representative observed, "it is important that we communicate even when we disagree." These representatives are using informal means to reach a unified California position within a formal setting that accentuates their differences.

At times informal contacts occur through the Golden State Roundtable, a group of public and private Washington representatives who meet monthly at lunch, or through meetings of the California State Society. Some groups also meet within subgroups and clusters by areas of interest. The representative for the League of California Cities serves as the point of contact for city representatives; the individual who staffs the County Supervisors Association of California performs the same function for county representatives. Similarly, those who work on education issues maintain contact with one another.

The national associations, despite their decline in staff and status, also play a role in maintaining networks. Most Washington-based California representatives are tied into one or another of the national groups (see Figure 12-2), many of which hold regular meetings that provide a venue for the exchange of information about upcoming issues and developments within the city.

However, few California representatives feel that they are able to use these national organizations as the focal point for advocacy and coalition development. They frequently find that the national organi-

Figure 12-2: National, State, and Local Interest Groups (partial listing)

Airport Operators Council International
American Association of Community and Junior Colleges
American Association of Port Authorities
American Council on Education
American Public Power Association
American Public Transit Association
American Public Works Association
American Water Works Association
Association of American Universities
Association of Local Housing Finance Agencies
Association of Metropolitan Sewage Agencies
Council of Chief State School Officers
Council of State Governments
Government Finance Officers Association
National Area Agencies on Aging
National Association of Counties
National Association of Regional Councils
National Association of Telecommunications Offices and Advisors
National Community Development Association
National Conference of State Legislators
National Governors Association
National League of Cities
U.S. Conference of Mayors

zations, because of their own internal dynamics, take positions that reflect a common denominator among the membership. California interests are often viewed as unique and requiring the special attention that is not possible within a national framework. As a result, these groups do not serve the umbrella function that some had envisioned for them.

Creating Coalitions

California representatives face two problems when it comes to building coalitions. First, the substance of policy issues often plays differently in the state than it does in other parts of the country. For example, the immigration pattern within the state has meant that California (and Los Angeles County in particular) has particular needs for assistance under the State Legalization Impact Assistance Grant (SLIAG) program that was created through the 1986 Immigration Reform and Control Act. While other states are impacted by this problem, none experiences it to the extent of California.

Second, representatives have to contend with the image of the state as a rich and successful giant that, while it values its independence and self-sufficiency, has consumed a disproportionate share of the federal pie. To some degree, the resentment is compounded by the size and power of the California delegation in Congress (and the expectation that the delegation will increase after the 1990 census).

Given this image, California representatives are often faced with a dilemma. On the one hand, they represent public organizations in the most populous state that—collectively—experiences the broadest range of urban, rural, geographic, industrial, agricultural, environmental, and social problems. On the other hand, if they deal with these issues as California problems, they face the ABC backlash. The challenge for the representatives is to devise a strategy that maximizes California support and at the same time minimizes the view that the issue at hand is unique to California. There are several ways that representatives have dealt with this dilemma. Some have chosen to stay close to the national organizations, believing that they can serve as a cover even though they may not be responsive to California needs. California representatives participate in a number of standing coalitions that, in some ways, operate more like networks than strategic coalitions. Among these are the Committee for Education Funding, the State and Local Government Pension Working Group, NOISE (the airport noise coalition), the Function 250 Coalition (a coalition that focuses on funds for science and research), and the State and Local Clean Air Coalition.

Others have sought to organize coalitions of non-California jurisdictions with similar problems. When Congress failed to appropriate funds under the SLIAG immigration program, Californians from the governor's office, the state education agency, and affected cities hammered out an agreement that served as the basis for a coalition; this was then expanded as an Informal Coalition on the Full Funding of SLIAG, including other states such as Texas and Florida as well as some national groups. Similarly, when the reauthorization process for the Vocational Education Program was underway, a provision in the Senate version of the bill would have created major problems for California's community colleges. Although the national organization representing community colleges supported the provision, the California representative organized a coalition to oppose the measure, involving twenty other states affected by the proposal.

Over the past few years California representatives have played a behind-the-scenes role in a number of policy areas. In one instance, a state agency paid for and provided staff for a lobbying effort that carefully avoided a public position that emphasized the impact of the proposal on California. Other coalitions have been created by representatives who have been able to package their California interests with those of their clients from other states. There seem to be some quiet, indirect ways of combating the ABC syndrome through personal relationships rather than formal coalition strategies.

The California Congressional Delegation

Not surprisingly, the major policy focus for the corps of California Washington representatives is the California congressional delegation. Most of the Washington representatives spend more than half their time lobbying on Capitol Hill, reflecting the shift that has occurred in policy making from the executive branch to the Congress.

The California delegation of forty-five members of the House of Representatives and two senators constitutes one of the most diverse delegations within the U.S. Congress. The twenty-seven-member Democratic group includes some of the most vociferous critics of a conservative Republican agenda; by contrast, the eighteen Republican members include several of the Republican administration's major supporters. The delegation reflects the multiple constituencies within the state itself. For the most part, members have been attentive to the special needs of their districts and maintain close relationships with the local governmental entities within them.

For the Washington representatives this diversity within the delegation is both a strength and a weakness. Some representatives note that it allows them to "shop around" for supporters, especially if the issue at hand is one that crosses district lines. Others, however, are concerned that the partisanship and geographical differences represented by the delegation minimize the ability of its members to see beyond their own districts concerning issues that affect the state.

Unlike those from some other states, many California members of the House bring knowledge of state politics to their national roles. A high percentage of the delegation cut their political teeth in Sacramento. The Los Angeles delegation, for example, includes seven members who served in the legislature and two former lieutenant governors. According to some observers, this experience has sensitized the members to the impact of national policies on the state. However, the Sacramento experience that is used as the point of departure may be somewhat outdated. As one representative put it, "the Sacramento of fifteen years ago is not the Sacramento of today."

The California delegation also contains a number of members who occupy important leadership positions, particularly in the House of Representatives. California Democratic members serve as chairs of education, health, appropriations, budget, and other committees and subcommittees; California Republicans also hold ranking minority positions in committees and subcommittees. While the Washington representatives rely on these individuals and cultivate their support, there is a sense of frustration that the forty-five-member California House delegation is not as powerful as might be expected, given its size. These representatives are not convinced that much will change, even after the 1990 census results are expected to add five to seven more seats to the California delegation. The problem, according to several observers, is that members focus first on their districts and then on national issues. There is little in the current system that pushes them to define issues in statewide terms. Although the two members of the Senate do have a statewide perspective, their committee assignments do not give them the opportunity to focus on the range of issues that affect the state.

This is an issue that has concerned Congressman Don Edwards, dean of the California Democratic delegation and chair of the congressional group called California Democrats. Edwards has developed a staff capacity to bring the large California Democratic group together, providing a forum for the discussion of issues that have a special California "spin." Over the past few years Edwards has attempted to broaden the focus of his activities to a bipartisan approach. According to one representative, "the California delegation is coming together more than it did before. We have had a change in congressional leadership that has made a difference." Some observers have commented that it has taken the delegation nearly a decade to get over the dissension spawned by the 1980 reapportionment engineered by the late Congressman Philip Burton of San Francisco.

The most frequently cited evidence of this changed environment is the congressional response to the 1989 Bay Area earthquake. Led by Congressman Vic Fazio, the delegation was able to push through a $2.8 billion relief package in five days. "We were able to develop a united front in Washington on this issue, despite the differences between our client jurisdictions within the state," noted one representative. Another commented, "After the earthquake, everyone jumped on every bandwagon. Congressman Anderson brought together the Army Corps of Engineers and FEMA. Congressman Stark focused on tax relief. Southern California supported northern California." While pointing to their success with the earthquake issue, one observer noted that members of Congress from around the country were "only willing to go so far on this issue. They were not willing to push the committee chairman on this measure." According to California Business magazine, Congressman Fazio prevailed only after the entire House accepted a Senate version penned by his own staff.[6] Despite the resistance, most of the representatives were pleased with the congressional response. Several noted that the favorable response was possible because the earthquake came on the heels of Hurricane Hugo: "We could focus the debate on disaster relief, not simply on earthquakes."

As they work on Capitol Hill, some of the representatives spend most of their time developing relationships with congressional staff. Several of the California groups use their Washington representatives to arrange formal presentations to their delegates. The City of Los Angeles, for example, holds an annual briefing on legislative issues for the Los Angeles congressional delegation. The 1990 report that served as the basis for the briefing focused on community development, housing, anti-drug efforts, transportation, the environment, and taxation. Similarly, the Metropolitan Transportation Commission in the San Francisco Bay Area develops an annual report to the Bay Area congressional delegation that outlines its recommendations involving federal legislation and budget allocations. While some of the representatives begin work with the California delegation, others find that this is not the best use of their time. In those cases, the California votes may be predictable and California members are not placed in the strategic or leadership positions

6. *Supra* note 3, p. 44.

within committees or subcommittees that allow them to be a part of the development of strategy.

Working the Agencies

Given the access provided by a president from California from 1981 to 1989, one might have expected the California representatives to focus on agencies of the executive branch. Although most of the representatives do spend part of their time dealing with agencies, that function is of less perceived importance than is time spent on Capitol Hill. To some degree, this emphasis mirrors the overall policy pendulum swing to the Congress, in terms of both new program design and the appropriations process.

To some extent, relationships with federal agencies depend on the point of access for Washington representatives. Because Governor Deukmejian was an early campaign supporter of President Bush, staff of the Office of the Governor had access to new appointees in the administration. This allowed the office to establish a dialogue with these individuals, offering assistance as well as letting them know of the governor's agenda. Representatives who specialize in particular policy areas often have long-term relationships with career staff members in federal agencies and are able to call on these contacts when needed.

For a number of representatives the problem is one of time. Because agency work can be more time consuming, they may try to find an alternative way to serve their clients. In some cases they may seek assistance from the national organizations. Larger jurisdictions and organizations often have specialist staff who have developed long-term relationships with agency officials. There are instances in which representatives become involved in cross-agency issues. For example, the attempt to develop a proposal for a Tijuana sewer system involved the Environmental Protection Agency, the Department of State, the Army Corps of Engineers, and the Office of Management and Budget.

Representatives who were involved with the agency side of the earthquake issue contrast the results and response they eventually received on Capitol Hill with that in the Federal Emergency Management Agency (FEMA). As one individual commented, "I went to a meeting at FEMA soon after the earthquake. There were incredible problems in the way that the FEMA staff was attempting to second guess the Californians. They had the attitude, let's get those guys."

To some extent, the shift of policy making power away from the federal bureaucracy assists those who are attempting to define issues in aggregate state terms. Agency decision making is often focused on the idiosyncrasies of a particular case, playing up the fragmentation and diversity within the state and hindering the creation of effective coalitions.

Summary and Conclusion

The corps of Washington-based representatives of California public organizations provides an important resource for the citizens of California. Over the past decade the group has increased in size, technical ability, and diversity. Although there are instances where issues appear to have fallen through the cracks, for the most part representatives have established networks and methods of information sharing that allow them to monitor the multiple decision points in the nation's capitol. Despite major differences in policy agendas, many representatives have devised informal coordination methods that allow them to agree to disagree about some issues and support each other on others. These relationships transcend traditional intergovernmental lines, providing an opportunity for state agencies and organizations, counties, cities, and special districts to manage their sometimes conflicting agendas.

The large and powerful California congressional delegation serves as a focal point for representatives' time and effort. Cooperation between the California Democrats and some of the congressional Republicans suggests that the delegation is reaching toward a statewide focus. The increase in the delegation that is expected as a result of 1990 reapportionment would bring the California congressional group to fifty members or more—approximately one-eighth of the entire U.S. Congress. This increase would be expressed not only in overall voting strength but also in assignments to committees and subcommittees.

While these developments are promising, they must be balanced against the negative image of the state in Washington and the conflicts among different interests within the state. Californians were discouraged by the loss of the semiconductor research consortium, the earthquake research grant, and the supercollider, and they contrast the well orchestrated campaign by business, government, and universities in Texas with the fragmented and uncoordinated California effort. Even a coordinated campaign, however, might not have helped. A united California agenda, in fact, might have elicited an intensified negative response from the rest of the country.

The second factor that is potentially negative involves the diversity that exists within the state itself. Californians may agree that they will not "wash their dirty laundry in the Potomac," but northern and southern California do have different interests, state organizations view their role differently from cities, counties, or special districts, and legislators are not willing to cede their authority to the governor.[7]

However, while some issues push toward fragmentation, emphasizing the differences rather than similarities among California jurisdictions, others, such as the earthquake issue and the question of defense retooling, appear to assist the move toward a unified California position.

Next Steps

Few who deal with California issues in Washington would disagree in principle with proposals to develop a statewide perspective. There are several ways to achieve this end. One approach would be simply to acknowledge the problem and support existing efforts to increase coordination and information sharing. A second approach would be to generate information on the impact of legislative and administrative proposals on California public organizations throughout the state.

A third approach would be to create a venue for the discussion of California impacts. Such a venue could either bring all of the official actors together (that is, Republicans and Democrats) or establish a forum with a "hands-off" relationship to official actors.

Over the past few years Congressman Don Edwards has been attempting to gain bipartisan support for the establishment of a California Institute, a body loosely modeled after several other state or multi-state think tanks in Washington. This effort is clearly

---

7. In addition, members of the congressional delegation bring their own concerns about protection of committee and subcommittee turf.

directed toward minimizing the fragmentation of positions within the state. For nearly three years, Edwards has been seeking the support of the eighteen-member Republican California delegation and recently has gained the endorsement of Congressman Bill Lowery, Senator Pete Wilson, and other congressional Republicans. In addition, Edwards has engaged the business sector in the effort.

The California Institute is designed to marshal the diverse resources in California and to make the California position clearer in national decision making. These could include the private sector, universities, research groups, elected officials, and other interested parties. The institute has been variously described as a brokerage organization, a research enterprise, and a clearinghouse. Its intent is clear—to keep California from being blindsided in the design of national policy and programs. Nevertheless, it is not always obvious how that intention will be implemented. Indeed, although most Washington representatives know something about the general idea of the institute, they are not clear about how its activities would affect them. Some are apprehensive that the institute could take on issues that would be politically or otherwise divisive.

The draft bylaws for the new organization call for:
- a board of directors that does not include any elected officials but is named by elected officials (House Republicans, House Democrats, California senators, and the governor would each appoint two directors);
- an agenda that must be agreed to by the entire board;
- an advisory group composed representatives from business, labor, and academia who would secure financing, among other duties;
- an executive director named by the board and responsible for day-to-day operations and staffing decisions.

The California Institute's creators have suggested that they are more concerned about the structure and decision process of the new organization than they are with the issues the institute might examine. Among the topics that have been mentioned, however, are defense sector conversion, relationships with the Pacific Rim, and long-term transportation issues. The institute would seek out policy areas that could be viewed as on the cutting edge, but would also deal with current projects of interest to both the private sector and elected officials. The institute is expected to avoid policy issues that divide the delegation, such as immigration relief or water programs. In addition, it is viewed as supplementing—not competing with—groups such as the California-based Council on Science and Technology. It has been suggested that the institute publish a yearly analysis of the impact of the federal budget on California.

Some Washington-based California representatives are skeptical about the proposal for a California Institute. They acknowledge the importance of devising new methods to reach an aggregate California position, but worry about creating an institution with a long-term focus in a political context with a short time frame. Others are concerned about developing a think-tank and research focus in an environment in which fluid and interpretive information is valued. Still others believe that the idea of a California Institute comes at a time of particular sensitivity to and resentment of the growing presence of Californians in Washington. As one individual commented, "The University of California is establishing a presence in Washington—a building and 150 interns who will be running around the Hill. We could have fifty-three members in the delegation. What will people think about the state then?"

Despite this concern, there is a sense that we are now facing a window of opportunity for the development of such an institute in a real spirit of bipartisanship. Reapportionment is still in the future, and the current governor is completing his tenure in office. Perhaps most important, the concept has gained broad political and private-sector support. While the proposal is not a panacea, it does provide a mechanism for balancing diversity and unity, and it offers a means of drawing on California expertise that may assist the corps of Washington representatives. Its genesis in the Congress suggests that it may be able to assist Californians in maximizing their impact on legislative decision making. It may be an idea whose time has come.

CONTRIBUTORS

Peter Asmus is a journalist specializing in public policy issues. He is co-author of *In Search of Environmental Excellence* and writes regularly on energy issues for state and national trade newsletters. His articles have been published in the *Los Angeles Times, Christian Science Monitor,* and *The Sacramento Bee.*

Katrina Burgess is assistant director of the California-Mexico Project at the University of Southern California. A graduate of Swarthmore College and USC's School of International Relations, she was previously assistant director of the U.S.-Mexico Project at the Overseas Development Council in Washington. D.C.

Bruce Cain is associate director of the Institute of Governmental Studies and professor of political science at the University of California, Berkeley. He received his Ph.D from Harvard University and taught at the California Institute of Technology between 1976 and 1989. He is author of the 1984 book *The Reapportionment Puzzle.*

Jeffrey Chapman is professor of public administration and director of the Sacramento Center of USC's School of Public Administration. His fields of specialization include public policy analysis, public finance, and urban and land use economics. His work has been supported by the National Science Foundation, the Rand and Duke University Public Policy Program, and the National Endowment for the Humanities. He is author of *Proposition 13 and Land Use: a Case Study of Fiscal Limits in California.*

Timothy Duane is an energy and environmental consultant with a doctoral degree in energy and environmental planning and a masters in infrastructure planning and management from Stanford University. His consulting clients include the Coalition for Energy Efficiency and Renewable Technologies, the U.S. Department of Energy, Pacific Gas & Electric, and the Natural Resources Defense Council.

John Kirlin is the Emery E. Olson Professor of Public-Private Entrepreneurship in the School of Public Administration, University of Southern California. Resident at the Sacramento Center, he has written on the politics of public finance, fiscal limits, urban management, and the design of public institutions and policies. He serves as a consultant in these areas to state and local governments and to businesses and civic organizations.

Eugene Lee is emeritus professor of political science at the University of California, Berkeley, where he served as director of the Institute of Governmental Studies for twenty years. A former vice-president of the university, he was also first chairman of the Commission on California State Government Organization and Economy and served in Washington, D.C. as staff consultant to the California congressional delegation.

Abraham Lowenthal is professor of international relations and director of the California-Mexico Project at the University of Southern California. He is also executive director of the Inter-American Dialogue in Washington, D.C. He has written or edited eight books and numerous articles on U.S.-Latin American relations; his most recent book is *Partners in Conflict: the United States and Latin America.*

Chester Newland is professor of public administration at the University of Southern California in Sacramento and Washington, D.C. This year he completed a six-year term as editor-in-chief of *Public Administration Review.* Dr. Newland is past national president of the American Society for Public Administration. His professional work has focused on public executive development, city management, federal management systems, public law, personnel administration, and labor-management relations.

Beryl Radin is professor of public administration at the Washington Public Affairs Center of the University of Southern California. Her major research and teaching interests focus on the implementation of national policies in a complex federal system. She has published many books and articles on education policy and human services policy and administration. She was selected as a Fulbright Scholar in India in 1990.

Michael Teitz is professor of city and regional planning at the University of California, Berkeley. He has studied regional and local economics and development policy for many years. In addition, he has been engaged in planning and policy for housing at the national, state, and local levels.

Fernando Torres-Gil is associate professor of gerontology and public administration at the University of Southern California, where he conducts research and teaches courses on public policy, health care, and ethnicity. He is also associate director of the National Resource Center on Minority Aging Populations and author of *Diversity in Aging: Challenges Facing the White House Conference on Aging*.

Donald Winkler is professor of public administration at the University of Southern California. He holds a Ph.D. in economics from the University of California, Berkeley, and has published widely on the finance of government, including educational finance, international flows of students, and the finance of capital infrastructure. He is currently on leave from the university and is working as an economist in public-sector management at the World Bank.

Linda Wray is a doctoral student in public policy and gerontology at the University of Southern California. She spent fifteen years in the public policy arena in Washington, D.C., serving as a policy analyst at Mathematica Policy Research, Inc., and as a congressional liaison at the Departments of Health and Human Services and Housing and Urban Development during the Carter Administration.